THE ADVAITA VEDĀNTA OF BRAHMA-SIDDHI

THE ADVAITA VEDĀNTA OF BRAHMA-SIDDHI

Allen Wright Thrasher

MOTILAL BANARSIDASS PUBLISHERS
PRIVATE LIMITED • DELHI

First Edition: Delhi, 1993

ISBN: 81-208-0982-3

Also available at:
MOTILAL BANARSIDASS
41 U.A., Bungalow Road, Jawahar Nagar, Delhi 110 007
120 Royapettah High Road, Mylapore, Madras 600 004
16 St. Mark's Road, Bangalore 560 001
Ashok Rajpath, Patna 800 004
Chowk, Varanasi 221 001

PRINTED IN INDIA
BY JAINENDRA PRAKASH JAIN AT SHRI JAINENDRA PRESS, A-45 NARAINA, INDUSTRIAL AREA, PHASE I, NEW DELHI 110 028 AND PUBLISHED BY NARENDRA PRAKASH JAIN FOR MOTILAL BANARSIDASS PUBLISHERS PRIVATE LIMITED, BUNGALOW ROAD, JAWAHAR NAGAR, DELHI 110 007

CONTENTS

INTRODUCTION vii

ABBREVIATIONS xi

I ANIRVACANĪYA 1-38

The Evidence of the Brahma-siddhi 1

The Evidence of the Sphoṭa-siddhi 15

Nirupākhya 18

The Evidence of the Vibhrama-viveka 20

The Possible Influence of Śaṃkara's Use of Anirvacanīya on Maṇḍana's 28

Maṇḍana's Development of the Theory 31

The State of Maṇḍana's Thinking in Writing the Vibhrama-viveka 35

II VIVARTA 39-50

III AVIDYĀ 51-75

The Causality of Avidyā 51

Avidyā as 'Beginningless' and 'Connatural' 57

Avidyā and Its Synonyms 58

Avidyā as 'Superimposition' 63

Śakti 65

Āvaraṇa and Vikṣepa 70

IV NIRVIKALPA JÑĀNA 77-100

Object of Nirvikalpa Jñāna 77

Verbality of Nirvikalpa 87

V ERROR LEADS TO TRUTH 101-109

APPENDIX A: Maṇḍana's Date 111

APPENDIX B: The Order of Maṇḍana's Works 129

REFERENCES 135

BIBLIOGRAPHY 161

INDEX 173

INTRODUCTION

The Vedāntin Maṇḍana Miśra is a seminal figure in the history of Advaita. An approximate contemporary of the great Śaṃkara, he differs from his views on many points, and at times directly opposes them. He is not uninfluenced by Śaṃkara, but his overall independence of him, the fact that his *Brahma-siddhi* is, along with the *Gauḍapāda-kārikās*, the sole work of the Vedānta system contemporary or prior to Śaṃkara to have survived, and his citations of the opinions of others on many disputed points, either in agreement or in disagreement, make him one of the most important witnesses we have for pre-Śaṃkara Vedānta. His works provide the earliest information we have from a Vedānta work on the concepts of *vivarta* 'unreal appearance', and *anirvacanīyatva*, the 'inexpressibility' of *māyā-avidyā* as real or unreal. He is, apparently, the first Advaitin to attempt to establish Advaita by means of a critique or ordinary sensory perception (*pratyakṣa*) which claims to show that perception does not prove the reality of difference, because it does not apprehend difference at all. He is one of our early witnesses for the theory of *sattādvaita*, the theory that all things are one because they are all *sat*, existent, and *sattā*, Being, is present in them all. Certain features of his doctrine, such as the inexpressibility of *avidyā*, the importance placed upon Being and bliss as characteristics of Brahman the critique of perception, the ascription to *avidyā* of two aspects, that of covering over the one true Brahman, and of projecting the manifold false world, and the concept of *vivarta* (not to exhaust the list) were taken over by Advaitins of the tradition established by Śaṃkara, although they are not to be found in Śaṃkara's own works. The great commentator on Śaṃkara's *Brahma-sūtra-bhāṣya*, Vācaspati Miśra, whose commentary, the *Bhāmatī* established a distinct and important school of interpretation within the body of Śaṃkara's followers, attempted, as far as possible, to harmonize Śaṃkara with Maṇḍana, on whose *Brahma-siddhi* he wrote a commentary, the *Tattva-samīkṣā*, which has unfortunately been lost.

It is not, however, my intent to discuss Maṇḍana's later influence, though a study of it would be very fruitful, perhaps indispensable, for an understanding of the later history of Vedānta. Rather my intent is to study certain topics in the doctrine of the *Brahma-siddhi*, "The Demonstration of Brahman", Maṇḍana's largest work, his most important, and the sole one dedicated as a whole to Vedānta. These topics are interrelated; they all have to deal with the nature and functioning of error, whether everyday error or the transcendental error *avidyā*, which makes us see the multiplicity of phenomena where there is nothing but the utter oneness of Brahman. They also demonstrate the number of different sources upon which Maṇḍana depended in erecting his own system. Chiefly, these sources are the metaphysical-grammatical tradition of Bhartṛhari's *Vākyapadīya* and the *Vṛtti* thereon, the Mīmāṃsaka Kumārila Bhaṭṭa, the Buddhist logicians Dignāga and Dharmakīrti, pre-Śaṃkara Vedānta, and perhaps Śaṃkara. In spite of the number and variety of these sources, Maṇḍana created a system the close coherence of whose parts is a cause of admiration, even if one does not always accept his conclusions.

The consistency of Maṇḍana's doctrine is visible even in those of his works which are not on Vedānta, that is to say, all but the *Brahma-siddhi*. Of these, three, the *Bhāvanā-viveka*, the *Vidhi-viveka*, and the *Mīmāṃsānukramaṇikā*, are on Mīmāṃsā, one, the *Vibhrama-viveka*, is a discussion of different theories of error from the standpoint of Kumārila's *anyathā-khyāti*, and one, the *Sphoṭa-siddhi*, a work of philosophy of language in the tradition of Bhartṛhari. Although these works in general agree with the positions of the *Brahma-siddhi*, and are interesting, original, and important in themselves, I have used them mainly to supplement what can be learned from the *Brahma-siddhi*.

To the body of this study I have added two appendices, whose conclusions are to some degree relied upon in the rest of the work. The first of these is on Maṇḍana's date, and the second on the order of his works.

Maṇḍana Miśra has, unfortunately, been little studied in proportion to his intellectual and historical importance. However, in addition to a number of articles written during this century by various scholars, several books on him have been published in the late 1960's. Madeleine Biardeau has published a complete French translation of the *Brahma-siddhi* along with a thorough study of its doctrine. Tilmann Vetter has published a German translation of the first *kāṇḍa* of the *Brahma-siddhi* along with extensive and illuminating notes. Finally, Lambert Schmithausen has published an edition and translation of his *Vibhrama-viveka*, containing also a long study on Maṇḍana's doctrine of error and the history of Indian theories of error prior to him. These works have made the task of a later student of Maṇḍana much easier. It would be impossible for me to call attention in the notes to every point for which I have been dependent upon them.

A few words are in order about the method employed here of making references to Sanskrit texts. For references to the *Brahma-siddhi* I give first the page number, followed by a period and by the line number. Thus '*BS* 11.13' means '*Brahma-siddhi*, page 11, line 13.' This same method has been followed for many of the other texts, in particular for the *Vidhi-viveka*, the *Vākyapadīya-vṛtti*, and Śaṃkara's works. I have not used the form 'p. 11, 1.13' except where it was necessary to avoid confusion with the citation of a passage in a work which I also have referred to by book, chapter, etc., which divisions I have likewise separated by periods. Thus '*BSūB* 1.1.17, 184.1-2' means '*Brahma-sūtra-bhāṣya* (of Śaṃkara), *Adhyāya* 1, *Pāda* 1, *Sūtra* 17; page 184, lines 1 to 2.'

The occasional references to *kārikās* in the *Brahma-siddhi* employ a Roman numeral for the *kāṇḍa*, a period, and the number of the *kārikā*. Thus *BS* III.2 is the second verse of the third *kāṇḍa*. When references are made to parts of a verse, the verse is divided into quarters rather than halves: thus '*VV* 68a-c' means the first three *pādas* of verse 68 of *Vibhrama-viveka*. No page reference is given to works entirely in verse.

All page references to the Sanskrit text of the *Sphoṭa-siddhi* are to Biardeau's edition, and of the *Vibhrama-viveka* to Schmithausen's. Page references to the *Vākyapadīya-vṛtti* are to K.A. Subrahmania Iyer's critical edition of *Kāṇḍa* 1 of the *VP* with the *Vṛtti* and Vṛṣabhadeva's *Paddhati*. It should be observed, however, that I use the customary numbering of the *kārikās* of *Kāṇḍa* 1, which is that followed in the earlier editions, in Biardeau's translation accompanied by the text, and in Iyer's own English translation. This numbering is given by Iyer in square brackets after his own numbering, beginning with verse 108. Iyer considers eight verses after V. 107 to belong to the commentary; therefore his numbering after V. 107 is 8 verses behind the older system. I use the older numbering purely for convenience sake, since Iyer's edition may not be available to all; Iyer gives his reasons for ascribing the verses to the commentary in pp. x-xii of his introduction. References to *Kāṇḍas* 2 and 3 of the *VP*, which are all to the *kārikās*, are to Abhyankar and Limaye's critical edition of the *VP kārikās*. All page references to Śaṃkara's works are to the Ānandāśrama Press editions, except those to the *Brahma-sūtra-bhāṣya*, which are to the Nirṇaya Sāgar press edition with *Bhāmatī*, *Kalpataru*, and *Parimala*. For further bibliographical details about all these books, see the bibliography.

I have occasionally regularized the punctuation of Sanskrit texts quoted, without thinking it necessary to note it on each occasion. In particular, I have used no apostrophe in the transliteration where an editor has used a single or double *avagraha* to represent the coalescence of two a-vowels in internal or external sandhi. In addition, to avoid confusion of single quotation marks with the apostrophe representing the *avagraha*, I have made all quotation marks within Sanskrit texts double.

I am indebted to many people for help in the preparation of this thesis and in the studies leading up to it. Above all, I owe thanks to Professor Daniel H.H. Ingalls, my first teacher in Sanskrit and my advisor for nearly a decade, who patiently discussed with me many problems in interpreting Maṇḍana's thought and in composing this study. Then to Pandit Vighnahari Bhalacandra Deo of the Deccan College, Poona, who in reading the *Brahma-siddhi* with me was a remover of obstacles in truth as well as in name. Also to other pandits of the Deccan College: to Pandit Shrinivasa Shastri, for giving assistance on particularly knotty points, to Pandit R. Srinivasan Raghavachariar of Tiruvarangam, with whom I read Vedānta and Mīmāṃsā, and to Pandit K.A. Sivaramakrishna Sastri, with whom I read part of the *Vākyapadīya* and its *Vṛtti*. Finally to Professor Masatoshi Nagatomi, who answered for me many questions on Buddhism and allowed me to use parts of his not yet printed translation of Dharmakīrti's *Pramāṇa-Vārttika*, and to Professor S.D. Joshi, who helped me with questions concerning the Sanskrit grammarians.

ABBREVIATIONS

AD	Ānandagiri
BG	Bhagavad-gītā
BGB	Bhagavad-gītā-bhāṣya
BH	Bhartṛhari
BS	Brahma-siddhi
BSV	Brahma-siddhi-vyākhye
BSū	Brahma-sūtras
BSūB	Brahma-sūtra-bhāṣya
BU	Bṛhadāraṇyaka Upaniṣad
BUB	Bṛhadāraṇyaka-upaniṣad-bhāṣya
BUBV	Bṛhadāraṇyaka-upaniṣad-bhāṣya-vārttika
BV	Bhāvanā-viveka
CU	Chāndogya Upaniṣad
CUB	Chāndogya-upaniṣad-bhāṣya
DK	Dharmakīrti
GK	Gauḍapāda-kārikās
GKB	Gauḍapāda-kārikā-bhaṣya
ĪśaU	Īśa Upaniṣad
JAHRS	Journal of the Andhra Historical Research Society
JAOS	Journal of the American Oriental Society
JBBRAS	Journal of the Bombay Branch of the Royal Asiatic Society
JORM	Journal of Oriental Research, Madras
JRAS	Journal of the Royal Asiatic Society
KaṭhaU	Kaṭha Upaniṣad
KB	Kumārila Bhaṭṭa
KS	Kuppuswami Sastri
LS	Lambert Schmithausen
M	Maṇḍana
MāṇḍU	Māṇḍūkya Upaniṣad
MB	Madeleine Biardeau
MBS	Tilmann Vetter, Maṇḍanamiśra's Brahmasiddhiḥ
MuṇḍU	Muṇḍaka Upaniṣad
NS	Naiṣkarmya-siddhi
P	pūrvapakṣa
PMM	M. Biardeau, La Philosophie de Maṇḍana Miśra

PV	Pramāṇa-vārttika
S	siddhānta, Sureśvara
Ś	Śaṃkara
ŚP	Śaṅkhapāṇi
SS	Sphoṭa-siddhi
SSMM	K.A. Subrahmania Iyer, Sphoṭa-siddhi of Maṇḍana Miśra
SV	Sambandha-vārttika
ŚV	Śloka-vārttika
TS	Tattva-saṃgraha
TSP	Tattva-saṃgraha-Pañjikā
TU	Taittirīya Upaniṣad
TUB	Taittirīya-upaniṣad-bhāṣya
TV	Tilmann Vetter
U	Upaniṣad
ViV	Vidhi-viveka
VM	Vācaspati Miśra
VP	Vākyapadīya
VPBH	K.A. Subrahmania Iyer, the Vākyapadīya of Bhartṛhari with the Vṛtti
VPBK	M. Biardeau, Vākyapadīya Brahmakāṇḍa
VPv	Vākyapadīya-vṛtti
VV	Vibhrama-viveka
YSū	Yoga-sūtras
YSūB	Yoga-sūtra-bhāṣya
WZKM	Wiener Zeitschrift für des Kundes Morgenlandes
WZKSO	Wiener Zeitschrift für die Kunde Süd-und Ost-Asiens
ZDMG	Zeitschrift der Deutschen Morgenländischen Gesellschaft

CHAPTER I

ANIRVACANĪYA

THE EVIDENCE OF THE BRAHMA-SIDDHI

1.1 9.11-10.2

One of the concepts for whose development Maṇḍana's testimony is most important is that of *anirvacanīyatva*, the 'inexpressibility' of *māyā-avidyā* as existent or non-existent, as identical to or different from Brahman. This concept, although not found in Śaṃkara, later became a commonplace of Advaita Vedānta. The first place where it appears in the *Brahma-siddhi* is BS 9.11-10.2. The *pūrvapakṣin*, a Vijñānavādin, has suggested (8.13-9.10) that as Brahman is eternal knowledge, there is nothing (no knowledge) that needs to be produced for liberation and nothing that needs to be stopped. This Siddhāntin says that it is *avidyā* that needs to be stopped. The *pūrvapakṣin* then says that if this *avidyā* is not the essence (*svabhāva*) of Brahman, there will be a second thing alongside the one Brahman, which the Advaitin cannot admit. If it is not another thing, it will be eternal like Brahman; how can it be stopped? It is in this context, rather than in the cosmological context of Śaṃkara,[1] that the word *anirvacanīya* is first used.

1.2

Maṇḍana says: "*Avidyā* is not the essence of Brahman, nor another thing; not absolutely non-existent, nor existent. It is just for this reason that it is called 'nescience' (*avidyā*), 'illusion' (*māyā*), 'false appearance' (*mithyāvabhāsa*). If it were the essence of anything, whether different or not different (from it), it would be ultimately real, and therefore not *avidyā*. If it were absolutely non-existent, it would not enter into practical activity any more than a sky-flower. Therefore, it is inexpressible. Besides, the adherents of every doctrine must agree to this, since it is thus: for the Śūnyavādins, if it exists as it is seen, it is not *avidyā*. If it is like a sky-flower, it cannot take part in practical activity. For him also who says (that everything is) just consciousness (*vijñā-*

na), if knowledge exists as it appears, (its) object cannot be denied, since he does not deny that the form of the thing known —such as blue or yellow—appears as external. If it were absolutely non-existent it could not appear as external any more than a sky-flower. For those also who teach (the existence of) external objects, cognitions like that of things that are not eternal as eternal, and errors such as that of silver (in regard to mother-of-pearl), could not be *avidyā* if the form that appears really existed. If it were absolutely non-existent there could be no practical activity based on it.

P: Perhaps the form that appears does not exist, but the appearance indeed exists, and that is what is called *avidyā*.

S: This is not valid. When that which appears is non-existent, its appearance also is hard to explain as being real. It may be an appearance, but it is simply an error to say in addition, 'the appearance of that'. Therefore, *avidyā* is neither existent nor non-existent. It is for this very reason that it can be ended—because it has no firm essence, since it is merely an illusion (*māyā*). If it were not so, but were firmly established in its own essence, how could it be changed: for change would mean the destruction of its essence. If it were void, it would (already) have ceased by itself. Thus there is neither the destruction of non-duality, nor the absence of something to be ended.[2]

1.3

Maṇḍana here makes some of his reasons for adopting the notion of *anirvacanīyatva* quite clear. If *avidyā* is ultimately real it can never be ended, and will form a second entity over and above Brahman. If it is absolutely non-existent there can be no bondage of *vyavahāra*, yet both bondage and *vyavahāra* seem to be real in some degree. This is but a logical development of the concept of two truths—practical (*vyavahāra, saṃvṛti*) and ulimate (*parinispanna, paramārtha*)—found in Mahāyāna Buddhism and Śaṃkara. The empirically existent, *vyāvahārika-sat* is not the *paramārtha-sat*, it is not fully existent. Yet it does have existence of a sort, and thus is not totally non-existent. Therefore, in Maṇḍana's terminology, it is neither existent nor non-existent.

1.4

Maṇḍana seems to be influenced here by the so-called

svavṛtti[3] to the *Vākyapadīya*, which elsewhere in the *Brahma-siddhi*, and in the *Sphoṭa-siddhi* as well, he gives abundant evidence of knowing.[4]

1.5

To begin with, he says: "*Avidyā* is not the essence of Brahman, nor another thing; not absolutely existent, nor non-existent." The *Vṛtti* to *VP* I.1 (8.3-9.3) says:

" 'Appears as the object'—Appearance (*vivarta*) is one thing's assuming other false divided forms in the likeness of diversity without ceasing to be itself, like the appearance of objects in dreams. Besides, it has been said: 'The false appearances of configuration and action are merely the activity of the power of *avidyā*'. They are inexplicable (*anākhyeyau*) as identical with or different from the Self which is knowledge (*vidyā*). For this is what makes *avidyā avidyā*."[5]

vivartate 'rthabhāvena: ekasya tattvād apracyutasya bhedānukāreṇāsatyavibhaktānyarūpopagrāhitā vivartaḥ. svapnaviṣayapratibhāsavat. uktaṃ ca. mūrtikriyāvivartau avidyāśaktipravṛttimātraṃ tau vidyātmani tattvānyatvābhyām anākhyeyau. etad dhi avidyāyā avidyātvam iti.

1.6

Although the passage does not explicitly say that the false appearances are not only neither identical to nor different from the Self, but also neither real nor unreal, the last sentence seems to imply it. Compare what was said in our passage from the *BS* (9.12): "It is just for this reason that it is called 'nescience', 'illusion', 'false appearance'." The *vivartas* seem to be equated with *avidyā*; they are not 'produced' by it, but rather 'the activity of the power of *avidyā*.' Compare also *VV* 28, to be discussed below (§1.43). "Therefore, the knowers of Brahman know that it is best (that error) is indescribable; otherwise nescience would cease to be nescience. If it (the error or its object) is real it is not false; if it is void its appearance would be inconceivable. They call that nescience inexpressible as existent or non-existent." Logically, if Brahman is the one thing that really exists, what is different from it does not exist, and what is neither the same nor different from it is neither real nor unreal.[5a]

1.7

That 'Harivṛṣabha' thought that *avidyā* is indescribable both as identical or different and as existent or non-existent is clear from the *Vṛtti* on *VP* I.4 (21.3-22.1):

"For the one Brahman, endowed with non-conflicting powers which are indescribable as identical or different (from it), and as existent or non-existent, being differentiated into unreal forms, has the false appearances (*vivarta*) of the knots which are the enjoyer, the enjoyed, and the enjoyment, which are without external reality and are different from each other."

ekasya hi brahmaṇas tattvānyatvābhyāṃ sattvāsattvābhyāṃ cāniruktavirodhiśaktyupagrāhyasyāsatyarūpapravibhāgasya svapnavijñānapuruṣavad abahistattvāḥ parasparavilakṣaṇā bhoktṛbhoktavyabhogagranthayo vivartante.[5b]

1.8

It appears that being *tattvānyatvābhyāṃ sattvāsattvābhyām anirvacanīya* is a trait that belongs to all the powers (*śakti*) of Brahman, and that *avidyā* has it in virtue of being a *śakti.*[6] Maṇḍana does not call *avidyā* a *śakti* of Brahman.[7] To allow Brahman a multiplicity of powers, or even a single power, would threaten the non-duality of Brahman and bring him close to a *bhedābheda* position which he rejects.[8] He could perhaps find some way to avoid this danger, but to talk even of a single *śakti* of Brahman would be out of line with his emphasis on *avidyā* as something belonging to the *jīva* rather than to Brahman, and his epistemological approach to the problems of difference. Still, dropping the concept of power, he adopts that part of Harivṛṣabha's presentation which suits his purpose.

1.9

It is striking that our first surviving statement that *avidyā* is indescribable in either way should be from a text of the *Śabdabrahman* tradition. Could this be why Śaṃkara did not adopt the idea? Hacker has said that this may be the reason that the idea of *vivarta* is not accepted by him, nor by his school for some time after him,[9] and both the texts quoted from the *Vṛtti* involve a technical use of *vivarta*. Ingalls has stated that Śaṃkara may have avoided the concept because it made the world, if not more real, at least less unreal than merely to refrain from saying whether it is real or not.[10] That the *Vṛtti* brings in the concept in connection with Brahman's powers would make Śaṃkara particularly wary.[11] It is a cosmological context, that of one Brahman becoming many, rather than Maṇḍana's epistemological one. Śaṃkara calls *māyā* a *śakti* of Brahman and identifies it with *prakṛti*, *nāma-rūpa* as the primordial substance of the world, and the like. To say that it is inexpressible as non-existent is to raise it to a higher level than he apparently wants to put it on; for him it is *avidyātmaka* or *avidyā-kalpita*, 'of the nature of ignorance' or 'produced by ignorance', which is more to say that it is unreal than to say it is indescribable. It is to take it out of the sphere of 'propaedeutic'[12] instruction into that of a final statement of what the world is. But if the multiform universe is not considered an 'objective' illusion, as Śaṃkara considered it,[13] and if *avidyā* (or, in Śaṃkara, *māyā*) is not considered a power of Brahman which allows him to appear as manifold, but rather as the subjective error of the *jīva*, this might not seem so much of a problem. The world as multiple is simply an error, and to say that an error is *anirvacanīya* is just to analyze what that means.

1.10

There is additional reason to think that this idea of the inexpressibility of *avidyā* arose in circles adhering to the doctrine of *Śabda-brahman*. Kamalaśīla, in his commentary (*pañjikā*) on verse 151 of the *Tattva-Saṃgṛha* of Śāntarakṣita,[14] presents arguments like those brought forward in the *Pūrvapakṣa* of the passage of the *BS* that we are considering, and even has his opponent refer to the concept of *anirvacanīyatva*. Yet this verse is not in the chapter against the Vedānta (Chapter VII, *Aupaniṣadātmaparīkṣā*), but in that against the *Śabda-brahman* (Chapter V, *Śabda-brahma-parīkṣā*). In the following, I follow Jha's translation.[15]

1.11

S: "Further, for you, apart from *Brahman*, there can be no Ignorance [*avidyā*]... under whose influence the *Brahman* would appear in the said form."[16]

Cf. *BS* 9.1: "If *avidyā* is not the essence of Brahman, there would be another thing than Brahman."[17]

1.12

TSP: "It might be said that—'When it is said that "It becomes cognised under the influence of Ignorance", what is meant is that It is of the nature of Ignorance...'

If so, then the implication is all the clearer that there can be no Liberation: when the Eternal One *Brahman* has the nature of Ignorance, there can be no cessation of that Ignorance, which forms the essence of *Brahman*—by virtue of which cessation there could be Liberation."[18]

Cf. *BS* 8.16-19: "The texts for the sake of it (liberation) and the activities for the sake of it would be pointless... since it is of the nature of *avidyā*, since, it being eternal, it could not abandon its former nature and take up another nature."[19]

And *BS* 9.8: "If (*avidyā*) were the nature of Brahman, how could it be made to cease, being eternal?"[20]

1.13

TSP: "If then, Ignorance is admitted to be something apart from *Brahman*—even so, it could not produce any effect upon *Brahman*, which is eternal and hence not susceptible to any addition to Its qualities. So that it cannot be right to assert that Its appearance (in Cognition) is due to the influence of Ignorance; and thus there being no connection between Ignorance and *Brahman*, there can be no *Birth and Rebirth*. Nor can it be right to assert that 'It could be described as being neither the same nor different:'[21] because all things must fall within one or the other of these two; otherwise it would not be a *Thing* (Entity) [*vastu*] at all. Nor can it be right to assert that 'it is because of its being a *Non-entity* that it is cognised in that form;' —as such an explanation would lead to absurdities."[22] The general context in which the concept of indescribability comes in is similar to that in the *BS*. although the Buddhist's opponent is not given a chance to elaborate on his reasons. It is a question of explaining how *avidyā* can have enough reality to cause bondage, yet not so absolute a reality as to prevent liberation, how it can exist, yet not exist, as different from Brahman.

1.14

Some other similarities between these two passages remain:
TSP: "... it has to be explained what the Brahman's form is

prior to the mystic state [*yogitvāvasthā*—the state of being a Yogin]. If It is always of the form of light effulgent, then there can be no state which is *non-mystic*; as *ex hypothesi*, Brahman is ever of the nature of the effulgent light of Self; so that the Liberation of all beings would be accomplished without effort.

It is possible that the following might be urged: 'Just as for you, Buddhists, during the state of Dream and the Like, the Cognition, though one, appears in a variegated form, so the Brahman also, even though one, appears diverse to persons whose chain of cognitions is not pure, through Ignorance.'

That cannot be right; because as a matter of fact, apart from *Brahman*, there are none whose 'Chain' is not pure, to whom the said form could appear as stated . . . As for us (Buddhists), Liberation is quite possible, as at that stage, there appears a distinct pure Cognition."[23]

Cf. *BS* 8.14-15: "But others say (that the attaining of Brahman is) defined as the production of a pure knowledge from which the contamination of the form of the object has been removed."[24]

BS 8.17-18: "If its nature is knowledge (activities for obtaining Brahman will be useless, because) there will be nothing to be stopped or to be gained, since *avidyā* is absent and knowledge is present."[25]

And *BS* 9.5-6: "And it (knowledge) is eternal in Brahman, and there is nothing other than Brahman whose non-apprehension might be stopped by knowledge of Brahman gained by effort."[26]

Notice also that the example of dream-cognition is given by the *VPv* in both passages quoted—though here in the *TSP* the *Śabda-brahma-vādin* attributes it to the Buddhist.

1.15

In spite of these close similarities and the fact that Śāntarakṣita and Kamalaśīla are both slightly later than Maṇḍana,[27] I do not think it likely that Kamalaśīla is opposing here the passage from the *BS* which we are discussing (*BS* 9.11-10.2). I think it much more probable that Kamalaśīla has preserved an argument from some lost work of the *Śabda-brahman* school. First, because he brings it in, as said before, in his critique of that school. Though Maṇḍana defends the doctrine of Brahman as *śabda* in the *BS*,[28] and the Buddhist could therefore conceivably include him in that school, the *BS* is clearly on the whole a work of Advaita Vedānta. Besides, this particular passage of the *BS* makes no mention of Brahman as *śabda*, and the passage which does discuss Brahman as *śabda* makes no reference to problems connected with liberation. Second, because Śāntarakṣita's *kārikā* and the beginning of Kamalaśīla's commentary mention the idea that 'the Yogins' can see Brahman.[29] Mentions of Yogins or even of Yoga are absent in the *BS*, but they are rather more typical of the *Vākyapadīya* and its *Vṛtti*.[30]

1.16

The fact that Maṇḍana in the *Vibhrama-viveka* ascribes the theory of the *anirvacanīyatva* of error to the Vedāntins (*brahma-vidaḥ*) shows that it was not confined to the *Śabda-brahma-vāda* at this time.[31] The presence in the *VV* passage of the term *vivarta* which some have ascribed to the grammatical tradition[32] makes it seem likely that there were groups where Advaita Vedānta and *Śabda-brahma-vāda* overlapped. It would then be difficult to know whether such concepts as *vivarta* and *anirvaca-nīyatva* arose in the latter school, and were taken over by a form of Advaita which Śaṃkara did not fully share (this might be confirmed by Kamalaśīla's putting the inexpressibility theory in the *Śabda-brahma-parīkṣā*); or whether they were Advaita-vedānta ideas taken over by the grammatical school (which might be supported by the greater use of such words as *vidyā* in the *Vṛtti* as compared with the verses of the *VP*[33]).

1.17 14.21-15.2

"S: The transmigrant is an agent and an enjoyer, and a succession (*saṃtati*) (of cognitions) cannot be an agent or en-joyer, because it is not a thing (*avastu*); or how could something non-existent be bound and released?

P: The succession is not absolutely non-existent, nor existent, rather it is existent through false imagination (*kalpanā*). The texts and activities are for its liberation.

S: Then it is something imagined that transmigrates and is released, and bondage and release which apply to something imaginary are themselves simply imaginary—why don't you agree to this when *we* say it? It has already been said that transmigration and release apply to something imagined, and do not exist in the highest, ultimate truth."[34]

1.18

This passage is part of Maṇḍana's answer to the difficulties raised in the Vijñānavāda *Pūrvapakṣa* to the previous passage (8.13-9.10). It makes it clear, I think, that for Maṇḍana the idea of indescribability was a way of stating the two-truths theory found in Mahāyāna and in Śaṃkara. He mentions 'ultimate truth' (*paramārtha*), and opposes it to what is 'imagined', that is, to what for the Vijñānavādin would be empirical reality (*saṃvyavahāra* or *saṃvṛti*). Bondage and liberation are real only through false imagination. Although the word *avidyā* is not mentioned, it is clear that it is equivalent to the Buddhist term *kalpanā*, for the place which Maṇḍana refers to at the end of the passage under discussion as saying that transmigration is not ultimately real is, according to Śaṅkhapāṇi (41.25-26), 12.6-7, which says: "Therefore the *jīvas* are transmigrant by *avidyā*, and are freed by *vidyā*."[35] The problem is much the same as in 9.11-10.2 (§1.1). *Avidyā* or *kalpanā* must be real enough to produce our (apparent) bondage, and yet be unreal enough to be ended by knowledge. Thus the texts and activities for the sake of liberation will not be useless on the ground that liberation is impossible nor on the ground that it is already here.

1.19 48.5-15

"Another explanation of the second half (of verse II.5) objects to the alternatives (or: 'mental constructions'—*vikalpa*) of difference and non-difference:

(P:) This division, being the essence of something or being other, which belongs to things (*vastu*), should not be transferred to difference, whose 'body' is formed by mental construction. For it is like this: (difference), which is indescribable as the same as the thing or different from it (*tattvānyatvābhyām anirvacanīya*), whose body is presented by mental construction based upon the influence of beginningless mental constructions, sets in motion the ordinary usage (*vyavahāra*). 'This is different from that; this is the difference of the two.' There is no such thing as 'difference', whose identity or difference might be considered.

S: To this (the second half of the verse) applies again: 'And with (difference not having) a positive form (*rūpa*), a thing cannot have difference.' If, then, difference has no form, no nature of its own—for it does not exist in reality, but is merely presented by acts of mental construction—then difference cannot belong to a thing, since with respect to the ultimate truth difference does not exist. For it is not logical for something, in virtue of an imagined nature, to possess that (nature) in ultimate reality, since (its possessing it) would just be imagined. Why don't you accept this when *we* say it. We too say this same thing: difference does not really exist; it is but the play of beginningless nescience."[36]

1.20

Here the problem is not that of bondage and release, but the problem of the nature of difference (*bheda*). Maṇḍana is trying to prove that perception merely posits, affirms, that it never negates, and therefore does not present difference. Specifically, he is replying to the objection (47.11-15) that difference being the nature of things, the act of perception that affirms the things also presents their difference. His counter-arguments (47.15-48.4) show the absurdities that result from identifying difference with the thing. Although his *pūrvapakṣa* may not be a fair presentation of the Buddhist position, it seems clear that he is opposing the Buddhists. The mention of 'mental construction' (*vikalpa*) and 'the influence of mental constructions' (*vikalpa-vāsanā*) reminds one of Dharmakīrti.[37] The formulation of *bheda* as *anirvacanīya* is not the Buddhist's but Maṇḍana's own. However, the Vijñānavādin would go so far as to say that difference is a *vikalpa*, that what is given in perception is the bare particular (*svalakṣaṇa*) without respect to difference or identity with anything else.[38] As in the passage just discussed (14.21-15.2, §1.17). Maṇḍana admits that what he is saying is close to what the Buddhist says. Maṇḍana puts his *abheda* (i.e. Brahman) in place of the Buddhist *svalakṣaṇa*. The last sentence, "Difference does not exist; it is but the play of beginningless nescience", equates the Vedāntic *avidyā* with the Buddhist *vikalpa*, as it was previously equated with *kalpanā* (§1.18). Again, as in the previous passage, the mention of 'ultimate truth' (*paramārtha*, 48.12), indicates that the *anirvacanīya* formulation is a development of the two-truths theory.

1.21

Note that the formulation here, where the topic is the universe presented by perception, is similar to that of 9.11-10.2 (§1.1), where it is the relation of *avidyā* to Brahman. In the earlier passage nescience is said to be neither the essence (*svabhāva*) of Brahman, nor different from it. Here the same is said of difference. Compare 12.5-7, where the vision of non-difference (*abheda-darśana*) is equated with *vidyā*, and the vision of difference with *avidyā*.[39]

1.22

It should also be observed that the argument does not pose the inexpressible as a third truth-value belonging to the world or to 'things' which have a certain, though ambiguous, reality, but rather as a definition of that which is not a 'thing' at all. A similar argument has already been quoted in the passage from Kamalaśīla (§1.13): "Nor can it be right to assert that 'It could be described as being, neither real nor unreal'; because all things must fall within one or the other of these two; otherwise it would not be a *Thing*, (Entity) [*vastu*], at all. Nor can it be right to assert that 'it is because of its being a Non-entity [*avastu*] that it is cognised in that form'; as such an explanation would lead to absurdities." That Kamalaśīla, who belongs to "the mixed school of Mādhyamika-Yogacāras or Mādhyamika-Sautrāntikas"[40] should reject this formulation confirms that Maṇḍana's *Pūrvapakṣin* here is not a real Buddhist, but an imaginary one whom he sets up to be forced into arguments which lead up to his [41]

1.23 51.10-15

"P (a Buddhist): (Difference is inferred) from seeing (an effect) that has not been seen before.

S: That is false, since we see successive effects even from a single thing.

P: If there is absolute non-difference, it is illogical that there be both seeing and not seeing of the effects, since there is nothing to distinguish them (*viśeṣa*).

S: In that case a difference in effects does not annul non-difference (of the cause); all that can be inferred is a distinguishing trait (*viśeṣa*), without destroying it (non-difference). And we do not disregard that—(if it is) the object of imagination (*kalpanā*); for it is illogical if it belongs to a real thing (*vastu-sat*), because it can be neither identical with that thing nor different from it."[42]

1.24

This passage tells us something very important about Maṇḍana's theory of indescribability. For him it is not so much a special sort of reality as it is the denial of reality. That the distinguishing trait can neither be identical with the thing nor different from it is as much as to say that it is unreal, illogical, the object of imagination (note the Buddhist terminology again). It cannot be identical to the thing, since it would be merely the thing, not a *viśeṣa*. It cannot be different, because there would be no connection between it and the thing, and therefore it would not be the *viśeṣa* of the thing.[43] It is therefore unaccountable and contrary to logic, and does not really exist.

1.25 53.12-17

"This conjunction with contradictory properties was just refuted as a cause of difference. For surely, as things which last for a long time, being connected with qualities that last for a limited time, have those properties (at one time) and do not have them (at another), and yet the word 'contradiction' is not applied to them, so it is with things large in size and infinite things (connected) with (properties) limited in exten.

P: How can something infinite have a finite property?

S: If it is something over and above (the thing), or indescribable, there is no occasion to doubt its possibility. Even if it is nothing beyond (the thing), it will be like (a property) lasting for a limited time belonging to something which lasts for a long time."[44]

1.26

Here the problem is something like that in the previous passage. As there the question was that of the relation of a thing to its *viśeṣa*, here it is the relation of the thing to its property (*dharma*). If the property is identical with the thing, it would be contradictory for an infinite thing to have a finite property; since it would be limited by the property's finiteness. If it is different or indescribable, this difficulty does not arise. Maṇḍana does not elaborate on the relation of indescribability, as his purpose here is to establish by an example that a single thing may have contradictory properties, in such a way that it will be acceptable whatever one's philosophical opinion on the relation of substrate to property. It is interesting, however, that he does not mention a fourth solution, the *bhedābheda* one that the property is both different and not different from its substrate. This may indicate that he considered it a particularly illogical solution, more so than denying one or both of the alternatives.

1.27 54.19-20

"...and since (seeing something not seen before) is the cause (of an inference) merely of a distinguishing trait, and since that, being indescribable as identical or different, is the object of imagination..."[45]

1.28

This is part of a summary of the previous arguments, and merely repeats what was said at 51.10-15 (§1.23). It therefore needs no separate comment.

1.29 60.3-9

"P: But, as you said, it is impossible that the cognition of difference should arise from anything other than a means of valid knowledge (and therefore if, as Maṇḍana says, it does not come from perception, on which all the other *pramāṇas* except *śabda* depend, and *śabda* itself teaches non-duality, from what can the cognition of difference come?)

S: But who says anything else? For the apprehension of difference does not exist in final reality. If it did, how could difference be denied? And if it is denied, how can it be apprehended? It is impossible that the thing apprehended should not exist, and yet be apprehended.

P: What is it then?

S: Nescience (*avidyā*), an error (*vibhrama*)—and if the object of knowledge exists as it appears there is no error, but right cognition. And if it does not exist (at all), its apprehension is not possible. Therefore it is not described as existing in ultimate truth, nor as not existing, since it is established in ordinary life (*loka*) in all doctrines, as was said above."[46]

1.30

The last sentence refers back to 9.11-10.2 (§1.1), as is indicated by the reference to 'all doctrines' (*sarvapravādeṣu*, cf. *sarva-pravādibhiḥ* of 9.14). Again, inexpressibility is less a truth-value of the object conceived as external though not finally real[47] than the description of what sort of reality we must ascribe to an error, and therefore to its object.[48] *Avidyā* is assumed to share the same level of reality as the object which qualifies it; neither is fully real, as in 9.11-10.2. In fact, in the final sentence of the present passage it is hard to see if he is discussing error or its object. Perhaps we may say that the *word* 'error' (*vibhrama*) and its synonym 'nescience' (*avidyā*)[49] apply equally to the false consciousness (consciousness of difference, consciousness of silver) and to its object (difference, silver).[50]

1.31 66.13-22

"For him (who thinks that) the thing (*vastu*) is one (but) made up of two (elements), the true nature (*ātman*) of the thing is not the universal (*sāmānya*) alone, nor the particularity (*viśeṣa*) alone, for then there would be two separate things (*vastu-bheda*). Therefore the nature of the thing is mixed, its form is the two combined. Now a mixed thing connot carry over some place else; rather that which carries over is not the form of the thing. And so what is being expounded—though relying on other words—is that the individuals (*bhedāḥ*) alone are real. Or else (another gloss on verse III.21cd) (it is expounded) 'on account of another word', namely 'one thing is made of two'—since if the thing that carries over is not the essence (*svabhāva*) of the thing, it is the object of imagination.

P: It may not be the thing, (but) it is not ruled out that it is an aspect (*aṃśa*) of it. Otherwise, the imagination would be without a cause.

S: But what is this thing called an 'aspect'? It is not, to begin with, the thing itself, since, if the thing were just that, difference would result. Neither is it a thing in itself different from the thing, since then there would be three things: the universal, the particularity, and that which possesses them. If it is neither the thing itself, nor yet another thing by itself, it remains that it is the object of imagination, indescribable as the same or different."[51]

1.32

Again, as in earlier passages, Maṇḍana examines the status of anything apart from the bare thing (in 48.5-13 difference, in 51.10-15 and 54.19-20, a distinguishing trait, and in 53.12-17 a property). As he did for difference and a distinguishing trait, he decides it cannot stand the test of logic, and is therefore unreal, *avastu*, merely the object of imagination.

THE EVIDENCE OF THE SPHOṬA-SIDDHI

1.33

The *Sphoṭa-siddhi* does not employ the word *anirvacanīya*, but it does use the similar term *anupākhyeya*, which can be translated etymologically by 'inexpressible', although here it seems to have the meaning of 'indefinite'. I give a translation of Verse 18 of the *SS* and part of the autocommentary. Maṇḍana is explaining how the sounds (*dhvani*) bring about the knowledge of the *sphoṭa*: each communicates the complete *sphoṭa* in a vague manner, and the impressions (*saṃskāra, bhāvanā*) left by the last sound combine with those of the previous sounds to produce a clear knowledge.

1.34

Verse: "The sounds, which differ by the effort (made to produce them) illuminate it by the succession of their cognitions and of the impressions (of the cognitions)."[52]

Commentary: "The earliear sounds produce in the listener, in whose mind there have not yet been produced any particular impressions, cognitions which (themselves) take an indistinct (*avyakta*) form, but sow the seeds of impressions conducive to the production of the later clear (*vyakta*) determination (of the word). The last (sound), on the other hand, produces as it were a more perfectly clear (*ativyaktatara*) cognition, into which a clearer (*sphuṭatara*) image of the *sphoṭa* enters, assisted by the seeds of all the impressions produced by the indistinct (*avyakta*) determinations produced by the previous sounds. Similarly, the genuineness of a precious stone, which is not definite (*anupākhyāta*) when it is first viewed, appears in course in the final cognition in the mind of a tester of precious stones who is examining it, when (his mind) has received the form of the impressions deposited by the cognitions whose form is undefinable (*anupākhyeya*). Otherwise there would be no distinct illumination (of the objects) afterwards any more than before, since there would be no difference (between the two cognitions).

Therefore this has been said:

(Verses): "Just as one arrives at mastery of a Vedic passage or a verse by repetition, but it is not fully grasped in each repetition.

So the form of a word, illuminated by the sounds, is ascertained by cognitions which are indefinable (*anupākhyeya*) (yet) conducive to grasping (the word).

By the last sound the word is ascertained in the intellect in which seeds have been sown by the sounds, and which has been ripened by repetition."

The impressions produced by the perception undefinable in form (*anupākhyeyākāra*) of the *sphoṭa* produce a cognition which determines that same (*sphoṭa*) more clearly (*sphuṭatara*) and so there is not the defect of diversity in respect to the meaning (in this theory) as there is for him who says (that the word is) the letters (i.e. the defect that it is the sounds alone which are cognised, yet their impressions produce the cognition of the meaning)."[53]

1.35

Here *anupākhyeya*, which we have translated by 'undefinable', is opposed to 'distinct', 'clear' (*vyakta*, *sphuṭa*), and parallel to 'indistinct', 'vague', 'unclear' (*avyakta*). The quoted verses are from the *Vākyapadīya* (I.82-84), indicating that the term is borrowed from Bhartṛhari. Maṇḍana does not appear to use it in any other sense than that in which Bhartṛhari does. In this passage from the *SS*, in the *VP* verses, and in the *Vṛtti* on the verses,[54] the predominant connotation seems to be that of vagueness; there is no clear suggestion that the sounds or their cognitions are other than real. However, the next verse of the *VP* (I.85), which Maṇḍana quotes in the commentary to *SS* 21, does call the sounds, or the objects of the false cognitions they occasion, 'non-existent' (*asat*):[55]

"When one thinks that the non-existent interior verbal elements (i.e. the syllable as distinct from the word. the word as distinct from the sentence which the sounds cause us to believe in) exist, that is just the incapacity of the perceiver; it is a means to the grasping (of the real word)."

> *asataś cāntarāle yāñ chabdān astīti manyate |*
> *pratipattur aśaktiḥ sā grahaṇopāya eva saḥ ||*

Nevertheless, the *VPv* on this passage[56] does not gloss *asat* by *anupākhyeya*, although it does use *anupākhyeya* in its commentary on *VP* I.83,[57] so it seems likely that Harivṛṣabha did not identify the two terms. Maṇḍana shows by his wording in *SS* 21 and the commentary thereon that he was aware of and followed the *Vṛtti* to *VP* I.85,[58] so we may assume that for him too the two words were unassociated. He does mention, in the commentary to *SS* 21, immediately after three verses quoted from the *VP*, which begin with *VP* I.85 which we have just translated, "a fixed contamination of knowledge by error (*viparyāsa*) by the imitation of the form of a non-existent (*asat*), object of apprehension."[59] Although this does confirm, by the use of *viparyāsa* for "error"[60], that Maṇḍana held a theory of *viparīta-khyāti* when he wrote the *SS*, it does not commit him to any theory of the inexpressibility of error, or even to any theory of what it means to be 'non-existent'.

1.36

Thus, although M. Biardeau likens the term *anupākhyeya* to *anirvacanīya* and says that for Bhartṛhari it had a "valeur ontologique,"[61] it is not clear that it has similar implications in the *SS*, the *VP*,[62] or the *VPv*. As Biardeau herself says, "Pour Maṇḍana *anupākhyeya* pourrait see référer plus simplement à l'indistinction d'une forme."[63] What K.A Subrahmania Iyer says of Bhartṛhari's use of it seems valid for Maṇḍana also: "The cognition produced by each sound, taken by itself, is unnameable (*anupākhyeya*), because it is not enough to identify the *sphoṭa*."[64] Beyond that it does not appear that it applied to a special ontological status belonging to errors. In Verse 19 and commentary, Maṇḍana supports the idea that each of the sounds gives us an indistinct knowledge of the *sphoṭa*, and together produce the final clear knowledge, by the examples of the false cognition of a rope in a dark place as a snake, or of an elephant seen afar off as a tree. The previous erroneous cognitions lead to the final correct cognition, and at no time is anything other than the rope or the tree in contact with the sight. This is based on *VP* I.89-90, which he quotes, and the *Vṛtti*, which gives the two examples mentioned—another confirmation of Maṇḍana's acquaintance with it and use of the *Vṛtti*. Biardeau comments: "On s'attendrait à ce qu'il appliquât aussi le terme *anupākhyeya* aux perceptions erronées du type de serpent ou de l'éléphant dans sa théorie de l'erreur, tout comme les disciples de Śaṅkara diront de la perception erronée qu'elle est *anirvacanīya*."[65] It may indeed be that he would apply the term *anupākhyeya* to these false perceptions, since he gives them as a parallel to the perceptions of the *dhvanis*, which are so-called, and since they are similarly opposed to the 'clear' (*vyakta*) final perception.[66] But neither Maṇḍana nor his authority, the *VPv* on these two texts, actually uses the word. In any case, it does not seem that here in the *SS* he wishes to call either sort of false perception "neither existent nor non-existent", since as we have shown *anupākhyeya* means rather 'indescribable', 'indistinct'. To be sure, the idea of error leading to truth is an important one in the *BS*,[67] which uses the same analogy of the tree and the elephant to illustrate it,[68] and the *BS* defends the *anirvacanīyatva* of *avidyā*. However, the term and concept of *anirvacanīyatva* do not come in where the *BS* uses the analogy. Finally, the *VPv* uses different terms when it deals with the 'indescribability' of *avidyā* or the other *śaktis*: instead of *anupākhyeya*, it used the word *anirukta*[69] or the (admittedly similar[70]) *anākhyeya*.[71] So we are not entitled to say that Maṇḍana used the term in the same sense as *anirvacanīya* and its relatives. Nor does his use of it give further evidence of his indebtedness to the *Śabda-brahma-vāda* in his developing his theory of *anirvacanīyatva*.

NIRUPĀKHYA

1.37

For Maṇḍana this term is quite different from *anirvacanīya* or *anupākhyeya*. Although, like them, its etymological meaning is 'indescribable', it means 'void of all positive qualities',[72] 'utterly non-existent': For instance, *BS* 93.21-94.2, where he is discussing the question of what is the object of the cognition of non-existence, he says, "If 'the absence of a means of valid knowledge' is thus called the object of the cognition and verbal expression 'is not', then what is wrong with 'the absence of an object of valid knowledge', that it should be abandoned and 'the absence of a means of right knowledge' be called the object? For there is no difference whatever between them in their non-existence (*nirupākhyatva*)."[73] The word is used to gloss *abhāva* in the verse glossed (III.47b, 93.17). Compare 97.18-19: "The fact appears that existent things have a like form insofar as they differ from the non-existent (*nirupākhya*). If not, they would be as different from each other as they are from the non-existent (*nirupākhya*)."[74] Biardeau interprets the word in the first of these passages to mean 'non-existent', in the second to mean 'inexpressible'.[75] Either is in a sense correct, in that it means a degree of non-being going beyond even what is the 'absolutely non-existent' (*atyantāsat*) as exemplified by the traditional examples of a hare's horn or a flower in the sky. It refers to that which is so plunged in the blackness of non-being that it cannot even be talked about.

1.38

This is confirmed by the use of the word in the *Vibhrama-viveka*, which can be discussed more conveniently here than in the section on its handling of the concept of *anirvacanīyatva*. Verses 133c-136d, which employ the term, are part of the refutation of the *asat-khyāti* (i.e. the Śūnyavāda of the Mādhyamika Buddhists), from the standpoint of the *anyathā-khyāti* of the Bhāṭṭa Mīmāṃsā. They say:

"The cognition that grasps non-existence (*abhāva*), depends on another entity as being different from that which is other than it. There is nothing utterly indescribable (*nirupākhya*). Therefore, except for another entity, there is no voidness of entities (*bhāva-śūnyatvam*) for the intellect, since a non-existence cannot be discerned (or: described—*anirūpaṇāt*), nor any error, say the wise. Indeed, even that which is cognised in a hare's horn is not utterly non-existent (*nirupākhya*); for a horn is apprehended there in connection with a hare. Now that is not a non-entity (*avastu*), since it has already been seen on a hooved animal."[76]

Nirupākhya is clearly the equivalent of *śūnya*, at least in the Hindu's understanding of *śūnya*. Cf. 141a-c: "There is no consciousness void (*śūnya*) of an object of knowledge, since that would involve the destruction of its essence, and since it would be totally indescribable (*nirupākhya*)."[77] This is still part of the refutation of the Śūnyavāda. Śaṃkara uses the word in a similar sense—'utterly non-existent'—when refuting Buddhist theories.[78] The *VPv* uses it, and *anupākhya*, in the same sense, twice when citing Buddhist doctrines.[79] But Maṇḍana seems to give the word a special twist by keeping some of its etymological meaning. For him the real is describable (which is not to say that all that is describable is fully real). Although he says that verbal knowledge of Brahman must be supplemented by (or perhaps transformed into) direct knowledge (*sākṣātkāra*), he nowhere says that Brahman is beyond words,[80] while even the hare's horn has a certain reality. At *BS* 18.17-20, in a passage defending the doctrine that Brahman is *śabda*, 'word', he includes the hare's horn in a list of *vyāvahārika* objects (*vyāvahārika* here meaning rather 'pertaining to verbal usage' than 'pertaining to practical activity'), which have no being beyond being *vivartas* of *śabda*.[81]

THE EVIDENCE OF THE VIBHRAMA-VIVEKA

1.39

In the *Pūrvapakṣa* section of the *Vibhrama-viveka*, at the end of the section setting forth *asat-khyāti* 'the cognition of the non-existent', i.e. the Śūnyavāda), occurs this statement of the theory of error known as *anirvacanīyakhyāti*, "the cognition of the indescribable':

"28: Therefore (referring to the previous arguments for *asat-khyāti*) the knowers of Brahman know that it is better that (error) is indescribable; otherwise *avidyā* would cease to be *avidyā*.

29: If it is existent, it is not false (*mithyā*); if it were void (*śūnya*) its appearance would be inconceivable. They call that *avidyā* inexpressible as existent or non-existent.

30: It is illogical to look for something real (*vastu*) whether internal or external, in it, since it would cease to be if there were a real object of knowledge (*vedya-vastu*).

31: Moreover, this diversity (*prapañca*) of name and form is described as just *avidyā*. But if one thing is cognised as another there can be no denial of diversity.

32: If (error) were merely the absence of cognition, there

would be nothing but void; what would diversity be based on? What it is logical to say is that that in which there is no diversity appears as possessed of diversity.

33: Granted, if (error) were apprehension that is not clear, (Brahman) would not by itself appear clearly. But if the substrate of superimposition does not exist, it would be impossible for (Brahman) to possess all forms.[82]

34: For if the consciousness has various forms, so that diversity belongs to its nature, there can be no liberation, or else it will be impermanent.

35: It is obvious that in an error in which there are many forms, such as mirages, several false (*asatya*) forms appear in a single cognition.

36: The form of the consciousness is not real (*bhūta*), nor is (error) superimposition or an apprehension that is not clear. Therefore the knowers of Brahman think that error is an appearance (*vivarta*)."[83]

1.40

This passage shows clearly that the theory that error is a cognition that can be expressed neither as existent nor non-existent (*anirvacanīya-khyāti*) was already known as a Vedānta doctrine in Maṇḍana's time (see the reference to 'the knowers of Brahman', i.e. Vedāntins, in 28b and 36d).[84] Since he rejects it here, in a work which he apparently wrote before the *BS* in which he accepts it (see below §§1.70-75), he was not its inventor. These verses likewise show that the doctrine was in existence before Śaṃkara's activity.

1.41

Certain of the expressions recall the *VPv*. Compare V. 28 with the *Vṛtti* on *VP* I.1, already quoted (§1.5):

"For this is what makes *avidyā avidyā*." V. 35cd uses the word *asatya*, 'false', for the forms appearing in a single erroneous cognition, while *VPv* I.1 makes mention of 'other false divided forms', (*asatya-vibhaktānya-rūpa*), and *VPv* I.4 mentions 'the one Brahman being differentiated into unreal forms' (*ekasya brahmaṇas-asatya-rūpa-pravibhāgasya*—21.3-4). Finally, V. 36c uses the word *vivarta*, characteristic of the *VPv*. The passage thus confirms what was said above (§1.16), that the doctrine of inexpressibility must have arisen in a grammatical tradition and been taken over before Maṇḍana's time by the Vedānta,[85] or have arisen in the Vedānta and been taken over into the *Śabda-brahmavāda* by the author of the *VPv* or a predecessor.

1.42

It is clear that this theory was put forward as an explanation for both empirical and transcendental errors, for the errors of the everyday world and for the basic error by which we see the manifold world instead of the one Brahman, although the primary emphasis is on the latter.[86] The word *avidyā*, which tends to be applied to transcendental error, is used more often than *vibhrama*, which tends to be applied to empirical error.[87] The problems of the existence of diversity and the possibility of liberation are raised. On the other hand, V. 35 discusses the mirage, an empirical error, and the arguments of V. 28-30 apply to either sort.

1.43

As in the *BS*. the object of error and the error itself are on the same level.[88] In V. 29ab, it is impossible to tell whether it is a question of the error or the object of error being real or void. In V. 31ab, 'the diversity of name and form' is not said to be 'formed' or 'based' on *avidyā* (*avidyā-kalpita* or *-nibandhana*), but simply to be '*avidyā*'.[89]

1.44

From the fact that Maṇḍana includes this theory under *asat-khyāti*,[90] it appears that his rejection of it was based at least in part on the belief that it was too close to the Buddhist doctrine of Śūnyatā. This is true even though its proponent attempts to differentiate it from that position by his rejection of the 'void' in V. 29 and 32. For the opponent does not clearly say that error must have a substratum, something objective to which it refers (*ālambana*).[91] He says (V. 30) that it is illogical to look for an object either external or internal in error. V. 32ab does not say that diversity must have a basis in Brahman, but rather that if error is just the absence of knowledge, there will be a universal void, because there will not even be any positive error, any *avidyā*, just pure absence of consciousness.[92] V. 32cd might seem to imply a substrate, if the (understood) 'Brahman' is not defined positively, but purely negatively, as 'that in which there is no diversity', or 'that in which the universe does not exist' (*aprapañca*). Besides, V. 35 and 36a, by talking of 'the forms of consciousness', imply a model of *avidyā* in which the one consciousness of Brahman has many unreal forms, rather than the model of the *BS*, in which the transmigrant soul imagines diversity and superimposes it on the one Brahman, which is the objective support of that error. The crucial word of V. 33, *adhyasya*, which I have translated, following Lambert Schmithausen, as 'substrate of superimposition',[93] is a conjectural reconstruction.[94] With this possible exception, the discussion concerns itself not with the objective substrate of error (i.e. the mother-of-pearl), but with the status of the 'object' of error, that is, of the forms that appear in the erroneous cognition (i.e. the silver). This particular Vedānta, with its seeming nearness to Śūnyavāda, its concern for the unreal forms of the one consciousness, and its apparent extreme apophaticism and denial of the universe of diversity, may have approached that of Gauḍapāda. However, it apparently diverged from Gauḍapāda's doctrine by its willingness to give error and its objects a slightly higher status that the *ajāti-vāda* does, and its relations to speculations amongst the Grammarians.

1.45

In any case, it is clear that Maṇḍana thought that the partisans of the theory of the inexpressibility of error did not take account of the necessity for error to have a substrate. In V. 27, concluding the presentation of the 'Buddhist *asat-khyāti*',[95] he lets the Mādhyamika say, "Therefore it is logical to conclude that it is simply an error. (What is) in accordance with the consciousness (we actually have is) that no cause (*nimitta*, i.e. no object) for it is possible."[96] Maṇḍana introduces the next verse, the 'Vedāntic *asat-khyāti*,'[97] with the word 'therefore'. This indicates that he thought that the *anirvacanīya-khyāti-vādin* held error to have no object, which to his mind would verge on Buddhist 'nihilism'.[98] In V. 37, the first verse after the presentation of *anirvacanīya-khyāti*, he has another *Pūrvapakṣin*, a Prābhākara, object, "It would be illogical for something non-existent to appear",[99] confirming that he sees no real difference between the Vedāntin and the Mādhyamika. V.

38 strengthens this conclusion: "This seems rather contradictory, to say that there is nothing and that it appears. If it appears, it has positive form (*rūpa*) and is not non-existent, since that contradicts the consciousness (we actually have)."[100] Whether Maṇḍana wrote the *VV* as a Mīmāṃsaka or a Vedāntin (see below §§1.70-1.75), he maintained the necessity of a positive substrate or support for all knowledge both in the *VV* and in the *BS*.[101] If this section is a fairly accurate presentation of the teaching of an actual work or school (and I see no reason to believe it is not), its failure to guard that substrate would be for him a sufficient reason to reject it.

1.46

It also appears that Maṇḍana rejected the theory of the inexpressibility of error for the additional reason that he was unwilling when writing the *VV* to accept any 'third truth-value' besides existence and non-existence. Although the introductory verse to his *Siddhānta*, V. 47, closely approximates the phraseology of V. 29 defending the inexpressibility of error ("If it exists unequivocally, what error is there; if it does not exist, what appears? In accordance with both [facts], the elder [Kumārila[102]] accepts [error as] cognition [of the thing] as other [than it is]"[103]), this verse does not show sympathy for the *anirvacanīya-khyāti-vāda*, but rejects it by giving *anyathā-khyāti* as a better solution for the same problems. It pre-supposes that the content of our erroneous consciousness exists, but not at the present place and time. This is demonstrated by V. 133cd: "The cognition that grasps a non-existence depends on another existence."[104] Compare the following verses and Vs. 130 and 148.[105] So far from accepting a three-levelled ontology, Maṇḍana only accepts a one-levelled one, in that non-existence is simply the existence of another thing.[106] This theory that non-existence is but relative, although deriving from the realistic Pūrva-Mīmāṃsā of Kumārila Bhaṭṭa,[107] prepares the way for Maṇḍana's later attempt in the *BS* to prove *Advaita* by showing that all things have the common form of existence, and that difference (*bheda*), defined as mutual non-existence (*anyonyābhāva*), is a purely relative and therefore mental concept, a thought-construct.[108]

1.47

Maṇḍana seems to reject consciously the distinction of empirical and final reality. In Vs. 122c-123a he says: "If you think that the non-existent appears with the form of existence (*bhāva-rūpeṇa*), then you have accepted *anyathā-khyāti*."[109] The opponent replies (V. 123b), "That also (the thing that appears as existent, e.g., the silver), is void."[110] That is to say, we do not say that a real thing appears at a place and time where it does not exist; for the silver itself is only provisionally real. Maṇḍana replies (Vs. 123cd) that having the form of existence (*bhāva-rupatā*) and being non-existent ('void'—*śūnya*) are contradictory.[111] If the thing is in the final analysis non-existent, it must be so from the start, unequivocally. Maṇḍana may have regarded the position that *avidyā* or *vyavahāra* is neither non-existent nor existent as a weak attempt to get out of the absurdity of calling it both: if the law of the excluded middle is not thrown out, to deny both is to affirm both.

1.48

It is interesting that the Buddhist terms that appear in Maṇḍana's own presentation of inexpressibility in the *BS*, *vikalpa* and *kalpanā,* do not occur here. This may indicate that Maṇḍana himself reworked the theory using these terms, and that he changed his views on error after writing the *VV*. The proponent of *anirvacanīyatva* seems concerned to distinguish his position from the Śūnyavāda (see the word *śūnya* in Vs. 29a and 32a), and a Yogācāra position (see Vs. 34-35 and also the reference in V. 30ab to 'something real, whether internal or external'). The lack of technical terms and the fact that the argument against the Yogācāra presupposes that the Buddhist thinks that the many forms of the *citi* are real[112] may indicate that either the work or school that Maṇḍana followed in this *Pūrvapakṣa* directed its attack upon an earlier and less sophisticated form of Yogācāra than that of Dignāga or Dharmakīrti, or, as Schmithausen suggests,[113] the Vedāntin misunderstood it (or, for that matter, distorted it for the sake of his polemic).

1.49

Unfortunately, the text of the section of the *VV* in which Maṇḍana refutes the *anirvacanīya-khyāti-vāda* is extremely corrupt. Verse 150 is clearly directed against the theory. The MS at least has no gaps, and the manner in which its readings should be emended is fairly clear. However, the state of the next two verses does not allow us to be sure whether the section ends with V. 151 or V. 152.[114] We will first translate and examine V. 150, and afterwards do the same with the next two verses in Kuppuswami Sastri's reconstruction, whose evidence will be much less weighty.

1.50

V. 150: "Thus *avidyā*, even though (*ca*) it is expressible (*nirvacanīya*), will not cease to be *avidyā*, since it makes the form of one thing appear as belonging to another."[115]

1.51

I do not think that Maṇḍana's use of *avidyā* here implies that he held any theory of *avidyā* as a sort of universal deluding power when he wrote the *VV*. It is merely a synonym for *vibhrama*;[116] his use of it is due to his opponent's using it. He rejects the idea that error is inexpressible. If everything, including that which appears in an error, is existent, a *bhāva*, everything is expressible, including that. As we saw in the section on *nirupākhya*,[117] to be inexpressible is to be unreal. Maṇḍana defends the reality of both the object (the silver) and the substrate (the mother-of-pearl) of error against a theory which denies the full reality of the former and ignores the reality of the latter.

1.52

Although Vs. 151 and 152 are each deficient by a *pāda*, Kuppuswami Sastri's reconstruction of them seems to me to be reasonable, and the discussion is so brief that all the information we can get is valuable. I will mark the parts in the translation which correspond to the gaps in the text by broken underlining.

V. 151: "This (*avidyā*[118]) is *the consciousness of it other than it is*: if it did not exist there would be no consciousness. What error could there be with respect to something like a sky-flower, what *avidyā* where (*avidyā*) is not known?"[119]

Pādas b and c clearly affirm that error must have a real substrate, which Maṇḍana holds both here in the *VV* (e.g., V. 141: "There is no knowledge void of an object of knowledge, because that would involve the destruction of it essence, ... and because the mind is not independent."[120]) and in the *BS* (e.g., 19.2: "There is no knowledge void of an object."[121]). Luckily, the text of these two *pādas* has but one doubtful reading, which is insignificant,[122] and one correction, which is clear.[123] I am unable to get any fully satisfying sense out of *pāda* d, but it may be objecting to the idea that the consciousness which cognizes the objects presented by *avidyā* is unreal. This is not impossible, since we have already seen that Maṇḍana seems to consider the *anirvacanīya-khyāti-vāda* perilously close to the Śūnyavāda. If *matā* in the MS, which Kuppuswami Sastri leaves unchanged, were amended to *matiḥ*, this interpretation would be supported; for it could then be translated, "What *avidyā* can there be where there is no cognition?"[124] However that may be, Maṇḍana seems to have kept in the *BS* the opinion that the consciousness which appears in error, of which error is the distortion, is real. *Avidyā* is dependent on *vidyā*.[125] Compare the next verse of the *VV*:

1.53

V. 152: "*Since* by its very nature *avidyā* is not separated *from vidyā*, in it there is the apprehension (of something) as it is not; *vidyā* is called *avidyā*."[125a]

Unfortunately, the lacuna in *pāda* b breaks up the argument more than in the preceding verse. In addition, 'as it is not' (*atattvena*) is a correction for the MS's *ātmatvena*, which, since the next verse belongs to a refutation of '*ātma-khyāti*' (note the presence of the word in the first half), raises the possibility that V. 152 also may be against the Vijñānavāda. However, I find it hard to get any sense at all either from the MS or from the reconstructed reading that would connect V. 152 to V. 153, so I will proceed on the assumption that it is against the *anirvacanīya-khyāti-vāda*. The emendation of the MS's *prabhijñota* to *prabhidyeta* in *pāda* a seems reasonable. The MS reading *ātmatvena* in *pāda* c can be easily explained by the assumption that the copyist was confused by the occurrence of *ātma*—in the next verse. Kuppuswami Sastri's reconstruction of the first half seems to be based on *pāda* d. It is supported by *BS* 13.11f.: "*Avidyā* is not without *vidyā*. It is thus: even the vision of difference is not devoid of illumination, for if that were absent not even difference would appear."[125] Maṇḍana thus may have thought that the inexpressibility formula (or his opponent's version of it) not only disconnected error from an object, but also set up *avidyā* as something separate from consciousness (notice the opponent in the *VV* does not use the *tattvānyatva* formula), having an independent though deficient and ambiguous reality. This problem does not occur in the *anyathā-khyāti-vāda*, because the consciousness does have a real contact with the substrate of error, and part of the cognition it has of it is real knowledge (the shell in fact is bright and shiny). Later, writing the *BS* from a purely Vedāntic standpoint, he could avoid this problem by considering not only the existence or non-existence of *avidyā*, but also its identity or difference to Brahman. By saying it is neither identical with nor different from, he could avoid giving it an independent reality.

1.54

Inexpressibility is mentioned once more in the *VV*, in Vs. 155-156b: "The externality of the object of error is not denied by the sublating (cognitions); (by them) one does not arrive at (its) internality, nor does one think of it as being indescribable. Rather one arrives at the fact that the external object does not belong to that place and time."[125b]

Maṇḍana argues from the nature of the cognition that removes the error to the nature of the error. When one realizes, "It is not silver, but mother-of-pearl", one does not think that what one saw previously is indescribable, or utterly non-existent, or existing only in the mind, but that it does not exist here and now. This passage adds nothing requiring further content to our knowledge of the theory of *anirvacanīya-khyāti* that he was opposing.

The Possible Influence of Śaṃkara's Use of Anirvacanīya on Maṇḍana's

1.55

It is possible that Maṇḍana was influenced in his use of *anirvacanīya* by a misreading of the places where Śaṃkara uses the *tattvānyatvābhyām anirvacanīya* formula.[126] If one did not notice that Śaṃkara in his *bhāṣya* on *BSū* 1.4.3 uses it as a gloss on *avyakta*—'undeveloped or unmanifested', as Thibaut translates[127]—and that the formula here is too far from the word *īśvara* for *tat* in *tattva* to refer to it, and that the *bhāṣya* on 2.1.14 says unequivocally that the Lord is other than name and form, which are described as *anirvacanīya*, Śaṃkara could easily have been taken to say that *nāma-rūpa*, also called *māyā-śakti* and the like, is neither identical with nor different from *īśvara*.

1.56

In *BSūB* 2.1.14 (462.9-16) the opponent asks how one can say that the origin, etc. of the world are from Brahman, when it is supposed to have no second thing besides it. Śaṃkara answers that the Lord has name and form, his power of illusion (*māyā-śakti*). which is *tattvānyatvābhyām anirvacanīya*. The context might lead one to think that he meant it was neither identical with nor different from Brahman. In addition, he calls this power 'the self, as it were, of the omniscient Lord', which might suggest or seem equivalent to the notion that it is neither the Lord nor other than He.

1.57

In *BSūB* 2.1.27 (476.26-477.4) the opponent says that the Advaitin cannot consistently maintain that Brahman is without parts, because if it is, it either changes as a whole, which would mean its destruction, or does not change at all, and so there will be no universe. But if part changes and part does not, the scriptures will be contradicted, and there will be a division of forms (*rūpa-bheda*) in Brahman. Śaṃkara counters this by saying that the division of forms is "made by *avidyā*, defined as name and form, both evolved and non-evolved, indescribable as this or that" (*avidyā-kalpitena. . .nāma-rūpa-lakṣaṇena vyākṛtāvyākṛtātmakena tattvānyatvābhyām anirvacanīyena*). Again, the context, the problem of getting from the one Brahman to the multiple world, might suggest that *tat-* in *tattva* refers to Brahman, even though the word *Brahman* does not appear before it (though it does immediately afterwards).

1.58

Although Śaṃkara, in his use of the terms *māyā* and *avidyā*, tends to distinguish them,[128] Maṇḍana identifies them.[129] This would have facilitated Maṇḍana's applying to *avidyā* what he might have understood Śaṃkara to have said about *māyā*. This would be made even easier by *BSūB* 1.4.3 (378.1), where Śaṃkara calls the 'seminal power' (*bīja-śakti*) *avidyātmikā*, '*avidyā* by nature' or 'consisting of *avidyā*' (which parallels another term in the series of epithets, *māyā-mayī*, 'made of *māyā*'), rather than *avidyā-kalpitā*, 'formed by *avidyā*' or 'imagined through *avidyā*', as at 2.1.14 (462.15) and 2 1.27 (477.1), thus seeming to identify the two concepts. He might also have been influenced in identifying the two by the *VPv*'s calling *avidyā* a *śakti* of Brahman, just as Śaṃkara calls *māyā* a *śakti*. All this is, however, very speculative and uncertain.

1.59

As has been observed already,[130] Śaṃkara may have refrained from calling either *māyā* or *avidyā sadasadanirvacanīya* on the grounds that this would have been giving it too much reality. Since we know from the *VV* that at least *avidyā*, if not *māyā*, was described thus in his time, his failure to do so cannot have been chance; it must have been a deliberate refusal.[131] His approach, as Paul Hacker has noted,[132] is more cosmological and theistic than that of later Vedāntins of his school. The word *māyā*, introduced to explain how the Lord can produce the manifold world, is at once his power and a sort of material cause of the world.[133] It would have seemed as substantializing a power of this sort to say that it was not non-existent. On the other hand, since his doctrine of *māyā* belongs to a 'propaedeutic' level,[134] it would be unnecessary to deny the real existence of *māyà* in the same breath in which it was taught. That would be implicit in the rest of his teaching. However, Śaṃkara does deny *māyā*'s reality in the three passages we have just discussed, by calling it *avidyātmikā* or *avidyākalpitā*. Making a similar distinction of levels, he accepts provisionally the doctrine of *bhedābheda* in parts of the *BSūB* and rejects it in others.[135] On the final level of instruction, he does not want to admit that the world as different from Brahman exists at all. He says, "As the space (enclosed by) jars, water-pots, or the like is not different (*ananyatvam*) from universal space, and as such things as the waters of mirages are not different from the salt desert flats and the like. . .so all this diversity of objects and agents of enjoyment and so on is non-existent as different from Brahman (*Brahma-vyatirekeṇābhāva*)" (*BSūB* 2.1.14, 455.1-456.1).[135a]

1.60

Maṇḍana, on the other hand, pays relatively little attention to Brahman as the personal Lord of the universe, producing it and ruling it by his power and will. He is less concerned with cosmology, more with epistemology. While Śaṃkara gives a practical religious teaching and worries little about total consistency in the details,[136] Maṇḍana gives a relatively more consistent scholastic system. He therefore almost totally lacks the propaedeutic level of instruction, and is obliged to give a more precise statement on *avidyā-māyā* within a tightly organized, more or less 'one-levelled' system. Therefore he must be sure from the beginning to say that *avidyā* is not existent.

1.61

Moreover, his epistemological approach lets him see the idea of inexpressibility in a different light. Because he does not call *māyā* or *avidyā* a *śakti* of Brahman, or say that it is the material cause of the world, he does not have to avoid substantializing it by refraining from saying it is not non-existent. He works in a different manner from Śaṃkara, less by separating the Self from *avidyā* and the world,[137] than by examining the world and finding Brahman in it, showing that difference (*bheda*) is not given even in our ordinary direct experience. For him, 'the universe is non-dual',[138] it 'has positive being through Brahman's positive being.'[139] It is possible that this helped to make him feel that it was not giving *avidyā* too high a status to call it neither existent nor non-existent.

Maṇḍana's Development of the Theory

The Theory in the Brahma-siddhi

1.62

In some places in the *Brahma-siddhi*, Maṇḍana defends the *anyathā-khyāti-vāda*, whereas he defends the *anirvacanīya-khyāti-vāda* in others. Should we conclude from this that he held that *anyathā-khyāti* is the best explanation for empirical error, and *anirvacanīya-khyāti* for transcendental error? If we do, we could say that it is possible that at the time of writing the *Vibhrama-viveka* Maṇḍana already accepted the Advaita Vedānta, along with the theory of the inexpressibility of error, but considered that theory inadequate or merely unnecessary for everyday error. He wrote three books on the Pūrva-mīmāṃsā, at least two of them before the *Brahma-siddhi*, and it appears that at least when writing the *Vidhi-viveka* he was already a Vedāntin.[140] His continuing interest in the Pūrva-mīmāṃsā is obvious in his extended discussion of Vedic injunction in the *BS*,[141] and is doubtless connected with his advocacy there of the *jñāna-karma-samuccaya-vāda*.[142] It is not impossible that he could have written a book on empirical error from the view of the Bhāṭṭa Mīmāṃsā while adhering to Advaita and to the inexpressibility of transcendental error. Before attempting to determine whether this is the case, however, we must see whether or not he divides the two sorts of error in the *BS*.

1.63

Schmithausen[143] maintains that *anirvacanīya-khyāti* is Maṇḍana's own theory as a Vedāntin in the *BS*, and that his prolonged defense of *anyathā-khyāti* in the *Niyoga-kāṇḍa* (*BS*, pp. 136-50) is brought in purely to refute a specific argument of the Prābhākara. This opponent says that the Veda teaches Brahman by enjoining meditation upon it, because what is an authority for an activity (meditation) qualified by something is an authority for the existence of what qualifies it (the Brahman). Maṇḍana says this is not so, because meditation is a sort of cognition, and there is the possibility of cognizing things as other than they are. Maṇḍana, Schmithausen says, could refute the Prābhākara on this point without departing from the Bhāṭṭa Mīmāṃsā. Therefore, he concludes, Maṇḍana's theory of error as a Vedāntin should be sought in such passages as *BS* 9.18-10.2.

1.64

But it seems more likely that Maṇḍana held to the theory of *anyathā-khyāti* even as a Vedāntin. In the *pūrvapakṣa* to the passage Schmithausen gives as an example, where it is clearly a question of transcendental error (see our discussion of the passage above, §§1.1-1.3), two possible definitions of *avidyā* are given

(9.2-10). The first is *agrahaṇa* or *tattvāgrahaṇa*, 'non-apprehension (of the truth)'. The second is *viparyaya-grahaṇa*, 'wrong apprehension', which is another name for *anyathā-khyāti*. Since Maṇḍana, when he gives alternatives, usually puts the one he prefers last,[144] this may indicate that this is the alternative he prefers. This instance is, however, inconclusive, because it is in the *pūrva-pakṣa*, and is not repeated in the *siddhānta*. On the other hand, it should be observed that Maṇḍana's conclusion does not clearly reject either of the two theories mentioned by his opponent.

1.65

In the next place in which he gives the two alternative theories (20.15-21), he again gives the final place to the theory of wrong cognition. The context is clearly a metaphysical one, because he is refuting the theory of Śūnyatā. In addition, he uses the word *avidyā* to the exclusion of others that, although they can be used for metaphysical error, tend to be used for ordinary error only. He says that if error is 'non-apprehension' (*agrahaṇa*), transmigration cannot be caused by it, because non-apprehension exists equally in liberation (since according to the Buddhist emptiness is the highest reality), and nothing will appear in this world, because *avidyā* is a pure absence of cognition.[145] Then he says that if there is a wrong cognition (*ayathārtha-grahaṇa*, 'apprehension not in accordance with the object'), this theory of universal emptiness is impossible, "for a positive thing, not appearing as it is, can appear with a superimposed form which is not really there, but if (all things are) void, on what can there be a superimposition?" Maṇḍana's placing *anyathā-khyāti* as the last theory mentioned indicates that it was the theory he preferred. In addition, his discussion of 'superimposition' (*adhyāsa*) here links up with his theory of the causality of *avidyā*, because he several times says that works or suffering and delusion are 'superimposed by *avidyā*' (*avidyādhyasta*).[146]

1.66

At 32.8 there begins a long discussion between a *pūrvapakṣin* who maintains that there is no connection at all between works and knowledge and an opponent to him who is not necessarily the *siddhāntin*,[147] but who may represent his ideas in part.[148] This opponent to the opponent states that although the arising of knowledge is by itself the cessation of nescience defined as non-apprehension, this is not true of 'false knowledge' (*viparyāsa-jñāna*, i.e. *anyathā-khyāti*), which is not an absence (*abhāva*), but a positive entity (*bhāva*) that must actively be put down by knowledge (cf. the *bhāva-rūpā avidyā* of later Vedānta). The destruction of *avidyā* is something 'to be accomplished' (*sādhya*) by *vidyā* (32.18-33.8). In the final *Siddhānta* (35.1ff.) this notion is implicitly adopted to the extent that repetition (*abhyāsa*) of knowledge is needed to end the influence (*saṃskāra*) of *avidyā*. Also, the word *viparyāsa* is used in 35.2 as equivalent to *mithyāvabhāsa*, 'false appearance' of 35.1, 4 and *mithyā-darśana*, 'false vision' of 35.4, indicating that he accepts it as a proper word for the error that makes us see duality.

1.67

To turn to the defense of *anyathā-khyāti* in the *Niyoga-kāṇḍa* (136.18-150.24), it appears that even there Maṇḍana is not solely concerned with refuting the Prabhākara's argument, but is also interested in the implications of this theory for transcendental error. At the end of his defense (148.22-150.24) he uses a problem connected with transcendental error in a proof of *anyathā-khyāti*. He says that the aim of the injunction of knowledge of the Self supposed by his opponent would have to be the dissolution of the form of that which is not the Self. But if the Self does not appear with the form of something other than it, what is there to be dissolved? The opponent replies that *avidyā* is twofold, that which covers (*ācchādika*), and that which projects (*vikṣepikā*). Of these, the dissolution of covering nescience is the fruit of the injunction. Maṇḍana replies that this is not so, since it is more the cessation of the projective nescience, of the apprehension of difference, which is productive of many and various sufferings, that we desire, than the cessation of the mere non-apprehension of non-difference, and the existence of projective nescience implies *anyathā-khyāti*.

1.68

It therefore seems clear that Maṇḍana in the *Brahma-siddhi* accepts the theory of wrong cognition even as a Vedāntin.[149] It would be strange for him to spend so much effort to defend it in the *BS*, after having already written a separate treatise on it, if he did not think it directly relevant to the totality of his system. Similarly, his critique of the Prabhākara theory of *niyoga*, after having written the *Vidhi-viveka* on the same topic, is part of his proof that the Upaniṣadic texts need not be injunctive for them to convey a meaning, a point essential to the Vedānta.

1.69

How then are we to reconcile the two theories of *anyathā-khyāti* and *anirvacanīya-khyāti*? Maṇḍana does not tell us himself, but I think we can say that the theory of wrong cognition accounts for the process of error, how it comes about, and its relation to the object before us (shell, rope, *abheda*, Brahman), and the theory of inexpressibility, the status of being of the false cognition along with its content (silver, snake, *bheda*, the world). Error, *avidyā*, misrepresents reality, shows it other than it is. Therefore it cannot be real. But it appears, and has some connection with reality, so it cannot be unreal. Therefore it can be described as neither real nor unreal. *Anyathā-khyāti* describes the process of superimposition of the unreal on the real. *Anirvacanīya-khyāti* explains what it is that is superimposed. Maṇḍana probably, after writing the *Vibhrama-viveka*, decided that the two theories must be reconciled. To have upheld Kumārila's theory unadulterated he would have had to accept the full existence, though at another place and time, of the thing falsely presented, which would have destroyed Advaita. To have dropped it in favour of the even more radically realistic *akhyāti* of Prabhākara would have destroyed Advaita even more completely. To have upheld the Vedānta theory of inexpressibility without the other would have been to forget the need for a real, positive substrate—one cause of his objection in the *VV*, as we have noted.[150] Therefore he embraced both theories.

The State of Maṇḍana's Thinking in Writing the Vibhrama-viveka

1.70

What were Maṇḍana's opinions when writing the *Vibhrama-*

viveka? Was he at all inclined to accept *anirvacanīya-khyāti*, or to divide error into empirical and transcendental? There are several possibilities. He might have been a pure Mīmāṃsaka, rejecting Advaita totally, and with it the theory of the inexpressibility of error. He might have accepted Advaita along with inexpressibility, but have written the *VV* from a purely Mīmāṃsaka point of view, without attempting to reconcile the arguments with the exigencies of defending Vedānta, or else he might have written the *VV* as part of his total system. Finally, he could have accepted Advaita, but rejected inexpressibility.

1.71

If he were a convinced anti-Vedānta Mīmāṃsaka when he wrote the *VV*, he would presumably have given the most up-to-date form of the opponent's theory available. Otherwise he would be failing in his duty as a defender of the Mīmāṃsā theory. Since he does not mention the best form of the theory of *anirvacanīyatva*, the one which he later defends in the *BS*, in which it is united with *anyathā-khyāti*, I think we can say that at the time of the composition of the *VV* it did not exist—presumably because he himself was yet to invent it. I do not think we can rule out the possibility that Maṇḍana did not accept Advaita at all at this time. Although the thought of the *VV* has many similarities to the *BS* and to the rest of his corpus,[151] there is nothing in it to indicate any inclination to the Vedānta, nor as we shall see below, to *anirvacanīya-khyāti-vāda*.

1.72

If in fact he were already a Vedāntin, he could have written his treatise on error from the purest Mīmāṃsā point of view, setting an example for his illustrious commentator Vācaspati Miśra of defending a system not his own with the best arguments he could give. But again, if this was what he was doing he was lacking in his duty as a defender of Kumārila's views, or else was not yet aware of the improved version of the theory he refutes. But I do not think it likely that he was writing without regard to his own views. His obvious piety for Kumārila, whom he refers to in the honorific plural,[152] does not keep him from major innovation—though not, to be sure, opposition—in the *VV* itself.[153] Besides, I have not been able to find in the rest of his work a place where he clearly refutes a doctrine put forward in the *BS*; and none of them, except perhaps the *Mīmāṃsānukramaṇikā*,[154] seems to be merely a commentary on a system he does not accept. Always he shows self-confidence and innovative intellectual energy.

1.73

If he were neither a thoroughgoing Mīmāṃsaka nor an Advaitin totally disregarding his own views in writing a work of Pūrva-mīmāṃsā, he could have intended the book to fit into his own system. In so far as he refutes in the *VV* the theory of inexpressibility of error which he accepts in the *BS*, this could only be done by dividing error into transcendental and empirical, and examining only the latter in the *VV*. But this is unlikely. In his presentation of the *anirvacanīya* theory, both sorts of error are included and no distinction is drawn between them.[155] Also, as observed above (§1.47), the *VV* seems to reject deliberately the idea of a provisional, *vyāvahārika*, truth. Finally, if he accepted the combination of *anirvacanīya* and *anyathā-khyāti* as he later did, we would expect him at least to show some sympathy for the theory of inexpressibility, but he shows none. As we noted before, (§1.46) the similarity in phraseology between V. 29 defending *anirvacanīya-khyāti* and V. 47 introducing his own *siddhānta* does not show that he considers them akin, but that he considers *anyathā-khyāti* a better answer to the same problems. The brevity of its refutation might show that he at least thought it relatively inoffensive and near to his own theory, were it not that the refutation, in the *siddhānta* section of the book, of the *ātma-khyāti*, which he clearly rejects, is even briefer (V. 153, if it is indeed against the *ātma-khyāti*, which Schmithausen doubts[156]); and that, as the refutation of *ātma-khyāti* has already been achieved in the *Pūrvapakṣa* section by the *asat-khyāti-vādin* (Vs. 5-8), so the refutation of *anirvacanīya-khyāti* has already been taken care of by the arguments against the *asat-khyāti-vāda*, by the *akhyātivādin* in the *pūrvapakṣa* (V. 38), and by the *siddhāntin* (Vs. 120c-149d).

1.74

Could he, being an Advaitin as well as a Mīmāṃsaka, have wished to refute the theory of inexpressibility of error in a book written in the tradition of Mīmāṃsā when he had already rejected it as an Advaitin? It is hard to tell. Nothing in the *VV* supports such a conclusion; nothing opposes it. As an Advaitin he might have rejected the *anirvacanīya* theory uncombined with *anyathā-khyāti* as being as bad as Śūnyavāda,[157] but a Mīmāṃsaka would have been just as eager to refute it for that and other reasons.

1.75

Therefore it seems to me the most probable conclusion that when he wrote the *Vibhrama-viveka* Maṇḍana totally rejected the doctrine of the inexpressibility of error.[158] We cannot tell whether he was at the time of the earlier book a doctrinaire adherent of the Karma-mīmāṃsā or whether he already held to some form of Advaita. Because he ignores in the *VV* the developed form of the theory that appears in the *BS*, we may assume that the *BS* is the later book, which is confirmed by an apparent quote of the *VV* in the *BS*.[159] It would be strange indeed if he should ignore the combined theory if it existed, or treat a simpler form after having expounded the more complex. He must have had a change of mind after writing the *VV*. If the former, his 'conversion' was from Mīmāṃsā to Advaita (which might find some small confirmation in the tradition of his conversion to Vedānta by Śaṃkara, though he could not have got the idea of *anirvacanīyatva* from him). If the latter, it was merely to *anirvacanīyatva*.

CHAPTER II

VIVARTA

2.1

Maṇḍana Miśra's use of the term *vivarta*—a term closely related to *anirvacanīya*—is both philosophically interesting and historically important, and so demands careful examination. We will begin by quoting and translating the passages of the *Brahmasiddhi* in which he employs it, giving some comments after each passage when most convenient, and then we will see what peculiarities can be observed in his usage, and what are his sources and innovations. *Vivarta* (or *vivartana*) and *vivartate* will be translated throughout by 'appearance' and 'appear', respectively.

2.2 7.23-8.10

An opponent has said that since the power of vision cannot operate on itself, and since one can infer from the object seen (i.e. from the fact that it *is* seen) a seer (different from the seen), the *śrutis* that state the oneness of all things with the Self cannot be taken literally (6.7-11). Maṇḍana gives several counterarguments to these objections (7.20ff.), and then says:

> api ca ekatva evāyaṃ draṣṭṛdṛśyabhāvo 'vakalpate, draṣṭur eva cidātmanas tathā tathā vipariṇāmād vivartanād vā; nānātve tu viviktasvabhāvayor asaṃsṛṣṭaparasparasvarūpayor asaṃbaddhayoḥ kīdṛśo draṣṭṛdṛśyabhāvaḥ; na hi cityāsaṃsṛṣṭaṃ cetitam iti yujyate. (P) ekāntaḥkaraṇsaṃkrāntāv asty eva saṃbandha iti cet, (S) na, citeḥ śuddhatvāt apariṇāmāt apratisaṃkramāc ca. (P) dṛśyā buddhiś citisaṃnidhes tacchāyayā vivartata iti cet, (S) atha keyaṃ tacchāyatā? (P) atadātmanas tadavabhāsaḥ; (S) na tarhi paramārthato dṛśyaṃ dṛśyate; paramārthataś cādṛśyamānaṃ draṣṭṛvyatiriktam astīti durbhaṇam. (P) yo 'pi manyate—dṛśyatayaiva dṛśyaṃ vyavasthāpyate, na saṃbandhena; darśanaṃ ca 'idam' iti parāgrūpaviṣayam. (S) sa vaktavyaḥ—satyaṃ parāgrūpaviṣayam; tat tv ekasyaivātmanas tathā tathā vipariṇāmād vivartanād vā darpaṇatala ivātmanaḥ; tathā hi darpaṇatalastham ātmānaṃ vibhaktam ivātmanaḥ

pratyeti; cites tu vibhaktam asaṃsṛṣṭam tayā cetyata iti duravagamam.

"Moreover, the relation of seer and seen is possible only if they are one, by the seer—the Self which is consciousness—modifying or appearing in this or that way. But if there is multiplicity, what sort of relation of seer and seen is possible between two things whose natures are different, whose forms are mutually unconjoined, which are unconnected? For it is illogical to say that something is cognized which is not conjoined with consciousness. (P) But there is connection by their both entering into the same mental organ (*antaḥkaraṇa*). (S) No, because consciousness is pure, does not change, and does not enter into (anything else). (P) If you say that the intellect (*buddhi=antaḥkaraṇa*) which is (really) an object of sight (not a seer) appears (*vivartate*) with the image of consciousness by proximity to it. (S) Then what is this 'having its image'? (P) Something which is not a thing appearing (*avabhāsa*) as that thing. (S) Then the thing seen is not really seen, and it cannot be said that something which is not really seen is different from the seer. (P) The thing seen is established as different by the very fact that it is something seen, not by its connection (with the intellect or the Self), and the object of sight is something of an exterior aspect—'this'. (S) He who thinks this should be answered as follows: it is true its object is something of an exterior aspect, but that (exterior aspect) could be of the one Self, by its modifying or appearing in this or that way, as of oneself (seen) in the surface of a mirror. For in a similar way one perceives oneself in the surface of a mirror as if different from oneself; whereas it is hard to understand how something different from consciousness and unconjoined with it can be cognized by it."

2.3

Several observations should be made about this passage before proceeding to the next. First, *vivarta* and *pariṇāma* are distinguished. Twice Maṇḍana gives both terms as options: *vipariṇāmād vivartanād vā*.[1] The fact that he gives them as options indicates not that they are interchangeable,[2] but that they are different.[3] Furthermore, after Maṇḍana points out that the consciousness (the Self) does not change (*apariṇāmāt*), and so cannot enter into the *buddhi*, the opponent suggests that the *buddhi* appears (*vivartate*) with the image of the consciousness. Since the possibility of a *pariṇāma* of the consciousness has already been rejected, *vivartate* must differ from *pariṇāma* in meaning. It should be noticed that Maṇḍana does not reject the second proposal of the opponent, that there is an appearance, a *vivarta* or *avabhāsa*, (note that these terms seem to be approximately synonymous, and cf. §2.9 below) of the Self in the *buddhi*. This shows that though he allows the option he prefers the hypothesis of a *vivarta*. It should also be remarked that *vivarta* here involves the idea of reflection. It is used in the development of the Sāṃkhya epistemology which the opponent proposes and Maṇḍana accepts, in which the *buddhi*, which is by itself something seen (*dṛśya*), a product of *prakṛti*, unintelligent and unluminous, cooperates in the production of an act of knowledge by reflecting both the external object and the light of the Self. (Cf. 15.25-16.4, where a similar epistemology is accepted.) However, as Maṇḍana modifies the teaching, this mirroring is not real, nor is the difference of the seen from the seer. He also uses the image of reflection in a mirror explicitly, at the end of the passage. To be sure, he uses it after giving both terms, not just *vivartana*, but he goes on to say that "one perceives oneself in the surface of a mirror *as if* different from oneself." The use of 'as if' (*iva*) shows that he rejects the possibility of a real *pariṇāma*. Finally, note that the word *vivarta* involves the idea that all things are appearances of consciousness, a sort of *Vijñānādvaita* unlike the Advaita of Śaṃkara.

2.4 18.1-3

api ca prakṛtirūpānvitā vikārāḥ; *vāgrūpānvitaṃ ca jagat*; *ato vāco vipariṇāmo vivarto vāvasīyate.*

"Moreover, modifications are accompanied by the form of their material cause, and the universe is accompanied by the form of speech. Therefore it is ascertained to be a modification or an appearance of speech."

2.5

This, like the quotes to follow, is part of a passage proving that everything is identical with the word (*śabda*) (16.23-19.13). Note again that the option is given of *vipariṇāma* or *vivarta*. The passage as a whole is directly inspired by the *Vākyapadīya* and the *vṛtti* thereon, to which it shows many close similarities both of thought and of wording.[4] What we have just quoted seems to be inspired in particular by *VPv* I.1 (6.1-7.1): *tat tu bhinnarūpābhimatānām api vikārāṇāṃ prakṛtyanvayitvāc chabdopagrāhyatayā śabdopagrāhitayā ca śabdatattvam ity abhidhīyate*. For further comments on the place of the grammatical tradition in the development of the concept of *vivarta*, see below.

2.6 18.17-19

tathā ca tadrūpopagrāhyaṃ jagat tadvivarta iti pratīmaḥ. api ca santy arthā vyāvahārikāḥ, yeṣāṃ na śabdavivartād anyat tattvam; tatsāmānyād itare 'pi tathāvasātavyāḥ; yathā 'kuryāt na kuryāt' iti vidhiniṣedhau, vākyārthaḥ, samūhaḥ, asantaś cālātacakraśaśaviṣāṇādayaḥ.

"And so we understand that the universe which is grasped under the form of it (speech) is an appearance of it. Besides, there are things which form part of ordinary linguistic usage, which have no other reality than an appearance of the word. Other things also must be considered to be the same, since they belong to the same category. For instance, injunction and prohibition—'One should do; one should not do'—the meaning of the sentence, a collection, and non-existent things such as a circle made by a torch or a hare's horn."

2.7

Maṇḍana goes on to prove that these things are unreal, having no reality but that of a *vivarta* of speech. The use of *vivarta* here without the alternative *vipariṇāma* shows that it is Maṇḍana's choice.

2.8 19.1-4

evaṃ vākyārthaḥ; saṃsargo na samsargivyatirekeṇa kaścit, na saṃsargī asaṃsargirūpātiriktaḥ, na jñeyaśūnyaṃ jñānam; na vikalpapratyayo vāgrūpoparāgarahita iti vāktattvam eva tathā tathā vivartata iti nyāyyam.

"The same is the case of the meaning of the sentence: Conjunction (which is the meaning of a sentence) is nothing over and above the things conjoined. The thing when conjoined is not distinct from its form when unconjoined. (But) knowledge (such as that conveyed by a sentence) cannot be void of an object, (and) a constructive cognition (*vikalpapratyaya*=*savilpakā jñāna*) cannot be lacking in the form of speech. Therefore, it is logical to say that the essence which is speech alone appears in this way or that."

2.9

Again Maṇḍana's use of *vivarta* without *vipariṇāma* shows his preference. This passage also helps to justify our translation of *vivarta* by *appearance*. At 18.25-19.1, at the end of the argument on prohibition and injunction, which, like this passage, aims at showing that certain things in verbal usage are but *vivartas* of the word, Maṇḍana says: *tasmāt pravṛttinivṛttyānuguṇyena śabdatattvam eva tathā tathāvabhāsata iti sāṃpratam.* "Therefore it is proper to say that the essence which is the word alone appears in this way or that, favouring activity or abstention from activity." The parallel in thought and expression between this and the last sentence of the passage under discussion here is perfect; some of the words are different, but they are replaced by synonyms. We must therefore conclude that *vivarta* and *avabhāsa* are synonyms. Cf. the remark on *vivarta* and *avabhāsa* on §2.3 above, and also §2.12 below.

2.10 19.11-14

sarvathā vāgrūpādhīno jñeyabodha iti sarvaṃ jñeyaṃ vāgrūpānvitaṃ gamyata iti tadvikāras tadvivarto vā; mṛda iva ghaṭādayaḥ, candramasa iva jalataraṅgacandramasa iti. anye tu—mṛdādidṛṣṭāntadarśanāt pariṇāmitāṃbrahmaṇo manyante; tad apākriyate—akṣaram iti.

"In any case the knowledge of the object depends on the form of speech. Therefore every object is known as accompanied by the form of speech, and so it is a modification or an appearance of speech, as pots and the like are of clay, as the moons in the waves of water are of the moon. But others, because we see (in *śruti*) examples like that of clay, think that Brahman undergoes modification. This is rejected by the word 'Imperishable' (in *BS* I.1)."

2.11

Again Maṇḍana gives the option (replacing *vipariṇāma* with its synonym *vikāra*). But it is clear that for him *vivarta* and *vikāra* are not synonymous, because he gives separate examples for the two terms: pots are modifications of clay, but the reflections of the moon in the waves are not modifications of it, but appearances of it. Maṇḍana does not make it absolutely obvious by his phrasing that the first example goes with *vikāra* and the second with *vivarta*, but both Śaṅkhapāṇi and Ānandapūrṇa agree that such is the case.[5] Besides, he goes on to reject both the idea that Brahman undergoes modification and the example of pots and clay which illustrates it. (Arguments against them are given in 19.15-22.) Maṇḍana prefers the idea of reflection, which allows for the appearance of many things which are based on one thing (which is therefore their *prakṛti* or *upādāna*[6]) without subjecting that thing to change.

2.12

There is additional justification for the translation of *vivarta* by 'appearance', supplementing the remarks in §2.3 and §2.9 above. Compare the following:

7.24: *draṣṭur eva cidātmanas tathā tathā vipariṇāmād vivartanād vā*
13.12: *para eva prakāśas tathā tathā prakāśate*
18.25-26: *śabdatattvam eva tathā tathāvabhāsate*
19.3: *vāktattvam eva tathā tathā vivartate.*

From these sentences it is obvious that Maṇḍana uses *vivartate* as equivalent to *avabhāsate* or *prakāśate*, 'appears'. Vasubandhu, in verse 18 of the *Triṃśikā*, has a similar construction:

sarvabījaṃ hi vijñānaṃ pariṇāmas tathā tathā /
yāty anyonyavaśād yena vikalpaḥ sa sa jāyate//[7]

"Consciousness is the seed of everything. Modification in this way or that proceeds through mutual influence; by it this or that determination is produced."

The possibility cannot be excluded that Maṇḍana knew this *kārikā* of Vasubandhu. Vasubandhu talks about *pariṇāma* rather than *vivarta*, although for him the two terms were not different in meaning. But this construction with *tathā tathā* I have not been able to find anywhere else with either *pariṇāma* or *vivarta* in Maṇḍana's other predecessors.

2.13

One of the peculiarities of the concept of *vivarta* in Maṇḍana is that, as we have seen, it involves the idea of reflection; as an 'appearance' it is specifically appearance in a reflecting surface. This is not paralleled in the development of the concept prior to Maṇḍana. The *VP* and *VPv* both use (on one occasion in each) the verb *vivartate* in such a way that it clearly means 'to appear', 'to shine'.[8] However, neither connects *vivarta* with the idea of reflection.[9] Probably Maṇḍana came to make the connection by specifying the notion of 'appearance' which was already associated with *vivarta*. He does not, like some later Advaitins,[10] say that the Ātman is mirrored in *māyā-prakṛti*. In the passage reproduced in §2.2 he does say that it may be mirrored in the *buddhi*. But this mirroring, he adds, is not real (*paramārtha*) and in any case he does not answer the natural question in what is the first mirroring, the *buddhi* being but a product of *prakṛti*. This can be explained by his usual unwillingness to substantialize *māyā* or *avidyā*, to make it a real power of Brahman or *causa materialis*. Besides, if everything is interior to the one consciousness, there is no separate medium in which the Self can be mirrored.[11] The analogy of the mirror-image is therefore not perhaps wholly consistent logically with the rest of Maṇḍana's system, but it does have certain advantages. It disassociates the concept of *vivarta* from Bhartṛhari's, which emphasizes not so much the unreality of the phenomenon as the unreality of its difference from Brahman, in which, as in the *bhedābheda-vāda*, there is a certain continuity between Brahman and its manifestations.[12] There is no continuity between the moon and its reflection. Maṇḍana's conception perhaps has more in common with the *VPv*'s definition: "Appearance is one thing's assuming other false divided forms in the likeness of diversity without ceasing to be itself, like the appearance of objects in dreams", (*ekasya tattvād apracyutasya bhedānukāreṇāsatyavibhaktānyarūpopagrāhitā vivartaḥ*—*VPv* I.1, 8.1-9.1). However, Maṇḍana protects himself against the danger of falling into a 'transformistic' *vijñānādvaita* by using the analogy of reflection rather than that of dream-images. This removes all possibility that the changes and diversity of the phenomena can in any way affect Brahman.

2.14

Nonetheless, it is probable that one of the influences upon Maṇḍana in his theory of *vivarta* was the Vijñānavāda, and with it a variety of Vedānta which taught that all phenomena are *vivartas* or *pariṇāmas* of the consciousness which is the Ātman. In every case of its use in the *BS*, *vivarta* is connected with consciousness. The passage 7.23-8.10, already quoted in §2.2, explicitly says that the relation of seer and seen is by the *vivartana* of the *cidātman*, although Maṇḍana says that this relation is not ultimately real (*paramārtha*).

In the passages which I have quoted from the long passage on *śabdādvaita*, the concept of *vivarta* is still associated with consciousness, because the arguments which Maṇḍana makes to show that everything is *śabda*, or a *vivarta* of it, proceed from the fact that all knowledge is accompanied by language. At 19.10-11, just before the last passage we quoted (in §2.10), he says, "The fact that consciousness is consciousness is dependent on the form of speech; or else consciousness is just a power of speech (or 'the power of speech'); some say that even when (speech) is withdrawn there is a subtle power of speech", (*vāgrūpādhīnam eva citaś cititvam. vākśaktir eva vā citiḥ; tatpratisaṃhāre 'pi sūkṣmā vākśaktir ity eke*). To be sure, Maṇḍana's arguments in the *śabdādvaita* passage are preceded by similar ones in the *VP* and *VPv*. Still, the resemblance of his phrasing to verse from Vasubandhu, and the doctrine of 7.23-8.10 (§2.2), which is not found in the *VP* and *VPv*, make it appear likely that the grammatical tradition was not the sole influence on Maṇḍana's conception of *vivarta*. Although, so far as I know, there is no other evidence that Maṇḍana was directly aware of Vasubandhu, it is clear that he knew both Dharmakīrti and Dignāga,[13] and so it is not impossible that he knew the earlier master of the Vijñānavāda.

2.15

The existence of a school or schools of Vedānta in which all things are *pariṇāmas* or *vivartas* of *vijñāna* is attested by the *Tattva-saṃgraha* of Śāntarakṣita and Maṇḍana's own *Vibhrama-viveka*. In the chapter on the doctrine of the Ātman held by the Vedāntins (*Aupaniṣadakalpitātmaparīkṣā*),[14] Śāntarakṣita presents their doctrine in these words:

nityajñānavivartto 'yam kṣititejojalādikaḥ/
ātmā tadātmakaś ceti saṅgirante 'pare punaḥ// 328//
grāhyalakṣaṇasaṃyuktaṃ na kiñcid iha vidyate/
vijñānapariṇāmo 'yam tasmāt sarvaḥ samīkṣyate// 329//

"'Others proclaim that (all) this, earth, fire, water, etc., is a *vivarta* of eternal knowledge, and that that (eternal knowledge) is the nature of the Ātman. There is nothing here which has the marks of an (eternal) object to be apprehended; therefore everything is observed to be a *pariṇāma* of consciousness."

I have left *vivarta* and *pariṇāma* untranslated, because to translate them as heretofore, by 'appearance' and 'modification', respectively, would make it appear that they might have different meanings, whereas it is obvious that for Śāntarakṣita, and presumably for the school of Vedānta he describes, they are synonyms. Either might be translated by 'modification' or 'development'. (This fact, as well as the fact that neither Śāntarakṣita's verses nor Kamalaśīla's *Pañjikā* on the chapter recalls either the wording or the arguments of the *BS*, shows that Hacker is wrong in speculating that Śāntarakṣita has Maṇḍana in mind here.[15]) This school of Vedānta is so close to Vijñānavāda Buddhism that Śāntarakṣita himself says that the only thing wrong with it is that it holds consciousness to be permanent (*nitya*—V. 330). Maṇḍana, on the other hand, saw that if consciousness is *nitya*, it cannot undergo modification.

2.16

In the *Vibhrama-viveka*, in the section setting forth as a *pūrvapakṣa* the *anirvacanīya-khyāti-vāda* (Vs. 28-36, §1.39), the last verse uses the term *vivarta*:

vibhrameṣu vivartatvam ato brahmavidāṃ matam// 36cd//

"Therefore the knowers of Brahman think that error is an appearance."

2.17

I have already remarked that this passage shows that the concept of *anirvacanīyatva* was already current in Maṇḍana's day in Vedānta circles, as well as in the grammatical tradition (§§1.40-41). It also shows that *vivarta* was used in an illusionistic sense within the Vedānta before him.[16] The Vedānta which Maṇḍana describes here and rejects later in the *VV* is a sort of *vijñānādvaita*, in which all things are forms of the one consciousness. But it is an illusionistic *vijñānādvaita*, in which the forms are unreal (*asatya*—V. 35, cf. V. 34). (For this reason, and because it teaches the inexpressibility or error as existent or non-existent, Maṇḍana's *pūrvapakṣa* here probably does not represent the same school, person, or book of Vedānta as the *pūrvapakṣa* in the *Tattva-saṃgraha.*) It attempts to disassociate itself from Vijñānavāda Buddhism, in which the unreality of the forms of consciousness is, if not denied, at least not strongly emphasized[17] (cf. §1.48). The passage as a whole is a discussion of error. The fact that this passage defending *anirvacanīyatva* ends by saying that error is a *vivarta* shows that for this school the two concepts were very closely allied, indeed that in its opinion a *vivarta* is necessarily *anirvacanīya.* (For the association of the two concepts in the *VPv*, see above, §1.5). The *BS* does not say that a *vivarta* must be *anirvacanīya*, but it cannot be concluded that Maṇḍana did not think that it did; for, as we have seen (§§2.3, 2.9, 2.12), *vivarta* seems to be synonymous with *avabhāsa,* and in *BS* 9.11-12 (§1.2) *mithyāvabhāsa* or *avabhāsa* as a synonym for *avidyā* or *māyā* is called *anirvacanīya.*

2.18

The image of a reflection is not used in this passage. Because it is not used in connection with *vivarta* anywhere else before Maṇḍana, as far as I know, it may be that it is Maṇḍana's own contribution to the theory.

2.19

Because the word *pariṇāma* is not used here, whereas it is common as a synonym for *vivarta* in pre-Maṇḍana works where *vivarta* is used, and because, this Vedānta being illusionistic, it could hardly believe in a *pariṇāma* of Brahman, it is probable that for this school the two terms were not synonymous. In addition, the casual way in which Maṇḍana gives the option of the two terms in the *BS* shows that he was not the first to distinguish them.[18] If he were trying to separate two concepts from each other by assigning to either of them one of two words which previously were equivalent in meaning, he would give a definition for each. There is reason to believe that even as early as the *VPv* *vivarta* and *pariṇāma* were sometimes distinguished, even though the *VPv* for the most part uses them interchangeably.[19] In the *vṛtti* on *VP* I.120, several things are mentioned which some have thought to be the cause of the world.[20] Among them is 'an appearance unconnected with birth and modification' (*janma-*

pariṇāmāsaṃsargaṃ vivartam—184.1). To be sure, the *pariṇāma* mentioned here may not be a *pariṇāma* of Brahman, but *pariṇāma* within the world after it has come into being by *vivarta*. It may be *pariṇāma* as one of the 'six modifications of being' (*ṣaḍ bhāvavikārāḥ*[21]), whence it is mentioned along with birth (*janma*). Still, it does seem that the two words are differentiated here. It would not make much sense to translate as we would have to, if we took them as synonyms, 'a modification unconnected with birth and modification'. The sentence is very obscure, and while *pariṇāma* may refer to modification within the world after its production, it gives better sense if we take it as referring to a modification of Brahman. Then the point would be that the world is brought about by an illusory appearance of Brahman, which does not really come into birth (cf. Gauḍapāda's *ajātivāda*) or undergo transformation. To the objection that the *VPv* usually seems to identify *vivarta* and *pariṇāma*, the reply may be given that it is not stating its own opinion here, but giving that of others. Besides, the *vṛtti* in at least one other place appears to deny modification in Brahman. Commenting on *VP* I.1, it quotes this verse (14.1-2):

tathedam amṛtaṃ brahma nirvikāram avidyayā|
kaluṣatvam ivāpannaṃ bhedarūpaṃ vivartate||

"So this immortal Brahman, which does not undergo modification, through nescience appears in the form of difference, having, as it were, come to be soiled."[22]

Vikāra is used instead of its synonym *pariṇāma*. It appears that it is distinguished from *vivarta*, even though elsewhere it is used where we would expect *vivarta*. But it is hard to pin 'Harivṛṣabha' down. As Madeleine Biardeau justly says, he continually shows a 'syncrétisme invertébré'.[23]

2.20

The following conclusions can now be drawn: In his theory of *vivarta*, Maṇḍana was influenced by Vijñānavāda Buddhism, in particular, perhaps, by Vasubandhu, by *śabdādvaita* as taught in the *VP* and particularly in its *vṛtti*, and by Vedānta. The word *vivarta* was already used in Vedānta before him, and he was therefore not the first to borrow it from the *śabdādvaita* for Vedānta. Although it was used by a number of writers interchangeably with *pariṇāma* or its synonyms, there was a school of Vedānta in existence before Maṇḍana which distinguished the two, a tendency visible already in the *VPv*, it seems. Maṇḍana removed those elements in the earlier theories which would have allowed the possibility that the forms of the consciousness might be real modifications of it, while keeping the association of *vivarta* with the concept that things are appearances of consciousness, the consciousness of the Self. He also retained the association of the term with *śabdādvaita*. Taking the fact that the word already could mean 'appearance' he specified it to imply reflection, and this seems to be an innovation on his part.[24]

CHAPTER III

AVIDYĀ

THE CAUSALITY OF AVIDYĀ

3.1

An examination of the words which Maṇḍana uses in the *BS* to signify the causality of *avidyā* and related concepts may allow us to understand better his idea of *avidyā*'s workings.

Words Used With Avidyā

3.2

avidyā-adhyasta	*śokamohādi* (126.16-17)
	śokādayaḥ (127.4)
	karmāṇi (129.12)
avidyā-ākṣipta	*rāga*, which is defined as *abhūtaguṇābhiniveśa* (3.17-18)
avidyā-upapradarśita	the three *aṃśas* in *bhāvanā* (43.23-34)
avidyā-upādāna	*bheda* (10.13)
	karmaphalavibhāga (129.11)
avidyā-kaluṣita	*jīvas* (12.3, 7-8)
avidyā-krīḍita	*prapañca* (20.7, 8)
avidyā-nibandhana	*sarga* (10.19)
	sargavibhāga (10.21-22)
	saṃsāra (20.13, 14; 21.20)
	the *vibhāga* of the individual souls and Brahman (21.11)
karmāvidyā-nibandhana	*saṃsāra* (21.12)
avidyāpūrvakarma-nibandhana	*saṃsāra* (21.18)
avidyā is the *bīja*	of *vyāvahārika jñāna* (63.2-3)
avidyā-vilasita	*bheda* (48.14-15)
avidyā is the *hetu*	of *bandha* (78.10, 129.9)
an *avidyāsaṃskāra* is the *hetu*	of *vibhramas* in *pratyakṣa* (40.9)

Words Used with Māyā

3.3

māyā-nibandhana	*nānārūpāvagama* (6.11)
māyā-gaṃya	*bheda* (125.17)

Words Used With Vikalpa

3.4

vikalpair upapradarśyate	*bheda* (48.11)
vikalpavāsanā-upādāna	*vikalpa* (48.7-8: *bheda* is *anādivikalpavāsanopādāna-vikalpaparidarśitaśarīra*)
vikalpa-paridarśita-śarīra	*bheda* (48.7-8; see previous example).
vikalpa-racita	*śarīrabheda* (48.6)

To this may be added two examples in which *buddhi* or *pratyaya* is clearly, from the context, equivalent to *kalpanā* or *vikalpa*:

That which is *buddhi-*

upadarśita	is *vyavahārāṅga* (62.16,17)
pratyaya-viracita	the object (*artha*) of cognitions in which qualities, universals, and the like are attributed to a substance conceived as different from them (62.17-18)

Words used with Mithyādarśana and Mithyābhimāna

3.5

mithyādarśana-ja	a *saṃskāra* which causes to be erroneous, even a cognition in which one is certain (*niścaya*) (35.12)
mithyādarśana-nimitta	the characteristics (*dharmas*) of a transmigrant (34.16)
mithyābhimāna-nimitta	*śarīrasaṃbandha* (34.21)
mithyādarśanābhyāsa-pariniṣpanna	a *saṃskāra* which causes wrong knowledge to continue even after the operation of a *pramāṇa* (35.15-16)

What Avidyā Produces

3.6

An examination of these tables shows that in Maṇḍana's opinion the most characteristic function of *avidyā* (or its equivalents) is to produce difference of one sort or another, or the apprehension of difference. In eleven instances the description of what it produces (in the right column) contains some word directly referring to difference, division, or multiplicity. Next to this in number are those in which *avidyā* is said to produce transmigration or bondage: they total six. Of course, for Maṇḍana bondage and the apprehension of difference are one and the same. In most of the remainder *avidyā* is said to produce some sort of psychic affliction, either passions (*śoka, moha, rāga*), or a *saṃskāra*, which produces error, or errors in perception. Thus the consideration of what *avidyā* produces shows to Maṇḍana the extreme importance of the concept of difference.

The Operation of Avidyā

3.7

The most common word for the causality of *avidyā* and its equivalents in the *BS* is a vague one: *nibandhana*. This is one of Maṇḍana's favourite words; he uses it for the most varied relations of causality or dependence.[1] It is best to translate it when used in compounds as vaguely as possible: 'based on' or 'caused by'. Maṇḍana probably acquired his taste for its frequent use from Bhartṛhari, who uses it with equal frequency.[2] Maṇḍana uses the equally vague words *racita, viracita, bīja* and *-ja* once each. Perhaps this shows an unwillingness to commit himself to a particular model for the causality of *avidyā*, or a disconcern with the problem. He uses words denoting efficient causality only thrice (*hetu* once and *nimitta* twice, the latter in a passage which seems to be quoting Śaṃkara [see Appendix A, §§8-12]), too few to commit him to the idea that *avidyā* is the efficient cause. (In this he is like Śaṃkara, who also uses *nimitta,* but avoids, by the use of other words, committing himself to *avidyā*'s being the efficient cause.[3]) Maṇḍana shows a certain partiality for the use of words meaning 'displayed by': *ākṣipta, paridarśita* and *vilasita*, each occurring once, and *upadarśita* and *upapradarśita* twice each, a total of seven instances of the use of words in this category. These no doubt are intended to suggest the unreality of what *avidyā* produces. In addition, they have a certain similarity to a term specially characteristic of Śaṃkara in this connection, *pratyupasthāpita*, and the like which are probably meant to show that between *avidyā* and its products there is, as Hacker says, 'ein Kausalverhältnis ganz eigener Art'.[4] Twice the word *avidyākrīḍita*, 'the play of *avidyā*', is used. (If one interprets *vilasita* as 'play' rather than as 'display', the number of occurrences in this category may be increased to three.) The word *adhyasta*, 'superimposed', is used three times, indicating that the idea of superimposition, *adhyāsa*, was not very important in Maṇḍana's conception of *avidyā*, although it is most important in Śaṃkara's.[5] Cf. our discussion of *adhyāsa* in §§3.23-26.

3.8

The word *upādāna*, used thrice, demands separate examination. In its first use it serves to identify the opinion that *avidyā* is without beginning or motive as belonging to the *avidyopādānabhedavādins*, 'those who teach that *avidyā* is the *upādāna* of difference' (10.13). Maṇḍana does not clearly rank himself among these, though he does not reject their doctrine of the beginninglessness and motivelessness of *avidyā*. Because he does not clearly include himself in this school, and because, as will be shown below, he does not restrict the word *upādāna* to the material cause, we cannot say that he considered *avidyā* the material cause of the world. In fact, we do not even know that the school he refers to understood *upādāna* in the sense of 'material cause'.[6]

3.9

In the next use of *upādāna* (48.7-8), a Buddhist opponent suggests that difference (*bheda*) is *anādivikalpavāsanopādānavikalpaparidarśitaśarīra*, "having a 'body' that is displayed by mental construction whose *upādāna* is the influence of beginningless mental construction". Again, this is not Maṇḍana himself speaking, although he puts the opponent's suggestion in such a way that he can take it over, and the phraseology may reflect the opponent's way of speaking more than Maṇḍana's. Compare 73.8-9, where a Buddhist opponent says that the appearance of non-difference has for its *upādāna* a beginningless *vāsanā*. (I have left this out of the above tables, because it is without doubt an opinion which Maṇḍana rejects, unlike the case of 48.7-8 under discussion.) The opponent in both passages is clearly Dharmakīrti. I am not aware of any passage where Dharmakīrti says exactly what Maṇḍana's *pūrvapakṣa* says in 48.7-8, but he does use the term *anādivāsanopādāna*,[7] and Vācaspati Miśra, in a discussion with a Buddhist in the *Nyāyavārtikatātparyaṭīkā*, has the Buddhist say that *vikalpas* are *anādivikalpavāsanopādāna*.[8] (Unfortunately, the possibility cannot be ruled out that Vācaspati was influenced in his wording here by the very passage in the *BS* that we are discussing.) In any case, *upādāna* would not have implied for Dharmakīrti a material cause like the *prakṛti* or *pradhāna* of the Sāṃkhya; it would mean rather a basis, a substrate. Therefore, 48.7-8 does not show that Maṇḍana believed that *vikalpas* are the material cause of *bheda*. In fact, when he restates the Buddhist's suggestion to say that it is the same thing that he himself teaches, he says: *bhedaḥ...vikalpair eva kevalam upadarśyate* (48.11), without using the word *upādāna* at all.

3.10

In the final use of *upādāna* with *avidyā* (129.11), which does represent Maṇḍana's own opinion, it is obvious that the word cannot be taken to mean 'material cause'. Maṇḍana says that *avidyā* is the *upādāna* of the division of works and fruits (*karmaphalavibhāga*), but in the very next line, he says that works are 'superimposed by *avidyā*' (*avidyādhyastāni hi karmāṇi*—129.12).

3.11

It was said above that in the *BS upādāna* does not mean 'material cause'. It is convenient now to examine the uses of the word in other contexts than that of the causality of *avidyā*. In *BS* 15.10-17, the word is again used by a Buddhist; it is applied to a *svalakṣaṇa* as the cause of the *svalakṣaṇa* that immediately follows it.[9] In 60.12-18, the Buddhist position is stated that only the particulars (*viśeṣa-svalakṣaṇa*) are real, and that non-difference (*abheda*) is a mental construct (*kalpanā*) which has them for its substrate (*upādāna*) and its object (*viṣaya*). Then Maṇḍana's *siddhānta* is stated: only non-difference is real, and mental constructions of difference have non-difference for their substrate and their object. This is illustrated by the simile of the moon and its reflections in the waves, which is not an instance of material causality. *Upādāna* seems to be about equivalent to *viṣaya* in meaning, and could best be translated by something like 'substrate' or 'real basis'. The passage 70.5-22, which is part of the discussion on the positions set forth in this passage, uses *upādāna* in the same way; it appears to be equivalent to *āśraya* in 70.21. In 72.4-21, part of the same discussion, the opponent gives as an illustration of his theory that *abheda* has *bheda* for its *upādāna* the simile of the forest and the trees: the reality is just the separate trees, they are the *upādāna* of the notion which collects them into a single whole and erroneously calls them 'a forest', as if they were one thing. Maṇḍana again uses the counter-example of the moon and the waves, and adds to it that of a face in a mirror or other surface. He says that the face is the *ālambana* of its reflections, and *abheda* the *ālambana* of *bheda* (72.12-13). Therefore *upādāna* should be translated so as to be synonymous with *ālambana*, 'basis'. Finally, at 125.18-126.4, *bhedavikalpa* is again said to have *abheda* as its *upādāna* and to be a mere appearance, as reflections are not real things that are really produced from the original and different from each other, but mere appearances, of which the original is the *upādāna*, or as words, sentences, and chapters are nothing different from the letters, which are their *upādāna*.

3.12

Because *upādāna* does not in general in the *BS* mean 'material cause', and because in two out of the three places in which it is used in composition with *avidyā* or a synonym it is not certain that what is said is Maṇḍana's own opinion, and because he more often uses other terms to express the causality of *avidyā*, it can be seen that Maṇḍana did not think of *avidyā* as being a *causa materialis* like the *prakṛti-pradhāna* of Sāṃkhya. In this he agrees with Śaṃkara and disagrees with most of Śaṃkara's followers, beginning with Sureśvara.[10] Maṇḍana does not want to substantialize *avidyā*, or to give it an existence separate from Brahman. But to make it a material cause would inevitably compel him to do so. Therefore he, for the most part, chose words to describe its causality which either were vague or suggested the unreality of its products.

AVAIDYĀ AS 'BEGINNINGLESS' AND 'CONNATURAL'

3.13

It is known that Śaṃkara almost never calls *avidyā anādi*, 'beginningless'. He uses *anādi* once in the *BSūB* with *adhyāsa*, and once in the *BGB* with *avidyā*.[11] He reserves the word *anādi* for *saṃsāra*, and calls *avidyā naisargikī* or *nisargajā*, 'inborn, connatual'.[12] Maṇḍana, on the other hand, calls *avidyā* both *anādi* and *nisargajā*. The following tables show his usage of these two words in the *BS*.

Anādi

3.14

avidyā	8.22, 10.14, 11.17, 22.13, 32.18, 28.14-15, 60.16
avidyāsaṃskāra	40.9
avidyānubandha (of *pratyakṣa*)	40.18
avidyā and *jīva*	10.12, 14
tamas	159.15
mithyādarśana	35.15
mithyādarśanābhyāsa	35.4
vikalpavāsanā	48.7
vibhrama	11.15
saṃsāra	21.18

Naisargika and its Synonyms

3.15

Naisargika	
avidyā	11.18, 12.9
rāgādinibandhanapravṛttayaḥ	27.5, 7, 11
Nisargajā	
avidyā	12.7, 43.23-24
pratyakṣādinibandhana vibhaktavastuparicheda	40.5
Svābhāvika	
avidyā	11.17, 25

3.16

It is clear from these two tables that Maṇḍana frequently calls *avidyā* (or its equivalents) *anādi*. In fact, he uses *anādi* with *avidyā* far more often than with *saṃsāra*, with which he uses it only once. Hacker, if I understand him correctly, says that Śaṃkara avoids using *anādi* with *avidyā* because it is slightly more emphatic than *naisargika*, and tends more to erect *avidyā* into an 'eternal metaphysical entity'.[13] If this is so, one would expect Maṇḍana to take the same precaution, because he shows an equal desire to avoid materializing *avidyā*. But a look at the table in §3.14 may show why he does not think it necessary to do so. In several cases it is not *avidyā* which is without beginning, but an 'impression' or 'influence' of error: *avidyāsaṃskāra*, *mithyādarśanābhyāsa*, *vikalpavāsanā*. To call such an impression beginningless is not to substantialize it.

3.17

Naisargika and *anādi* are not synonyms, in Maṇḍana's usage. At *BS* 11.17 he uses both *anādi* and a synonym of *naisargika* in one sentence: *svābhāviky anādir avidyā nirhetuḥ*, 'Avidyā is connatural, beginningless, and causeless.' (This is part of the *pūrvapakṣa*, but based on what Maṇḍana has just been saying.) Śaṅkhapāṇi's comment is illuminating: *avidyā tv anaditvāt svābhāvikīti nirhetuḥ*, 'But *avidyā* is connatural because it is beginningless, and therefore it is without a cause' (34.26). We may say that the concept of the beginninglessness includes that of connaturality, and that this is why, although they are not synonymous, the two words are used together only once.

Avidyā and Its Synonyms

3.18

Avidyā has a number of synonyms in the *BS*. An investigation of them will show that he considers *avidyā* more in epistemological terms than as a material cause or a power of Brahman. It is equivalent to *māyā* and to *mithyāvabhāsa*, 'false appearance': *evam eveyam avidyā māyā mithyāvabhāsa ity ucyate* (9.12). It is also used interchangeably with *kalpanā*, 'imagination' or 'mental construction': *yat tu kasyāvidyeti, jīvānām iti brūmaḥ*. (P) *nanu na jīvā brahmaṇo bhidyante*; *evaṃ hy āha—'anena jīvenātmanānupraviśya'* (*CU* 6.3.2) *iti*. (S) *satyaṃ paramārthataḥ, kalpanayā tu bhidyante*. (P) *kasya punaḥ kalpanā bhedikā*? (10.3-5). Note that the same question is asked about both *avidyā* and *kalpanā*, 'Whose is it?' This shows that the two terms are equivalents. Another synonym of *avidyā* is *vibhrama*, 'error'. Compare 11.15-16, *anādau vibhrame hetvanveṣaṇam asāṃpratam eva*, and 11.17, *nanu svabhaviky anādir avidyā nirhetuḥ*. (Cf.60.6-7: *kiṃ tarhīdam? avidyā vibhramaḥ.*[14]) It is clear from this that *vibhrama* is not restricted to everyday errors, but can be employed for the basic error that causes bondage.

Bhedadarśana, 'the vision of difference', is another term used interchangeably with *avidyā*: *atha bhedadarśanena brahmaiva saṃsarati, abhedadarśanena ca mucyate; tatra sarvavibhāgapratyastamaye yugapat sarvamokṣaprasaṅgaḥ. tasmād avidyayā jīvāḥ saṃsāriṇaḥ, vidyayā mucyante* (12.4-7). *Viparyāsa*, 'error' (but implying the theory of *anyathā-khyāti*[15] is employed as a synonym of *avidyā* at 33.1-3: (Objector to the *pūrvapakṣa*:) *'anādir aprayojanā cāvidyā' ity uktam* (cf. 10.14); *tatra ca hetvanuyogo niravakāśaḥ; viparyāsatatsaṃskārayoś ca parasparahetuphalabhāvena vyavasthānān na doṣaḥ. Mithyādarśana*, 'false vision', is also synonymous with *avidyā*. Compare the following two sentences: *tathā nirvicikitsād āmnāyād avagatātmatattvasyānādimithyādarśanābhyāsopacitabalavatsaṃskārasāmarthyān mithyābhāsānuvṛttiḥ* (35.4-5); and *śakyo hi āmnāyād evānādir avidyāsaṃskāro vibhramahetuḥ pratyakṣādiṣu saṃbhāvayituṃ niścetuṃ ca dehātmābhimāna iva*. Finally, there are *ajñāna* and *mithyājñāna*, 'Ignorance' and 'false knowledge'. Verse IV.6cd in the *kārikās* (158.6), *api cājñānataḥ sukhī duḥkhī jivaḥ prakaśate*, is glossed thus in the prose: *api ca 'śoky aham' 'duḥkhy aham' 'dhanādini mama naṣṭāni' iti viśuddhabrahmātmano jīvasya mithyājñānam.*

3.19

The following words have been shown to be synonymous with *avidyā* in Maṇḍana's usage: *māyā*, *mithyāvabhāsa*, *kalpanā*, *vibhrama*, *bhedadarśana*, *viparyāsa*, *mithyādarśana*, *ajñāna*, and *mithyājñāna*. With the exception of *māyā*, they all refer to false knowledge, a quality of the knowing subject, rather than to anything objective. Even *mithyāvabhāsa*, 'false appearance', which might be thought to suggest what Hacker, in speaking of *vivarta*, calls 'an objective illusion',[16] usually in the *BS* connotes the subjectivity of the appearance. Maṇḍana says that *mithyāvabhāsas* may continue even after the truth is known from a *pramāṇa*, because of the strength of the accumulated *saṃskāras* of previous *mithyāvabhāsas*, as the error of seeing a double moon or of confusion about the cardinal points continues even after a qualified person has told one the truth (35.1-5). The *mithyāva-bhāsa* that molasses is bitter which a sick person may have continues even though he knows it is sweet (35.23-24). However, Maṇḍana does use one example of an 'objective illusion': actors on the stage produce emotions by a *mithyāvabhāsa*, even though the spectator knows the events represented are not real (35.22-23). But even in this case the reference may be to the false appearance in the spectator's mind, rather than to that on the stage. Therefore *mithyāvabhāsa*, like the other synonyms of *avidyā*, is something belonging to the subject (specifically to the *jīva* rather than to Brahman). Once again we see Maṇḍana's determination to avoid hypostatizing *avidyā* by making it something 'external' to the seer, such as a *śakti* of Brahman or the material cause of the world.

3.20

This is probably the reason that Maṇḍana does not often use the term *māyā*. In fact, it is never used in the *BS* except for some particular purpose. Twice it is used to gloss *RV* 6.47.18 (=*BU* 2.5.19)—*indro māyābhiḥ pururūpa īyate*—when that text is adduced as a proof of *abheda*: at 6.10-11 and 125.16-17. Once, in the sentence at 9.12, just quoted in §3.18, it is one of a list of synonyms: "It just is for this reason (that it is neither entirely real nor entirely unreal), that (nescience) is called 'nescience', 'illusion', 'false appearance'." At 10.24-11.1, it is used in an illustration against the objection that Brahman cannot be the cause of the world, because if it were, the inequalities of enjoyment in the world would show that it had the faults of inequity and cruelty. Maṇḍana says, among other things, that a magician (*māyākāra*) shows no partiality or dislike in making various illusory people appear with their limbs intact or cut off. At 13.22 *māyā* again comes in an illustration. It is not true, Maṇḍana says, that something unreal cannot produce an effect, because magic (*māyā*) can occasion delight or fear. Finally, *māyā*, or rather *māyāmātra*, is used to solve certain problems concerning the nature of *avidyā*. In the passage beginning at 9.11, Maṇḍana attempts to show that the adherents of all schools must agree that *avidyā* is *anirvacanīya*. In conclusion he argues that it is only because *avidyā* is neither existent nor non-existent, because it has no fixed essence but is merely an illusion (*māyāmātratvāt*), that it can be ended. If it were not so, it would be either existent, in which case it would be firmly established in its own essence and could not change or be destroyed, or it would be non-existent, and would never have been there. It seems that Maṇḍana employs *māyāmātra* to mean simply 'illusory', but in the argument here this implies ambiguity (it is neither existent nor non-existent), and instability (it can be ended). The illusory, because it is illusory and not real, is free from the necessity of other things either to exist or not. *Māyāmātra* can be used to imply these things, whereas none of the other words of this class (*avidyā*, *mithyā* and its various compounds, *asatya*, etc.) can. None of them is a convenience word meaning simply 'illusory'.

3.21

The use of *māyā* and *māyāmātra* in 10.9-11 is somewhat similar. The opponent has pointed out that if *avidyā* (or *kalpanā*) belongs to the *jīvas*, there will be mutual dependency—the division of the *jīvas* from Brahman depends on *avidyā*, and *avidyā* is based on the *jīvas* (10.5-8). In reply, Maṇḍana says:

atra ke cid āhuḥ—vastusiddhāv eṣa doṣaḥ—nāsiddhaṃ vastu vastvantaraniṣpattaye 'lam, na māyāmātre; na hi māyāyāṃ kācid anupapattiḥ; anupapadyamānārthaiva hi māyā; upapadyamānārthatve yathārthabhāvān na māyā syāt.

"On this point some say: This fault applies to establishing a real thing—a real thing cannot produce another real thing if it has not already been produced itself—but not to a mere illusion. For it is not impossible at all in the case of an illusion, because an illusion is precisely something whose object is impossible. If its object were possible it would not be an illusion, because it would be in accord with the object."

Again the illusory is illogical and free from the laws that govern real things. *Avidyā*, *kalpanā*, and the like cannot suggest this as well as *māyā* and *māyāmātra* can. In both these instances *māyāmātra* is, as in Śaṃkara's use of it, "just a traditional expression inherited by him, meaning simply 'illusory'."[17] But Maṇḍana uses it where no other expression will do.

3.22

We see that Maṇḍana seldom uses *māyā*, and never without some specific reason, even though he lists it as a synonym of *avidyā* and we might therefore expect him to use both words interchangeably. Śaṃkara uses it much more often than Maṇḍana does, although much less often than he uses *avidyā* and *nāmārūpa*.[18] The difference between the two Vedāntins can be explained in part by Maṇḍana's relative disinterest in Brahman as *Īśvara*. Maṇḍana, like Śaṃkara,[19] identifies Brahman and *Īśvara*, but is little concerned with Brahman's 'personal' side and does not often use the word *Īśvara*. At least as early as the *Bhagavadgītā* and the *Śvetāśvatara Upaniṣad māyā* was associated with *Īśvara*. For example, see *ŚveU* 4.10ab: *māyāṃ tu prakṛtiṃ vidyān māyinaṃ tu maheśvaram*, "Know that *māyā* is *prakṛti*, and the Great Lord is the possessor of *māyā*"; and *BG* 4.6:

ajo 'pi sann avyayātmā bhūtānām īśvaro 'pi san/
prakṛtiṃ svām adhiṣṭhāya saṃbhavāmy ātmamāyayā//

"Even though I am unborn and my being is eternal, even though I am Lord of beings, resorting to my own *prakṛti* I take birth by my own *māyā*."

It should also be observed that *māyā* is identified with *prakṛti* in the quote from the *ŚveU*, and, if not identified, at least closely associated with it in that from the *BG*. Maṇḍana therefore had two reasons to avoid the word *māyā*. First, its connection with *Īśvara*. Not only was Maṇḍana uninterested in Brahman as *Īśvara*, and therefore in concepts and problems related to Brahman in its personal aspect, but the theistic overtones of the concept of *māyā* (clearly visible in Śaṃkara's use of the word[20]) tended to convey the idea that it is a *śakti* of Brahman (as it is in *BSūB* 2.1.14, 462.16). Maṇḍana saw no reason to let one or more powers intervene between Brahman and the phenomenal world (see §3.28-29), and, in addition, for *māya-avidyā* to be a power of Brahman would conflict with his doctrine that the locus (*āśraya*) of *avidyā* is the *jīva* rather than Brahman. Second, *māyā*'s association with *prakṛti* (whatever may have been the precise meaning of either of these words in the *ŚveU* and *BG*) tended to substantialize it and make it into a material cause of the world rather than an epistemic defect, into an entity at least distinct from Brahman, if not independent of it. Therefore, Maṇḍana avoids the use of *māyā* as much as possible.

AVIDYĀ AS 'SUPERIMPOSITION'

3.23

It has already been pointed out (§3.7) that Maṇḍana uses the word *adhyasta*, 'superimposed', to denote the causality of *avidyā* only three times. *Adhyāsa* itself only appears once in the *BS*, at 20.18-19. Maṇḍana is arguing against the Śūnyavāda. He says that if one accepts *anyathākhyāti*, *śūnyatā* is impossible, "for a positive thing, not appearing as it is, can appear with a superimposed form which is not really there, but if it is void, on what can there be a superimposition?" (*bhāvo hi yathāvad aprakāśamano 'dhyastāvidyamānarūpaḥ prakāśate*; *śūnye tu kvādhyāsaḥ*.) It appears from this sentence that in Maṇḍana's usage *adhyāsa*, superimposition, implies the *anyathā-khyāti* theory of error.

3.24

The same conclusion results from an examination of the passages of the *BS* in which *samāropa*, another word meaning 'superimposition', is used. Most of them are part of Maṇḍana's argument that an injunction of knowledge does not establish the truth of the content of that knowledge, because knowledge may be erroneous, and not merely a failure to observe something about its object, as the Prabhākaras say, but an active misrepresentation of the object, that is, an *anyathā-khyāti*. (See 135.17 [III.114ab] and gloss 136.14-16, 137.21 [III.123ab] and gloss 138.19-20, 151.19-20, 152.3-6.) In one of the two remaining cases of its use in the *BS*, it means the metaphorical use of a word (134.9). In the remaining case it is applied to the 'superimposition' of a serpent on a rope (131.2). This use does not directly involve *anyathā-khyāti*, but it does show, as the passage using *adhyāsa* just quoted also does[21] (cf. §1.44) that the theory of error as superimposition requires that error must have a substrate.

3.25

Āropa, another synonym of *adhyāsa*, is likewise used in the context of *anyathā-khyāti*. In 94.10-22, Maṇḍana says that error is not a mere absence of apprehension, because the misapprehension of a piece of shell as silver cannot occur unless there is cognition of both the locus of superimposition (*āropasya viṣaya*—the shell) and the thing superimposed (*āropaṇīya*—the silver). The concept of superimposition is associated with *anyathā-khyāti* in the *Vibhrama-viveka* as well. In verse 25 the Śūnyavādin opposes *anyathā-khyāti* on the grounds that error cannot be a superimposition (*adhyāropa*), because 'superimposition' can mean only a metaphorical use of a word. But in a metaphorical use of a word, we are conscious of the difference of the thing identified and that with which it is identified, whereas in error the two things are not discriminated. (This argument is answered in 147cd. Cf. also Schmithausen's commentary on 25, *VV*, p. 99.) In 36b the *anirvacanīya-khyāti-vādin* says that error is neither *adhyāropa* (*anyathā-khyāti*) nor indistinct apprehension (*asphuṭa-graha*). In 66d-67b Maṇḍana says that if *akhyāti* were true, if error were merely the absence of discrimination of two things, there would be no need to have the contact of a sense with an object, or the perception of the object, to have an error of perception. On the other hand, the necessity for the contact of the sense with an object and of the apprehension of the object is explainable if error is the superimposition (*samāropa*) on a perceived object of some other thing.

3.26

It appears from all this that the concept of error as *adhyāsa* has two uses. It forms part of the defense of *anyathā-khyāti*, and in doing so also emphasizes that error must have something real as its object. However, outside of this context, *adhyāsa* and its synonyms are, as we have seen, little used in the *BS*. Śaṃkara, on the other hand, defines *avidyā* as *adhyāsa* (*BSūB* 1.1.1 [Introd.], 39.2-40.1). Why did Maṇḍana avoid the concept outside of certain contexts? Probably because he saw that to define *avidyā* as a superimposition of one thing on another would require, or at least tend towards, the acceptance of the real existence of the thing superimposed. This would destroy non-dualism. Śaṃkara's followers later came to the same conclusion, and rejected the concept of *avidyā* as *adhyāsa* which Śaṃkara, perhaps affected by an early period as an adherent of the *Yoga-darśana*, had put forward.[22]

Śakti

3.27

As has been noted many times in these pages, Maṇḍana Miśra does not accept that *māyā-avidyā* is a *śakti*, a 'power', of Brahman. He avoids using the word *śakti* in the sense of a power in some sense distinct from, but residing in, Brahman. He does not call Brahman or *Īśvara sarvaśakti* or the like, whereas Śaṃkara does so frequently. He does use *śakti* (or *sāmarthya*) more or less as an equivalent of the Buddhist *arthakriyā*, or the capacity to produce an *arthakriyā* (see, for instance, 53.3-54.14), but *śakti* in this sense is nothing distinct from the object which possesses it, it is no separate *thing*, but merely an aspect of its possessor. Similarly he talks of *dṛkśakti* as the Ātman's capacity for vision or *īśana-śakti* as Brahman's capacity to rule, but not as anything different from Ātman or Brahman.

3.28

Maṇḍana seems aware of schools of Vedānta which attribute several *śaktis* to Brahman, although when he refutes them he does not indicate that they are Vedānta schools. He inserts his refutation of them (*BS* 55.23-56.19) in the midst of a long argument against the Buddhist attempt to prove difference (*bheda*) by the fact that things produce different *arthakriyās*. He has said, in 54.15-55.22, that just as a single fire has various effects, such as heating and cooking, so the one Brahman can produce all effects. (He attributes Brahman's ability to do this not to its *śakti* or *śaktis*, but to its 'greatness' [*mahiman*—54.16] or 'extra capacity' [*sāmarthyātiśaya*—54.24, 55.21]. It is probably deliberate that he does not use the word *śakti*.) The *pūrvapakṣin* replies that the difference of effects is dependent on the difference of the fire's powers, and so it is not so that multiple effects proceed from a single cause. Maṇḍana says that if it is indeed the fire that is the cause, then in fact there are several effects from one cause. If the opponent should say that it is only the powers that are the cause, how is it that it is contradictory for one thing to be linked with several effects, but not contradictory for it to be linked with several powers? Moreover, if you say that the *śaktis* are not different from their possessor, then you have said that one thing can be many. It is absurd to say that the oneness of the cause is not contradicted by the multiplicity of powers, which is in the same substrate as the oneness, but that it *is* contradicted by the multiplicity of effects, a multiplicity which resides in other things than the cause. If you say that the powers are different from their substrate, illogicalities follow, no matter how you define 'substrate' (*āśraya*).

3.29

For Maṇḍana, then, there is no need to make *śaktis* intervene between Brahman and the multiplicity of the world. Śaṃkara's answer to this is more complex; he compromises with the *bhedābheda* tradition which ascribes a number of powers to Brahman. He often calls Brahman *sarvaśakti* or *sarvaśaktisamanvitam* (e.g., *BSūB* 79.2-80.1, 86.2, 102.2). In some places he says that Brahman can produce various effects because it is joined with various powers (*BSūB* 2.1.29, 478.8-9; and 2.1.24, 474.9-12). In the dissolution between world-cycles the universe exists in Brahman as a 'seminal power' (*bījaśakti—BSūB* 1.3.30, 336.6; 1.4.2, 377.8-9). But this seminal power is 'made of *avidyā*' (*avidyātmikā*) and is burnt up by *vidyā* (*BSūB* 1.4.3, 377.17-378.2). In *BSūB* 2.1.30 Śaṃkara says that Brahman has different powers, and in 2.1.31 he adds that this division of powers is formed by *avidyā*. A *śakti* of a cause is identical with the cause, and the effect is identical with the *śakti* (*BSūB* 2.1.18, 468.1). This is typical of Śaṃkara's accommodation of *bhedābhedavāda*: he first admits a variety of powers to explain the diversity of Brahman's effects, and then denies that the powers, or their diversity, or their distinction from Brahman, is real. Maṇḍana, here as elsewhere, has a more 'one-levelled' system: Brahman, the one cause of all things, can produce all multiplicity directly, without the intervention of *śaktis*.[23] Of course, elsewhere the real existence of these effects is denied. The 'special capacity' (*sāmarthyaviśeṣa*=*sāmarthyātiśaya*) of Brahman is not to produce many real things, but to *appear* as many (*ekasyaiva vastunaḥ sāmarthyaviśeṣān nānāvabhāso 'bhyupeyatām—BS* 61.13-14, cf. 73.12-14).

3.30

Maṇḍana also speaks of *dṛkśakti*, 'power of seeing', *vākśakti*, 'power of speech', and *īśanaśakti*, 'power of ruling'.

In each case *śakti* denotes a capacity of a thing, an aspect of it, rather than something distinct from it but resident in it, as for instance a quality is. In *BS* 6.7-8 the *pūrvapakṣin* denies Advaita on these grounds:

"The seer and the seen cannot be identical, because the power of seeing must have external objects, because it cannot operate upon itself" (*dṛkchakteś cārthavattvāt svātmani vṛttivirodhāt*). At 7.22-23 Maṇḍana replies: "The power of seeing has an object, because it itself serves (that purpose); and there is no contradiction in its operating upon itself. It is like a lamp, or, as has already been said, like the fruit of a means of valid knowledge." (*dṛkchakteś cārthavattvaṃ svātmopayogāt, na ca svātmani vṛttivirodhaḥ pradīpavat pramāṇaphalavac cety uktam.*) The last sentence refers us back to 3.26-4.15.[24] There the objection was raised that if the bliss that is in Brahman can be known, there will be duality, because knowledge requires an object and an agent. But if it is not the object of knowledge, it is as good as non-existent, and not an aim of man. Maṇḍana replies that it is not true that the fruit of a means of valid knowledge (i.e., valid knowledge) is not the object of knowledge, because if it is unknowable everything else will be unknowable (since it is by valid knowledge that we know things). On the other hand, it is not the object of knowledge, because, if it were, there would have to be another means of valid knowledge to know it, which would have its own fruit. But this would result in a *regressus ad infinitum*, and in any case we do not see any second fruit. Therefore it is the object of knowledge in so far as it is self-luminous, but is not the object of knowledge, in so far as it is not like an external object. Similarly, the agent of knowledge is known, because if it were not known one would not have the idea, 'I know this'. But it is not the object of knowledge, in so far as it is not an external object distinct from the knower. Its being known consists in its self-luminosity. Similarly Brahman and its bliss are the object of knowledge in that they are self-luminous.

3.31

The word *śakti*, then, when it occurs in *dṛkśakti*, does not imply any duality, any operation of the agent of knowledge on an object of knowledge different from it. The seer, the power of seeing, knows itself by being self-luminous. To the *dṛkśakti* of the *Brahma-siddhi* we may compare the *dṛkśakti* and *citiśakti* of Patañjali's *Yoga-sūtras* and the *Yoga-sūtra-bhāṣya* of Vyāsa. For Patañjali and Vyāsa, *dṛkśakti* or *citiśakti* is identical with *puruṣa*, *cit*, *caitanya*, or *draṣṭṛ*.[25] In *kaivalya* the *citiśakti* stands by itself,[26] and the *puruṣa* is self-luminous.[27] In this context *śakti* does not imply anything distinct from consciousness itself. Nor does it suggest that consciousness is ever merely potential. Consciousness is eternally actual; it is only potential in so far as particular determinations of it arise or cease by adventitious conjunction with external *prakṛtic* phenomena.[28] To say *citiśakti* rather than *citi* indicates that there is an unchanging subject and source of all particular cognitions which can exist without them or their objects. The *puruṣa* has the 'power' to lend its light to the knowledge of the evolutes of *prakṛti*, but in *kaivalya* it no longer does so, it is merely the 'power of consciousness'. Similarly, in the *BS dṛkśakti* means the immutable agent of knowledge, which is self-luminous and needs no external object.

3.32

Śakti seems to have similar connotations at 19.10-11: *vāgrūpādhīnam eva citaś cititvam. vākśaktir eva vā citiḥ, tatpratisaṃhāre 'pi sūkṣmā vākśaktir ity eke*, "The fact that consciousness is consciousness depends upon the form of speech. Or else consciousness *is* the power of speech, even when it is withdrawn there is a subtle power of speech, some say." This is inspired by the *Vākyapadīyavṛtti*. Although the *VPv* in places says that Brahman has several powers, I do not think that *śakti* here means a power of *vāc* as *Śabda-brahman*, because the passages which Maṇḍana follows here do not employ *śakti* in this sense. See, to begin with *VPv* 1.123 (189.4-5): "Thus, according to some teachers, the activity of knowledge continues in a sleeping person like the activity in waking, except that the seeds of the impressions of language assume a subtle activity." (*tathaikeṣām ācāryāṇāṃ suptasyāpi jāgradvṛttyā sadṛśo jñānavṛttiprabandhaḥ. kevalam tu tadā sūkṣmāṃ vṛttiṃ pratilabhante.*) Also, 1.124 (190.6): "Even in the state of unconsciousness, (knowledge) continues to be accompanied by the qualities of speech, in a subtle way." (*vāpy asañcetitāvasthā tasyām api sūkṣmo vāgdharmānugamo 'bhyāvartate.*) Finally, 1.126 (193.9-10): "Therefore there is no activity of consciousness which is not joined with the power of speech. Others say that the form of the activity of consciousness *is* the form of the principal word." (*tasmāc citikriyārūpam alabdhavākśaktiparigraham na vidyate. vāktattvarūpam eva citikriyārūpam ity eke.*) *Vākśakti* is used only once in these three passages. I think Maṇḍana's employment of it is in part due to the influence of its use in the *Yoga-sūtra-bhāṣya*. *Vākśakti* is the power of speech—and therefore of consciousness—which is permanently present and actual, self-luminous, but does not always manifest itself in particular cognitions.

3.33

Śakti is used on one other occasion for an eternally possessed capacity which does not require any external object. Maṇḍana has said (126.12-127.5) that when one's true form as Brahman has become manifest in liberation, one obtains all the bliss, knowledge, and lordship that are in Brahman. An opponent objects (127.5-7) that in Brahman, in which there is no duality or diversity, there is nothing to be known or ruled, and so it is impossible for it to have knowledge or lordship. Scriptural expressions such as 'omniscient' (*MuṇḍU* 1.1.9) and 'Lord of all' (*MāṇḍU* 6) must be reconciled with this fact. Maṇḍana replies: 'Its being a lord is not brought about by that which is to be ruled, nor its being a knower brought about by that which is to be known. Rather by its already existent form of knowledge and its already existent power of ruling it attains the object to be known and assigns tasks and gives commands to that which is to be ruled. It is like light or burning. For the sun illumines that which is to be illuminated by its already existent form of light, but its form of light is not dependent on the thing to be illuminated, nor is fire's power of burning dependent on the thing to be burnt.' (*neśitavyakṛtam īśvaratvam, jñeyakṛtaṃ vā jñātṛtvam; kiṃ tu siddhena jñānarūpeṇa siddhayā ceśanaśaktyā jñeyam avāpnoti, īśitavyaṃ ca viniyuṅkte praśāsti ca, prakāśadāhavat; siddhena hi prakāśarūpeṇa prakāśyam prakāśayati vivasvān; na tu prakāśyādhīnaṃ tasya prakāśarūpam, dāhyādhīnā vā agner dāhaśaktiḥ*—127.7-11.) *Śakti* again signifies not a power to some degree distinct from its possessor, but an aspect of its possessor, a capacity that it always has, irrespective of the presence or absence of an external object upon which to exert it. Brahman's power of ruling and fire's power of burning are permanent and independent of objects of their activity. So, although Maṇḍana does not actually use the word *jñānaśakti*, is the power of knowledge.[29] This brings us back to the *dṛkśakti* or *citiśakti* discussed in §§3.30-31. It seems highly probable that it is the *Yoga-sūtra-bhāṣya* of Vyāsa that influenced Maṇḍana in this use of the term *śakti* in the terms *dṛkśakti*, *vākśakti*, and *īśanaśakti* to imply a capacity permanently possessed by the Self or Brahman whether particular manifestations or objects of it are present or not.

3.34

From all this it may be seen that Maṇḍana Miśra does not admit the existence of one or more powers of Brahman. He specifically rejects the existence of several powers of Brahman as being superfluous and illogical. He avoids using the word *sarva-śakti*, 'having all powers', because it might suggest the *bhedā-bheda* doctrine of the multiplicity of Brahman's *śaktis*. On several occasions when he does use the term *śakti*, he gives it a peculiar shade of meaning, so that it signifies a permanent capacity of a thing which it may or may not exercise on external objects, but not anything distinct from the thing itself.

Āvaraṇa and Vikṣepa

3.35

The doctrine of two *śaktis*, 'powers', of *avidyā*, the *āvara-ṇa-śakti*, 'power of concealing (Brahman)', and the *vikṣepa-śakti*, 'power of projecting (the appearance of the multiple universe)', is a commonplace of later Advaita Vedānta. It is missing in Śaṃkara.[30] It is present, however, in Maṇḍana Miśra, and is closely connected with his adherence to *anyathā-khyāti* —a good example of the tight coherence with which the different elements of his system fit together.

3.36

In *BS* 21.8-22.7 a number of arguments are given to show that there may be a fear of a released person's coming back into transmigration. Amongst these is the argument that Brahman is reached in deep dreamless sleep, but we observe that one comes back from that state (21.21-22). No *śruti* is quoted, but the doctrine that Brahman is reached in deep sleep may be found in

CU 6.8.1, 8.3.2-5, and 8.11.1, and *PraśnaU* 4.4. To this argument Maṇḍana replies at 22.16-17: "But in deep sleep only (*avidyā*'s) projection ceases; its influence and the non-apprehension do not cease. Otherwise (deep sleep) would not differ from the fourth (state, above waking, dreaming, and deep sleep, as described in the *MāṇḍU* and Chapter 1 of the *Gauḍapāda-Kārikās* thereon). It is called 'attaining Brahman' only because projection is absent" (*suṣupte tu vikṣepamātraṃ nivṛttam, tatsaṃskāro 'grahaṇam ca naiva nivṛtte; anyathā na turīyād bhidyeta; vikṣepamātrābhāvāt tu brahmaprāptyabhidhānam.*) Brahman is not really attained in deep sleep, because it is not known in that state, since deep sleep is pure unconsciousness, the non-apprehension of Brahman or of anything else.[31] Maṇḍana, apparently following his policy of using the word *śakti* as little as possible, talks of *vikṣepa* rather than *vikṣepa-śakti.* He does not use the word *āvaraṇa* or a synonym, but the opposition of *vikṣepa* to *agrahaṇa* shows that an idea conveyed by the latter is equivalent to that conveyed by *āvaraṇa,* the absence of knowledge of Brahman.

3.37

This passage seems to show the influence of the *Gauḍapāda-Kārikās*. *GK* 1.12 and 13 state the difference between deep sleep and the fourth state (*turīya, turya*), in which there is no *avidyā* and Brahman is experienced.

nātmānaṃ na parāṃś caiva na satyaṃ nāpi cānṛtam/
*prājñaḥ kiñcana saṃvetti turīyaḥ sarvadṛk sadā//*12//
dvaitasyāgrahaṇaṃ tulyam ubhayoḥ prājñaturyayoḥ/
*bījanidrāyutaḥ prājñaḥ sā ca turye na vidyate//*13//

"*Prājña* (the Self in the state of deep sleep) knows nothing, neither itself nor others, neither the true nor the false, but *Turīya* is always all-seeing.

Non-apprehension of duality is common to both *Prājña* and *Turya*. *Prājña* is joined with seminal sleep, but this does not exist in *Turya*."

Deep sleep differs from the fourth state by being a total unconsciousness. Gauḍapāda does not talk about *āvaraṇa-śakti,* but about the absence of cognition, as Maṇḍana talks about *agrahaṇa*. Cf. *GK* 1.15:

anyathā gṛhṇataḥ svapno nidrā tattvam ajānataḥ/
viparyāse tayoḥ kṣīṇe turīyaṃ padam aśnute//15//

"Dream belongs to him who apprehends reality other than it is; sleep belongs to him who does not know reality. When the error in both of these is destroyed one attains the fourth state."

Gauḍapāda recognizes two sorts of error or ignorance—non-apprehension of the truth and wrong apprehension. Non-apprehension corresponds to the *āvaraṇa-śakti* of later Advaita, and wrong apprehension to *vikṣepa-śakti.* Thus a natural link is set up between the two different theories of error *akhyāti* and *anyathā-khyāti* and the two forms of *avidyā.*

3.38

To return to the *BS* passage under discussion before proceeding, it should be observed that Maṇḍana says that both non-apprehension and the *saṃskāra* of *avidyā* persist in deep dreamless sleep. Presumably it is the function of the *saṃskāra* to bring a sleeper back to the diverse consciousness of the waking or dreaming states. Gauḍapāda, in *GK* 1.13, quoted just above, says that in deep sleep the Self is joined with 'seminal sleep' (*bīja-nidrā*). From *GK* 1.15 we know that *nidrā* refers to non-apprehension of the truth. (Cf. *GK* 1.11, quoted in the next *BS* passage discussed.) It is the cause of returning to particular cognitions, as Śaṃkara says in his commentary on 1.13.[32] Maṇḍana's saying that not only non-apprehension, but also a *saṃskāra*, persists in deep sleep is perhaps due to his thinking that if nothing but non-apprehension persists, there can be no explanation why only certain cognitions and not others should arise upon returning to the waking or dreaming states.

3.39

The connection of the doctrine of the twofold *avidyā* with the doctrine of error, and Maṇḍana's dependence on Gauḍapāda in this doctrine are noticeable in another passage where he uses it, *BS* 149.16-150.24. This forms part of Maṇḍana's refutation of those who would maintain that there is an injunction for the knowledge of Brahman. Among other reasons for rejecting such an injunction, Maṇḍana argues that there is no necessity that the cognition prescribed by an injunction be a true one. It could be false, because error is not merely the absence of apprehension (*agrahaṇa*), but an apprehension actively wrong (*viparyaya-grahaṇa*, i.e. *anyathā-khyāti*). In 149.10-16, Maṇḍana argues that there can be no purpose in an injunction of knowledge unless error is wrong cognition, not mere non-cognition. For the injunction must have as its end the dissolution (*pravilaya*) of that which is not the Self, because it is by dissolving what is not a thing itself that we arrive at the knowledge of the thing. But if the Self does not appear with the form of that which it is not, what is there to be dissolved? In 149.16-19, the opponent suggests that *avidyā* is of two sorts, that which covers over the light (*ācchādika* = *āvaraṇa*), and that which projects (*vikṣepikā*). Projective nescience is found in the waking and the dreaming states, where we have cognitions of various objects. Covering nescience is found in deep, sleep, where we do not know anything. It is defined as dissolution (*laya*). The fruit of the injunction of knowledge is the cessation of the covering nescience. The opponent does not say so explicitly, but the point of making the distinction and saying that the fruit of the injunction is the cessation merely of one sort of *avidyā* is to avoid Maṇḍana's argument that knowledge may be actively erroneous, substituting something else for the external object it refers to. If the nescience that is to cease by the knowledge enjoined by the Veda is merely non-apprehension, as covering nescience is, the cognition which removes it must be apprehension of the object, and must therefore be true. The knowledge given by the injunction, and the cognition produced by following the injunction, cannot be false. So, at least, the opponent thinks. Maṇḍana replies, beginning at 149.19, that it is not *ācchādika avidyā* whose termination is desired so much as *vikṣepikā*. In dreamless sleep we no longer experience the various sufferings that we endure in waking and dreaming, and therefore *śruti* often praises this state as blissful (cf. *śruti*'s calling deep sleep the attainment of Brahman, mentioned in the *BS* passage in §3.36). It is the cessation of that *avidyā* that projects manifold sufferings that we want. Besides, you cannot have a division of sorts of *avidyā* unless you accept that error is actively wrong knowledge (*viparyāsa*). If error is merely non-apprehension, it will be the same in all three states, waking, dreaming, and sleeping. Therefore there are two *avidyās*, related as cause and effect. Both the cause, non-apprehension of Brahman, and the effect, apprehension of the world, are present in dreaming and waking, but in deep sleep only the effect is present. As Gauḍapāda says (*GK* 1.11):

"*Viśva* (the Self in the waking state) and *Taijasa* (the Self in the dreaming state) are held to be bound with both the cause and the effect. But *Prājña* (the Self in deep sleep) is bound with the cause, while neither is present in the fourth state."

kāryakāraṇabaddhau tāv iṣyete viśvataijasau/
prājñaḥ kāraṇabaddhas tu dvau tau turye na sidhyataḥ//

3.40

The quotation of Gauḍapāda, the connection of the doctrine of twofold *avidyā* with the four states of the Self, and the connection of the doctrine with the theory of error all show Gauḍapāda's influence. Although Gauḍapāda does not use the words *vikṣepa*, *āvaraṇa*, or *ācchādika avidyā* in the passage from *GK* from which we have quoted several verses (*GK* 1.11-16), it appears that Maṇḍana's terminology is influenced by his. *Laya*, 'dissolution', mentioned by Maṇḍana's opponent as the mark of covering *avidyā*, is ascribed to deep sleep in *GK* 3.35, 42, 44 and 46.[33] Forms cognate to *vikṣepa* appear in contrast with *laya* in all of these but 3.35. One must restrain the mind when it is distracted (*vikṣipta*), and awaken it when it is in *laya*, in deep sleep. When it is neither, then the mind is Brahman. The root *vi-kṣip* here means 'to distract', not 'to project', but the connection between Gauḍapāda's use of it and Maṇḍana's is still close. Gauḍapāda's use approaches the phenomenon of being conscious of the manifold objects of the universe from the side of the mind, which is distracted from its repose in itself to pay attention to various objects. Maṇḍana's use approaches the same phenomenon from the side of the objects, whose multiplicity is projected by *avidyā* even though it does not really exist.

3.41

A comparison with two other passages in the *BS* will further illustrate how Maṇḍana's doctrine of twofold *avidyā* fits in with the rest of his theory of error. As Maṇḍana follows Gauḍapāda in saying that covering nescience is the cause of projective nescience, so at *BS* 143.23-144.3 he says that an erroneous cognition (*viparīta-khyāti*) is occasioned by ignorance of the truth (*tattvājñāna-nimitta*). In *BS* III.152-54 (145.15-20), and gloss

146.4-5, he says that the presence or absence of faults that cause error can just as easily be the means for discriminating non-apprehension and apprehension on the theory of error as wrong cognition (*viparīta-khyāti*) as on theory of non-cognition (*akhyāti*). In fact, if error is wrong cognition (*viparyaya*), the faults will be even more effective in producing error, and therefore their presence or absence will be better as a criterion of true knowledge or error. For on the theory of wrong cognition they not only obstruct the effect that is desired, i.e. knowledge of the truth, but produce the opposite, i.e. a false cognition.[34] The examples do not, of course, explicitly mention the two forms of *avidyā*, but they give a fine illustration of the parallelism of Maṇḍana's thinking on error in general to his theory of the nature of *avidyā*, transcendental error.

CHAPTER IV

NIRVIKALPA JÑĀNA

Object of Nirvikalpa Jñāna

4.1

One of the most important and distinctive elements in Maṇḍana Miśra's system is his analysis of perception (*pratyakṣa*). He attempts to show that *bheda*, difference, is not given in perception, but is a mental construction, a *vikalpa*, a relative concept that follows the direct apprehension of the bare object (*artha-mātra*). It is the form of being (*sad-rūpa*), which is perceived everywhere, that is the true nature of objects, not their difference. Maṇḍana is the first Vedāntin whose works have survived to incorporate such an analysis of perception into his system, showing part of his importance in the history of Vedānta.[1] It is therefore important to know whether the *sat* or *sattā*, 'being', and the *abheda*, 'non-difference', presented in *pratyakṣa* are identical with Brahman, or whether Maṇḍana merely wishes to show that because perception does not apprehend difference, it cannot be summoned to testify against Advaita.

4.2

It might seem that the *abheda* discussed at great length in the *Tarka-kāṇḍa* of the *Brahma-siddhi* is not identical with Brahman, because it is never explicitly identified with Brahman in that *kāṇḍa*. Therefore it might be thought that Maṇḍana's aim is solely that which he states in the introduction to his study of perception (44.4-9), to demonstrate to him who refuses to believe that scripture supercedes perception in authoritativeness when the two are in conflict, who believes that perception is the stronger of the two means of knowledge, that we do not know difference from perception any more than from scripture. His intent would be merely to remove an objection, accepting for the time being the opponent's opinions, rather than to teach a doctrine of his own, to deny that perception apprehends *bheda* rather than to show that it apprehends the *abheda* that is

Brahman. However, if we take into account not only what he says in the *Tarka-kāṇḍa*, but also what he says in the rest of the *BS*, it can be seen that Maṇḍana holds that Brahman is in fact given in every perception.[2]

4.3

First, it should be observed that Maṇḍana identifies *sāmānya*, 'universal', with *abheda*, and *viśeṣa*, 'particular', with *bheda*. For instance, in *BS* 60.10-19, he gives four alternative analyses of the fact that our cognition sees in the object (*vastu*) both an aspect that is common to other objects and an aspect that is peculiar to itself. The universal (*sāmānya*) and the individual (*vyakti*) may be two separate things, as those who teach *saṃsarga* (=*samavāya*) say. Or the object may be one, but made of universal (*sāmānya*) and particular (*viśeṣa*), as the Jainas and Bhāṭṭas say. Or the particulars (*viśeṣa*) may be the object, and non-difference (*abheda*) a *vikalpa* based on it, as the Buddhists say. Or finally (Maṇḍana's own opinion), non-difference (*abheda*) is true, and mental constructions of difference (*bheda*) are based upon it. Here *sāmānya* is more or less equivalent to *abheda*, and *viśeṣa* to *bheda* and *vyakti*. Similarly, at 63.8, it is said, "The universal runs through various particulars" (*sāmānyaṃ bhedāntarānuyāyi*). Here *bheda* is better translated 'particular' than 'difference', and it is clearly opposed to *sāmānya*. Finally, at 64.8-10 Maṇḍana says: 'The particulars are different, on account of their contradiction in form, which is synonymous with mutual non-existence. Even though they differ, the universal is not different, because it is the opposite." (*rūpavirodhād dhy anyonyābhāvaparyāyād viśeṣā bhidyante*; *bhidyamāneṣv api teṣu sāmānyam abhinnam, viparyayāt.*)

4.4

The particular universal which is everywhere present, and which Maṇḍana calls upon to establish universal *abheda*, is *sattā*, being. At 58.20-22, he says: 'Moreover, because the form of mere being is cognized everywhere, it is not true, in the case of objects that have being as their nature, that true knowledge of that which is wrongly thought of as different does not arise in respect to that which it is thought to be different from; for both have being as their nature, and the existence of a means of valid knowledge always (has the form) '(It is) existent', and it is the absence of a means of valid knowledge that is the cause of the knowledge of reciprocal non-existence (i.e. of difference).' (*api ca sanmātrarūpe sarvatra pratīyamāne tatsvabhāveṣu vastuṣu netarābhimata itarābhimatapramāṇānutpādaḥ, satsvabhāvatvāt tayoḥ; 'sat' iti ca sarvatra pramāṇasadbhāvāt; pramāṇābhāvāc cetaretarābhāvajñānam iti*). Everywhere, he goes on to explain (58.22-59.19), we see this one undivided form of being. We recognize it as one and the same thing in all cases, not as a number of different things which resemble each other. Note that *sat* is the 'nature' (*svabhāva*) of everything, that which in the final analysis it is. It also seems to be identical with 'the bare object', 'the thing in itself' (*arthamātra*). The opponent objects (58.22-24): 'But there is no non-different form whatever of objects, because it would be known from recognition, and one who sees merely an object (*artha-mātra*) does not have, with respect to another object, a recognition, 'this is that', as one who sees one cow has with regard to another cow.' (*nanu nārthānāṃ kiṃcid abhinnaṃ rūpam; pratyabhijñānād dhi tad gamyeta; na cārthamātraṃ dṛṣṭavato 'rthāntare sa evāyam iti pratyabhijñāsti, yathā ekāṃ gāṃ dṛṣṭavato gavāntare.*) The bare thing (*artha-mātra*), shorn of any further description or relations, which are nothing but mental constructions, is identified with being. Similarly, at 72.17-19, Maṇḍana says: "The difference of the universe is false, because it is pervaded by non-difference, like the moons in waves. For each of them is accompanied by non-difference, (because we call it) 'the moon'. So also in the case of the difference of the universe, in each case it is accompanied by non-difference—'this', 'that', 'object', 'thing'." (*abhedānuviddhatvāt pratyekaṃ viśvasya bhedo mṛṣā; yathā jalataraṅgeṣu candramasaḥ; tatra hi pratyekaṃ candramā ity abhedānvayaḥ, tathā viśvasya bhede 'pi pratyekam 'idam' 'tat' 'arthaḥ' 'vastu' ity abhedānvayaḥ.*) The most rudimentary and vaguest word that can be attached to a thing, which does not signify any comparisons or relations, denotes what is basic and real in it, that which is found in all things. In 71.8-15, Maṇḍana says that he has shown that the universal and the particular cannot be two different things (*vastudvaya*), nor can they together compose the thing. Therefore we must suppose that one of them is unreal. But in error, such as that of mother-of-pearl mistaken for silver, we never see that the appearance of the bare thing (*vastu-mātra*) is absent, whereas the appearances of the particulars, such as silver, may be absent. 'The bare thing' is contrasted to the particulars (*viśeṣa*); it is therefore, presumably, a sort of universal. Paradoxically, the pursuit of the final reality in the highest abstraction, the most inclusive concept, the *mahāsāmānya*, *sattā*, and in the greatest concreteness, the bare object without any determinations, coincide. They are two ways of approaching what is common to all things. This may in part reflect the influence of Bhartṛhari, who, in accommodating both sides in the debate over whether words refer to the universal or to the substance (*dravya*), says that Brahman as the ultimate reality and the ultimate reference of all words is both the *mahāsāmānya* and the *pāramārthika dravya*.[3] Maṇḍana, however, prefers to use *vastu* or *artha* rather than *dravya*, which he only uses to mean 'substance' in the sense of a substrate in which other things reside.[4] Still, *vastu* is given by Bhartṛhari as a synonym of *dravya*.[5]

4.5

At 71.1-2, Maṇḍana says: "Perception is first, without mental construction, and has for its object the bare thing. The constructive cognitions which follow it plunge into particulars." (*vastumātraviṣayaṃ prathamam avikalpakam pratyakṣam*; *tat-pūrvās tu vikalpabuddhayo viśeṣān avagāhante*). I have not translated, 'The first perception is without mental construction, and has for its object the bare thing', because Maṇḍana does not, as far as I can see, distinguish two sorts of *pratyakṣa*, *savikalpa* and *nirvikalpa*. In fact, he seems deliberately to choose another term for the second cognition than *savikalpa pratyakṣa*, viz., *vikalpa-buddhi*, 'constructive cognition'. In the next two lines, 71.3-4, *pratyakṣa-buddhi* is opposed to *vikalpa-buddhi*.[6] I have not been able to find any place where he uses the term *savikalpa pratyakṣa* or an equivalent in stating his own position. He does use it once in the context of an opponent's opinion. See below, §4.10.

4.6

By this he shows his dependence on the doctrine of perception and mental construction of Dignāga and Dharmakīrti, and his rejection of Kumārila's contention that a cognition may be *savikalpa*, may take into account an object's similarities to and differences from other things, without ceasing to be perception. For Maṇḍana, as for the Buddhists, *pratyakṣa* is always *nirvikalpa*. As he says at 60.1, 'The knowledge of difference (which is, of course, a *vikalpa*[7]) is not perception' (*pratyakṣataiva bhedajñānasya na*...). However, for him it is the universal, the non-difference, that is directly given, the object of *pratyakṣa*, rather than the particular, the *svalakṣaṇa*, the difference. Maṇḍana is quite aware of the similarity of his conception to those of the Buddhists;[8] a number of times he phrases his presentation of his opinion and theirs so as to bring out the symmetry of the two opposing views.[9] Although he makes his Buddhist opponents say that difference is given in perception, he is dependent on them even in refuting this doctrine; for his theory that difference, being a relative concept, is not given in perception, but is rather a mental construct subsequent to perception, and therefore unreal,[10] is but a modification of the Buddhist theory that perception apprehends the *svalakṣaṇa* without any relations.[11] Likewise, his doctrine that perception grasps only something existent (*sat*) (see 58.20-22, translated above, §4.4), and that perception always posits and never negates,[12] resembles the Yogācāra Buddhist doctrine that perception is pure affirmation, and negation an inference and a mental construct.[13]

4.7

Maṇḍana was not, however, the first Vedāntin to hold this doctrine. In the *Śloka-vārttika*, *Pratyakṣa*, 114-16, Kumārila describes a similar doctrine of perception, which the two commentators Umbeka and Pārthasārathi Miśra agree in attributing to the Vedānta.[14] They are as follows:

> *mahāsāmānyam anyais tu dravyaṃ sad iti cocyate/*
> *sāmānyaviṣayatvaṃ ca pratyakṣasyaivam āśritam//114//*
> *viśeṣās tu pratīyante savikalpabuddhibhiḥ/*
> *te ca kecit pratidravyaṃ ke cid bahuṣu saṃśritāḥ//115//*
> *tān akalpayad utpannaṃ vyāvṛttānugatātmanā/*
> *gavy aśve copajātaṃ tu pratyakṣaṃ na viśiṣyate//116//*

"114: Others say there is a highest universal, which is called 'substance' and 'being', and so they hold the object of perception to be the universal.

115: The particulars, on the other hand, are cognised by the constructive cognitions. Some of these are peculiar to each individual, and some reside in many.

116: Perception, which arises without taking into account those (particulars) as peculiar or common, does not differ as it arises in regard to a cow or a horse."

4.8

The point of the second half of 115 is that below the *mahāsāmānya*, the *summum genus*, *sattā*, there are some particulars which are common to many, such as cowness or horseness (these are *sāmānya-viśeṣas*, 'particular universals') and some which are peculiar to one individual (*viśeṣa* as 'ultimate particularity'[15] in the Nyāya-Vaiśeṣika sense). A hierarchy of universals under being as the highest universal is accepted by the Nyāya-Vaiśeṣika, Bhartṛhari, and Kumārila,[16] as well as by Maṇḍana himself.[17]

4.9

The *pūrvapakṣa* of the *ŚV* shows the same preference for *vikalpa-buddhi* over *savikalpa pratyakṣa* that Maṇḍana does. Kumārila's reply (Vs. 117ff.) makes it additionally clear that his opponent does not accept the apprehension of particularity to be *pratyakṣa*;[18] he directs his efforts to showing that this subsequent cognition is also perception, because the sense remains in contact with the object.[19]

4.10

Maṇḍana enrolls himself in the ranks of those who proclaim the universal to be the object of *nirvikalpa pratyakṣa* by quoting as the opinion of an opponent the first half-verse of Kumārila's reply. He says: "As for those who say that the difference of entities is established precisely by our sight of them; for it has been said by (Kumārila), denying that the object of *nirvikalpa pratyakṣa* is the universal, 'That is not right, because in each individual a different form is apprehended'...they have already been refuted."[20] (*ye tv āhuḥ—darśanād eva bhāvānām bhedaḥ sidhyati*; *tathā hi—nirvikalpasya pratyakṣasya sāmānya-*

viṣayatvam apākurvatoktam—"tad ayuktaṃ pratidravyaṃ bhinnarūpopalambhanāt" (*ŚV*, *Pratyakṣa*, 117ab) *iti;...te prāg eva pratyuktāḥ.*--*BS* 58.6-9). Although Maṇḍana here uses the term *nirvikalpa pratyakṣa*, I do not think this shows that either he or the school represented by Kumārila's *pūrvapakṣa* believed that *pratyakṣa* could ever be *savikalpa*. He is merely using Kumārila's own terminology. Kumārila says that *pratyakṣa* may be divided into *nirvikalpa* and *savikalpa*, and that difference is perceived in both. See the second half of the verse quoted by Maṇḍana: 'It does not follow from the fact that it cannot be described (in *nirvikalpa pratyakṣa*) that difference is not there' (*na hy ākhyātum aśakyatvād bhedo nāstīti gamyate*—*ŚV*, *Pratyakṣa*, 117cd).

4.11

It has been shown that for Maṇḍana perception is always *nirvikalpa*, that it apprehends the object by itself, without any relation to other objects, as 'this' or 'an object' or 'being', and that its object is the *sāmānya*, or *abheda*. As already observed, he does not say anywhere in the *Tarka-kāṇḍa* that this *abheda* is Brahman. However, it seems likely from what is said in the other *kāṇḍas* that he does think so. For instance, at *BS* 37.19-24 he says:

"V. I.3: Because all differences are absorbed in it, it is described as a universal, as gold is indicated by the absorption of its differences, such as bracelets, etc.

"Commentary: And because it is described by means of the cessation of particulars, therefore Brahman is described by other men well-versed in the knowledge of Brahman as having the form of a universal: 'This is the great, unborn Ātman, defined as Being'; likewise: 'Being alone is the womb of all difference, the highest material cause.' Similarly, the essence of gold, which is described by the absorption of its particulars, such as bracelets, rings, etc., is called a universal."

> *saṃhṛtākhilabhedo 'taḥ sāmānyātmā sa varṇitaḥ/*
> *hemeva pārihāryādibhedasaṃhārasūcitam//*I.3//

yataś ca viśeṣapratyastamayamukhena tannirūpaṇam, ato 'nyair brahmavidyābhiyuktaiḥ sāmānyarūpam brahma nirūpitam—'sa eṣa mahān aja ātmā sattālakṣaṇaḥ' tathā 'sattaiva sarvabhedayoniḥ prakṛtiḥ parā' iti. yathā suvarṇatattvaṃ kaṭakāṅgulīyādiviśeṣopasaṃhāreṇa nirūpyamāṇaṃ tatsāmānyam iti.

4.12

This passage shows the influence of Bhartṛhari and the *Vākyapadīya-vṛtti*. Of the two quotes within it, the first is based on *BU* 4.4.24-25: *sa vā eṣa mahān aja atmānnādo vasudānaḥ. vindate vasu ya evaṃ veda.* (24) *sa vā eṣa mahān aja ātmājaro 'maro 'mṛto 'bhayo brahma. abhayam vai brahma. abhayam hi vai brahma bhavati ya evaṃ veda.* (25) "Truly, this is the great, unborn Ātman, the eater of food, the giver of wealth. He who knows this gets wealth. Truly, this great unborn Ātman, without old age, without death, immortal, fearless, is Brahman. Truly, Brahman is fearless. Truly, he who knows this becomes the fearless Brahman." The adjective *sattā-lakṣaṇa*, 'defined as being', however, is not found in the *BU*; it comes from the *VPv* 1.145: *...ṛṣayaḥ kecit pratibhātmani vivartante sattālakṣaṇaṃ mahāntam ātmānam avidyāyoniṃ paśyantaḥ pratibodhenābhisaṃbhavanti* (226.4-5). "Some seers appear in *pratibhā* itself; seeing the great Ātman defined as being, the womb of *avidyā*, they unite themselves with it by direct knowledge."[21] Cf., in the *kārikās*, *VP* 3, *jāti* (1), 34cd: *sā (jātir) nityā sā mahān ātmā tām āhus tvatalādayaḥ.* "That (universal, being) is eternal; it is the great Ātman; (the abstract suffixes) *-tva* and *-tal*, etc., express it." The second quote may be inspired by *VP* 3, *Dravya* (2), 15: *vikārāpagame satyaṃ suvarṇaṃ kuṇḍale yathā/ vikārāpagame satyaṃ tathāhuḥ prakṛtiṃ parām//*, "As, in an ear-ring, it is the gold that is true when the modifications have disappeared, so, they say, it is the highest material cause that is true when the modifications have disappeared." The simile in this verse, it might be added, is the same as in Maṇḍana's argument, although, to be sure, it is a commonplace in the Vedānta tradition. It is not possible to know with certainty whether the two quotes in the *BS* are loose quotes of the *VP* and *VPv* or distillations of their meaning, or whether they are direct quotes from some lost text. (If the former, *sarvabhedayoni* in the second *BS* quote might be inspired by *avidyāyoni* in the quote from *VPv* 1.145.) In any case, it is probable that the *śabdādvaita* tradition was one of the influences on Maṇḍana in the formation of his doctrine in this area.

4.13

It is noteworthy that 'universal', in this passage, does not carry so much the meaning of an abstraction, a concept, as that of an ultimate material cause. Although Maṇḍana, or rather the 'quotations' he gives, talk of *sattā*, employing the abstract suffix, the example he gives is of a material cause, gold. Just as, as observed above (§4.4), the search for the ultimate concreteness and that for the most inclusive universal coincide, so here the most inclusive universal is discussed as if it were the final substance.[22] Maṇḍana shows a certain freedom in the use of the term *sāmānya*, 'universal'. Immediately after the passage in the *BS* that we are discussing, in 38.1-5 the objection is raised that no true universal can be without particulars (i.e. without instances). But in Brahman there are no particulars, and so, if you say it is a universal, it cannot exist. Maṇḍana replies that in that case we are using the term 'universal' metaphorically; all we mean is that it is described by the denial of particulars. But the cursory way in which he deals with the objection suggests that he is not much troubled by it, and does not admit the opponent's definition of 'universal'. The fact that he continues to use the word, and does not again say that it is applied to Brahman only metaphorically, points toward the same conclusion. For him, a *sāmānya* is whatever is common to several things, whether one considers it abstractly, as in the case of *sattā*, or concretely, as in the case of gold.

4.14

In any event, it is clear that Brahman, as a *sāmānya*, is identical with *sattā*. Therefore it must be given in perception. This is confirmed by the evidence of the final chapter of the *BS*, the *Siddhi-kāṇḍa*. At 156.4-20, an opponent contends that the Upaniṣads cannot teach us about Brahman. For a word cannot convey information unless its connection with its reference is known, and the connection cannot be known unless the reference itself is known. But Brahman is not known. Therefore we cannot know its connection with the word that denotes it. Neither can a sentence about it convey information, because the understanding of a sentence is preceded by the understanding of the individual words. Maṇḍana's first reply (157.1-9) is that a sentence can convey information about some object not already known by combining a universal already known with a particular set of characteristics. Now, we already know the universals of a cause and being. Scripture can tell us about Brahman as a particular sort of cause, or a particular being, by adding certain other characteristics to these. Then he gives a second suggestion (157.14-21):

"Or else, say that Brahman is not totally unknown in ordinary experience, because it is knowable in every cognition, because no object of cognition except Brahman exists, and cognitions of particulars are always accompanied by the form of the universal, and it has been explained that Brahman is the true thing that is left over when particulars have been absorbed, and because of the example, 'The modification is a name that has its basis in speech; the truth is just "clay" ' (*CU* 6.1.4). What then is taught by the (scriptural) word? The non-existence of phenomenal diversity (*prapañca*). Here both the meaning of the term 'phenomenal diversity' and negation are already known; by their conjunction the non-existence of phenomenal diversity is taught. But this is said to be based upon Tradition alone, because perception etc. are associated with *avidyā*. For, because they do not take (Brahman) as their object under the form where all difference has disappeared, the disappearance of difference is knowable from Tradition (alone)."[23]

4.15

If Brahman is given in all cognitions whatsoever, it is clear that it must be given in perception. What constructive cognitions do, presumably, is to add other things to Brahman as it appears in perception. Compare the definitions of the transmigration and release in *ViV* 277.3-4: "Transmigration is the appearance of the Self as associated with phenomenal diversity. Release is the appearance of the Self as without phenomenal diversity, its abiding in itself" (*saprapañcātmatattvāvabhāso hi saṃsāraḥ. niṣprapañcātmāvabhāso hi mokṣaḥ svātmani sthitiḥ*). Brahman, as that which remains when all particulars are absorbed (Maṇḍana refers back in this passage of the *ViV* to *BS* I.3 and its commentary, just quoted, §4.11), is both the most basic thing and that which exists everywhere; therefore it is that which is known everywhere. Here he states the situation according to the order of being; elsewhere, in the passages from the *Tarkakāṇḍa* we have discussed, he states it in the reverse order, the order of knowledge: 'being' (*sat*), or 'the bare object' (*vastumātra*) is known everywhere; therefore it is the most basic thing, that exists everywhere. A similar sort of argument is used in the passage proving that Brahman is 'word' (*śabda*), *BS* 18.1-19-13: *śabda* must be the *prakṛti* of everything, because nothing can be known except by knowledge which has a verbal form.

4.16

It is hardly surprising that Maṇḍana should teach that Brahman is known in ordinary perception, even though it is, as he says, "associated with *avidyā*" (*avidyā-saṃbhinna*); for this is implied by his doctrine of *anyathā-khyāti*, according to which the object to which an erroneous cognition refers, e.g., a piece of mother-of-pearl, is from the beginning in contact with the observer's sense, and is cognised wrongly. See, for instance *VV* 81cd: *ābhāsate kathaṃcic ca tan, nātyantaṃ na bhāsate*, "And that (piece of mother-of-pearl) appears in some way; it is not so that it does not appear at all." It is also implied by the doctrine that *avidyā* is not without *vidyā*, which I have discussed elsewhere (§§5.1, 5.6).

Verbality of Nirvikalpa

4.17

In most theories of *savikalpa* and *nirvikalpa jñāna*, *nirvikalpa jñāna* is non-verbal. However, it is not clear that it is not verbal in Maṇḍana's theory. He has not, unfortunately, set forth his theory of *savikalpa* and *nirvikalpa* cognition in one place in a clear and systematic way; we are obliged to gather what we can from the various places where the two sorts of knowledge are touched upon. Still, this effort is worthwhile, because his ideas on the verbality of *nirvikalpa jñāna* are, as we shall see, highly unusual, and throw light on his concept of the ontological status and the function of the Vedic revelation.

4.18

In the passage of the *Brahma-siddhi* attempting to prove that Brahman is *śabda*, word, Maṇḍana Miśra first offers arguments from scripture (*BS* 16.23-17.1). Then (18.1-19.13), he offers an argument from reason: modifications are accompanied by the form of their material cause (*prakṛti*), and the world is accompanied by the form of the word, and we know that the world is accompanied by the form of the word by the fact that it is cognized by knowledge having a verbal form. Maṇḍana offers several arguments to prove that all knowledge is verbal; we need not set forth all of them here. But some of what he says is relevant to our investigation. For instance, he says that "knowledge from a word is not like that from (a sense-organ) such as the eye, because if one is not aware of it (the word), there is no knowledge of the object (whereas one is not ordinarily aware of the eye while seeing through it)" (*na śabdāc cakṣurādivat pratipattiḥ, tadasaṃvedane 'rthe pratipattyabhāvāt*—*BS* 18.3-4). If all knowledge is verbal, and there is no consciousness of any other object without the consciousness of the word, then we must assume that *nirvikalpa* also is verbal.

4.19

This seems to be confirmed by what is said a few lines further down (*BS* 18.13-17). Maṇḍana says:

"Even the movement towards, for instance, their mother's breast, disregarding other things, that babies show could not be if they did not determine it as 'this'; unless it has been determined whether something is a post or a man there is no activity based on (its being) one or the other. Now, there is no determination without the coloration of words. Therefore even they (children), possessing the influences of words from previous births, have knowledge that is determined by being coloured by the form of speech."

bālānāṁ api ca yeyam anyaparihāreṇa stanādau pravṛttiḥ, sā na "idam" iti aniścinvatāṃ bhavitum arhati; nāniścite sthāṇau puruṣe vānyataranibandhanā pravṛttiḥ; na ca niścayaḥ śabdānurāgaśūnya iti teṣām api pūrvajanmaśabdabhāvanābhājāṃ vāgrūpoparaktameva jñānaṃ niścīyate.

4.20

Although *niścaya*, here translated as 'determination', in Buddhist usage is sometimes equivalent to *vikalpa*,[24] it is probable that Maṇḍana considers the knowledge, present in a baby, which he describes here to be *nirvikalpa*. This appears first of all from a consideration of his sources in writing the passage on *śabdādvaita*, the *Vākyapadīya* and the *Vākyapadīya-vṛtti*. In *VP* 1.121-26, Bhartṛhari says that all knowledge is verbal. In the first of these three verses, 1.121, he says: "All knowledge of how to do things in the world depends upon the word; even a baby has such (knowledge), by having the impressions (of words) deposited in previous (births)." (*itikartavyatā loke sarvā śabda-vyapāśrayā/ yāṃ pūrvāhitasaṃskāro bālo 'pi pratipadyate//*) The *Vṛtti* comments: "Even in babies there arises knowledge, based on vague words, in regard to these or those purposeful activities, because speech is present in them even at their birth, because there have been deposited the impressions of the previous habitual exercise of words."[25] (*samāviṣṭavācāṃ ca svajātiṣu bālānām api pūrvaśabdāveśabhāvanāsaṃskārādhānāt tāsu tāsv arthakriyāsv anākhyeyaśabdanibandhanā pratipattir utpadyate*—*VPv* 186.5-187.2). I have translated *anākhyeya*, literally 'indescribable' or 'inexpressible' by 'vague', following Iyer's translation[26] and the analogy of *anupākhyeya* (see above, §1.33-35), so that it refers to the indistinction and inarticulateness of the words in the baby's mind. It could be translated with equal justification as Biardeau does,[26] by 'unutterable' ('non proférable'), so that it refers to the fact that the words cannot be communicated to others. Of course, these two interpretations are not mutually exclusive; what is vague within the baby's mind also cannot be uttered so as to communicate it to others.

4.21

The *Vṛtti* on *VP* 1.124 tells us what form these *anākhyeya śabdas* take. It says: "Even the first light that falls upon external objects illuminates merely the individual form of the thing by a vague operation (of speech), as 'this' or 'that', because it does not grasp the special causes." (*yo 'pi prathamopanipātī bāhyeṣv artheṣu prakāśaḥ sa nimittānām aparigraheṇa vastusvarūpamātram idaṃ tad ity avyapadeśyayā vṛttyā pratyavabhāsayati*—*VPv* 190.4-5). As we saw above (§4.4), in *BS* 72.17-19, 'this', 'that', or 'thing' is a name for the bare thing, which equals the *sat* or *abheda* which is present everywhere and which forms the object of *nirvikalpa pratyakṣa*. The *vastusvarūpamātra* of this passage in the *VPv* is very like Maṇḍana's *vastu-mātra*. *Nimitta*, which I have translated rather freely by 'special causes', seems to refer to such things as universal, particularity, relations, and the like, which figure in a *savikalpa* cognition. So, at least Vṛṣabhadeva thinks.[27] Finally, the fact that this knowledge ('light') is said to be first might indicate that it is *nirvikalpa*. As in the passage under discussion, *BS* 18.13-17, there is mentioned a subtle verbal knowledge in the form of 'this'. This knowledge while verbal is not complex or relational, and is therefore not a *vikalpa*.

4.22

The *Vṛtti* is perhaps justified in attributing to Bhartṛhari the idea that such *anākhyeya śabdas* as 'this' and 'that' are the cause of a rudimentary sort of knowledge which leads to activity by a passage in the second *kāṇḍa* of the *VP*. First, Bhartṛhari says that a *pratibhā* ('intuition') is the meaning of the sentence (2.143). Then he adds:

"144: Others say that this (*pratibhā*) is totally inexpressible, just 'this' or 'that'; established as existing within each individual, it is not explicable even by its maker."

idaṃ tad iti sānyeṣām anākhyeyā kathaṃcana/
*pratyātmavṛtti siddhā sā kartrāpi na nirūpyate//*144//

After a few words more on *pratibhā* as the sentence-meaning, he says:

"146cd: No one transgresses it in regard to how things are to be done.

147: All men look to it as a means of valid cognition; even animals understand their undertakings by means of it.

149: Who changes the song of the male koel in spring? By whom are bugs and other animals taught to form nests and the like?"

*itikartavyatāyāṃ tāṃ na kaścid ativartate//*146//
pramāṇatvena tāṃ lokaḥ sarvaḥ samanupaśyati/
*samārambhāḥ pratīyante tiraścām api tadvaśāt//*147//
svaravṛttiṃ vikurute madhau puṃskokilasya kaḥ/
*jantvādayaḥ kulāyādikaraṇe kena śikṣitāḥ//*149//

If this rudimentary knowledge is present in animals, it is presumably present in babies as well. In fact, in *VP* 2.117, the word is said to be the cause of the intuition of both babies and animals (*abhyāsāt pratibhāhetuḥ śabdaḥ sarvo 'paraiḥ smṛtaḥ/ bālānāṃ ca tiraścāṃ ca yathārthapratipādane//*). It must be admitted, however, that 2.144ab might be translated in another manner, thus: "This (*pratibhā*) is not in any way expressible to others as 'this' or 'that' "; or, "This is not in any way expressible to others, so that one could say, 'This is what it is'." Both Biardeau and Iyer take it more or less in this way.[28] On the other hand, it does not contradict our interpretation significantly if *anyeṣām* is taken to mean 'to others' rather than 'according to others', as we took it. The half-verse could then be translated, "This (*pratibhā*) is inexpressible to others; it is simply 'this' or 'that'."

4.23

The tentative conclusion reached in paragraph 4.21, that for Harivṛṣabha the object of *nirvikalpa jñāna* is the bare object, which is designated by vague words merely as 'this' or 'that', may be contradicted by *VPv* 1.123:

"As the influence of words exists in a state of reabsorption, nothing can be done with regard to objects of knowledge by (the use of) the *avikalpa* knowledge, even if it has been produced. It is like the case of a man hurrying along: even if there is knowledge from the contact (of the senses) with the grass, clods of earth, etc., still that is only a certain state of knowledge. (But) in that (state) in which the seeds of the influence of words come forward and the powers of the expressible (*ākhyeyarūpa*) and of the vague (*anākhyeyarūpa*) words, which communicate the objects and are limited to particular objects, become manifest, the thing, being given form and taken up by knowledge, penetrated by words and in accordance with (their) powers, is accompanied by knowledge and appears with a clear form, and is then said to be (truly) 'known'."[29]

4.24

This is the only place where the *VPv* distinguishes *savikalpa jñāna* and *nirvikalpa jñāna* by using either of those terms or a synonym (the *VP kārikās* never do so).[30] But it seems here that the 'vague' or 'inexpressible' (*anākhyeya*) words belong to the second state, which we must suppose, from its opposition to *avikalpa jñāna*, to be *savikalpa*, just as much as do the 'expressible' words. The syntax of these sentences is exceedingly contorted, and the meaning of certain locutions rather obscure. The *Vṛtti*'s apparent division of knowledge into non-verbal *nirvikalpa* and verbal *savikalpa* contradicts the very verse it is glossing, which says that *all* knowledge is penetrated and accompanied by words.[31] The contradiction could be resolved if we could somehow read the text so that it would say that *savikalpa* and *nirvikalpa* are both verbal, but *savikalpa* involves 'expressible' words, while *nirvikalpa* involves 'inexpressible' words. But I do not see how this can be done, and there are not even any variant readings for this passage in the critical text. Perhaps the key to Harivṛṣabha's ideas lies in the fact that he says, "even if *avikalpa* knowledge is produced" and "even if a man hurrying along has knowledge (although he is not paying attention)". Perhaps for Harivṛṣabha the primary meaning of *avikalpa jñāna* is non-verbal knowledge rather than determinate, complex, relational knowledge, whether verbal or not. But he does not believe that non-verbal knowledge exists, nor that someone hurrying along a path, paying no attention to what he sees, and using no words whether expressible or not, has any knowledge at all. He merely grants the possibility of *avikalpa jñāna* for the same argument, and then goes on to show its inferiority: nothing can be done by the use of it. For his own part, he accepts the fact that there are two sorts of knowledge, a prior non-relational one and a subsequent relational one. But for the opposition of non-verbal/non-relational to verbal/relational, he tacitly substitutes an opposition of verbal/non-relational to verbal/relational. The first knowledge uses 'vague', 'inexpressible' words, such as 'this' or 'that', and the second 'expressible' words. But he does not call the two knowledges *avikalpa* and *savikalpa* (which helps to explain why neither of these words, or a synonym, appears anywhere else in the *VPv* to designate one of the two opposed sorts of knowledge). Thus we could harmonize what he says here in *VPv* 1.123 with what he says in *VPv* 1.124 (§4.21).

4.25

In any case, for our purposes it is less important what Harivṛṣabha meant by his passage than what Maṇḍana did with it. He was manifestly inspired by *VPv* 1.123, for further on in the *śabdādvaita* passage of the *BS*, he mentions the example of a man walking along and looking at grass etc. (*BS* 19.8-10). But, for the reasons given above (§4.18), I think that Maṇḍana considered a baby's knowledge of his mother's breast as 'this' to be *nirvikalpa*. This is rendered more probable by the fact that another of his masters, Kumārila, explicitly compares *nirvikalpa jñāna* to the knowledge that a baby has. *Śv*, *Pratyakṣa*, 112 says: "There is a first, *nirvikalpa* knowledge, which is (mere) observation, like the knowledge of babies, the dumb, etc., produced from the bare thing." (*asti hy ālocanā jñānaṃ prathamaṃ nirvikalpakam| bālamūkādivijñānasadṛśaṃ śuddhavastujam||*). In Kumārila, this knowledge is non-verbal, but Maṇḍana, following Bhartṛhari and Harivṛṣabha, would think that there is verbal knowledge in the form of 'this', even in babies or the dumb. Therefore Maṇḍana probably regarded *nirvikalpa jñāna* as verbal.

4.26

The next place in the *śabdādvaita* passage of the *BS* that is relevant to the problem of the object of *nirvikalpa jñāna* is 19.1-4:

"The same is the case of the meaning of the sentence: Conjunction (which is the meaning of a sentence) is nothing over and above the things conjoined. The thing when conjoined is not distinct from its form when unconjoined. (But) knowledge (such as that conveyed by a sentence) cannot be void of an object, (and) a constructive cognition (*vikalpapratyaya*) cannot be lacking in the form of speech. Therefore, it is logical to say that the essence which is speech alone appears in this way or that."

evaṃ vākyārthaḥ; saṃsargo na saṃsargivyatirekeṇa kaścit, na saṃsargī asaṃsargirūpātiriktaḥ; na jñeyaśūnyaṃ jñānam; na vikalpapratyayo vāgrūpoparāgarahita iti vāktattvam eva tathā tathā vivartata iti.

The cognition of the meaning of a sentence is necessarily a complex cognition, and therefore *savikalpa* and verbal. The point of this argument is to show that the sentence-meaning is something which has no existence besides being a *vivarta* of speech, like injunction and prohibition and the like, and thereby to lead to the generalization that all whatever things are but *vivartas* of speech (cf. §2.4-11). Since in saying that constructive cognitions must be verbal, the passage is merely basing itself on what is more or less generally accepted, it does not imply anything further about Maṇḍana's own doctrine, in particular that he thought that *nirvikalpa* was non-verbal.

4.27

Maṇḍana goes on to say that "even if there is knowledge of the notes of the scale or of cows and the like before the word, still, it is not the same as after the advent of the word; for the apprehension is indistinct before, but afterwards clearer and distinct. And so cowherds, shepherds, etc. assign (each animal) a name so as to be able to distinguish them."[32] (*yady api ṣaḍjādiṣu gavādiṣu ca prāk śabdāt jñānam asti, tathāpi na tādṛk, yādṛk śabdaniveśād uttarasmin kāle*; *aviviktā hi prāk pratipattiḥ, sphuṭatarā vivekavatī paścāt. tathā ca gopālāvipālādayo vivekajñānasiddhaye saṃjñāṃ niveśayanti—BS* 19.4-8.) This however, is according to Śaṅkhapāṇi merely a concession to those who hold that *nirvikalpa* is non-verbal, the concessive nature of the statement being indicated by the words 'even if' (*yady api*).[33] That Śaṅkhapāṇi is right is shown by the conclusion of this passage: "The fact that consciousness is consciousness depends upon the form of speech. Or else consciousness *is* the power of speech; even when it is withdrawn there is a subtle power of speech, some say. In any case, the knowledge of the object depends upon the form of speech." (*vāgrūpādhīnam eva citaś cititvam. vākśaktir eva vā citiḥ*; *tatpratisaṃhāre 'pi sūkṣmā vākśaktir ity eke*; *sarvathā vāgrūpādhīno jñeyabodhaḥ...—BS* 19.10-12.) The fact that Maṇḍana adds to the statement that consciousness is the power of speech, and that that power remains in a subtle state even when it is withdrawn, the words 'some say' (*ity eke*) do not indicate that he is putting a distance between his own opinion and that of the grammarians on this point.[34] For the *ity eke* is derived from his source, the *VPv*, which attributes the idea that the seeds of the impressions of language assume a subtle activity in sleeping to 'some teachers' (*ekeṣām ācāryāṇām*), and the idea that the form of the activity of consciousness is the form of the principal word to 'some' (*ity eke*). (See §3.32 for Skt., translation, and discussion of these texts.) (Therefore, since the *VPv* attributes both these ideas to 'some', and both are mentioned in the *BS*, I take *ity eke* in the *BS* to include within its scope everything beginning with the word *vākśaktir*, not just with *tatpratisaṃhāre*.) The attribution of a doctrine to 'some' or to 'others' is not a necessary sign in either the *VP*, the *VPv*, or the *BS* that the author doubts the opinion. In the present connection, the *VPv*, although in the place just mentioned it attributes the doctrine that in sleep the impressions of language assume a subtle activity to *eke*, elsewhere states as its own the almost identical opinion that in unconsciousness verbal knowledge continues in a subtle way (see §3.32 again). If it is Maṇḍana's own opinion that consciousness is the power of speech, and that it persists in a subtle state even when it is withdrawn, his attributing it to 'some', and his going on to say "in any case, the knowledge of the object depends upon the form of speech", indicate merely that he does not want to get away from the main point, that all knowledge is verbal. But if all knowledge is verbal, *nirvikalpa jñāna* must be verbal also. Although, as we have seen, the *VPv* is somewhat ambiguous on this topic, there were some *Śabdādvaitins*, according to Jayanta Bhaṭṭa, who made the principial word (*vāgrūpaṃ tattvam*) the object of *nirvikalpa jñāna*,[35] so Maṇḍana, if he does teach that *nirvikalpa jñāna* is verbal, is not a totally isolated figure.

4.28

BS 71.2-5 seems to imply the association of *nirvikalpa* with non-verbality and *savikalpa* with verbality:

"P: Perception grasps a qualified form, but that difference, because it is not touched by words, is not noticed as it is in a constructive cognition.

S: That is illogical, because it is contradictory. It is a contradiction to say that particularity appears in a perceptual cognition but is not noticed."

syād etat—viśiṣṭarūpopagrāhy eva pratyakṣam; sa tu bhedaḥ śabdenāsaṃsparśān na tathopalakṣyate, yathā vikalpabuddhau. tad ayuktam, vipratiṣedhāt; na copalakṣyate pratyakṣabuddhau viśeṣah prakāśate ceti vipratiṣiddham.

The opponent is probably Kumārila. The mention of the absence of words in *pratyakṣa* reflects his beliefs rather than Maṇḍana's, and Maṇḍana does not take up the point in answering him. (On the other hand, as has been mentioned above [§4.5] the terminology in this message conforms to Maṇḍana's opposition of *pratyakṣa* to *vikalpa-buddhi* rather than to Kumārila's opposition of *nirvikalpa pratyakṣa* to *savikalpa pratyakṣa*.)

4.29

In *BS* 33.15-18, in the midst of an argument between a *pūrvapakṣin* who represents a current within Śaṃkara's school which considered the knowledge of Brahman gained from the reading of the Veda to be sufficient for liberation, and an opponent to the *pūrvapakṣin* who does not entirely represent Maṇḍana's own opinions (see Appendix A.8), the opponent to the *pūrvapakṣin* suggests:

"Another knowledge than verbal knowledge is required (for liberation), a direct (*pratyakṣa*) knowledge in which the grasping of division is swallowed up, beyond all *vikalpas*; for it is of this knowledge that Brahman is the object, not of verbal (knowledge) which grasps the conjunction of the meanings of different words. Deeds, meditation, and so forth are needed to produce this (knowledge)."

> *atha matam—śābdajñānād anyad api pratyakṣam jñānam iṣyate vigalitavibhāgodgrāhaṃ sarvavikalpātītam; tasya hi brahma gocaraḥ, na śābdasya vibhaktapadārthasaṃsargodgrāhiṇaḥ; tadutpattau karmopāsanādyapekṣeti.*

Here it is quite clear that verbal knowledge involves complexity, relation, and therefore *vikalpa*. However, as we said, this is the opponent to the opponent speaking, not Maṇḍana himself. When Maṇḍana closes the argument by stating his own position (*BS* 35.1-36.3), he does not use the same terminology. Instead, he says that even when one has ascertained the truth from a means of valid knowledge such as *śruti*, false appearances may continue because of the *saṃskāra* of error that is still there, and this must be countered by producing an opposite *saṃskāra*, by repeating the knowledge of the truth already acquired. Maṇḍana does not say verbal knowledge involves *vikalpas* or division. He says several times in *BS* 35.1-36.3 that *śabda* gives real knowledge of Brahman directly by itself, and it is this same knowledge that must be repeated to remove all traces of false cognition. He does approach close enough to the other's doctrine to talk of "a knowledge to which the (Vedic) word is a means" (*śabdasādhanajñāna—BS* 36.2), but he does not define this knowledge in the terms which the opponent to the *pūrvapakṣin* uses. In fact, he does not define it at all. Therefore we cannot say that he opposes this knowledge to verbal knowledge as *nirvikalpa* to *savikalpa*.

4.30

At the beginning of the *Niyoga-kāṇḍa*, Maṇḍana announces the intention of the *kāṇḍa*—to show that the Veda teaches Brahman as an already existent truth and not as the object of an injunction of knowledge. He then lists the three sorts of knowledge that might be the object of an injunction, each of which he takes up in the course of the *kāṇḍa*. He says:

"There are three knowledges of Brahman: the first from the word; another, after having gained knowledge from the word, having a continuous stream of that (verbal knowledge), called *dhyāna, bhāvanā, upāsanā*, etc.; another, which gains its perfection from the second one, in the form of direct apprehension, in which all *vikalpas* have been swallowed up."

tisraś ca pratipattayo brahmaṇi; prathamā tāvac chabdāt, anyā śabdāt pratipadya tatsantānavatī dhyānabhāvanopasanādiśabda-vācyā, anyā tato labdhaniṣpattir vigalitanikhilavikalpā sākṣāt-karaṇarūpā—BS 74.10-13.

Maṇḍana does not actually say here that the final knowledge is utterly non-verbal, he merely says that it is without any *vikalpas*.

4.31

At the beginning of the prolonged discussion of the possibility that a cognition of the third sort could be the object of a Vedic injunction, the opponent says:

"We do not say that it is an awareness of the truth that arises from language that is enjoined, but one in which the apprehension of the difference between the intellect and its object has disappeared. Therefore it is without duality, either because there is no second awareness of the same sort or because it lacks the duality of agent and object of valid cognition, and so it is different from that (verbal awareness).... For the essence of the Self is not the object of verbal knowledge, because it is in the form of sentences that language is a means of valid cognition. And the object of (the sentence) is the conjunction of the meanings of various words, because it is understood in accompaniment with them. How can the knowledge produced from (the sentence), in which appears the connection of diverse separate objects (*artha-mātra*), take for its object the essence of the Self, in which there is no multiplicity of phenomena, which is unsoiled by the slightest bit of duality?

S: This also is worthless, because this non-dual awareness of the essence of the Self, free from the slightest touch of duality, is (the self's) abiding in its own form on account of the absence of the error of limitation." (*BS* 115.13-21)[36]

4.32

The opponent clearly says that verbal knowledge involves duality and relation. It must therefore, although he does not here use the word *vikalpa*, involve *vikalpas*. Maṇḍana's reply, however, does not take up the question of the verbality of the *nirvikalpa jñāna* (or, to use the terminology of later Advaita, *nirvikalpa samādhi*) of Brahman. The possibility is left open that to Maṇḍana's mind even the final, non-dual knowledge of Brahman is still verbal, because its object is Brahman, which is also *śabda*. Just as Brahman as 'being' and 'the bare thing' is the object of *pratyakṣa*, which is *nirvikalpa*, so Brahman as the highest *śabda* is the object of a *nirvikalpa* verbal knowledge. Verbal knowledge is not necessarily relational: a baby's knowledge of its mother's breast apprehends it merely as 'this'. (Of course, we are not to assume that the word 'this' is actually uttered by the baby in its mind in the form of articulate syllables; the word takes a more subtle form.) So the highest knowledge of Brahman, in which there is no duality, no relation, no *vikalpas*, may still be verbal.

4.33

To say that Maṇḍana holds or assumes this is consistent with the picture he gives of the process of advancement towards liberation. He does not envisage a sudden break with the previous stage anywhere along the route, between the initial verbal knowledge and its habitual repetition or the repetition and the final liberating knowledge. Rather he envisages a gradual deepening of the original verbal knowledge until it is transformed into direct awareness. As he says *BS* 154.5-8:

"Thinking over the same thing results in a direct awareness of it...and it is observed in ordinary life that repetition of knowledge causes clarity of right cognition. For by especially intense concentration even a non-existent thing comes to be experienced, how much more so something that exists."

sākṣātkaraṇaphalaṃ hi tattadanucintanaṃ... dṛṣṭā ca jñānābhyāsasya saṃyagjñānaprasādahetutā loke. bhāvanāviśeṣād dhi abhūtam apy anubhavam āpadyate, kiṃ punar bhūtam.

4.34

In Maṇḍana's theory of error, previous erroneous cognitions, as for instance the erroneous perception of distant trees as elephants, may be a means towards the final, correct cognition. Yet it is the same external object of error, the trees, that is in contact with the senses throughout the process.[37] If the process of advancement towards *mokṣa* is put into the same framework, it is Brahman as *śabda-tattva* that is known at the beginning, when instruction about it is received from the Upaniṣads, and at the end, when direct awareness is reached. The example of the trees and the elephants is introduced by Maṇḍana to show that the fact that perception precedes *śabda* as a means of valid cognition does not imply that *śabda*, being dependent on it, is weaker than it. A correct cognition may follow an erroneous one and depend on it, yet it is obviously stronger. Maṇḍana applies this example to the opposition of perception, which is false, to *śabda*, which is true; he does not, it is worth noting, apply it to an opposition of verbal knowledge as false to direct awareness as true. Knowledge of Brahman is present from the time that it is first obtained from the Veda until the final direct awareness, and it is always knowledge of the same object, the Brahman which is also *śabda*.

4.35

It should, finally, be noticed that Maṇḍana never says that the Vedas are unreal or in the realm of *avidyā*. Śaṃkara, on the other hand, does say so. He says: "Perception and the other means of valid knowledge (which depend on it, such as inference), and the sacred texts are in the realm of *avidyā*" (*avidyāvadviṣayāṇy eva pratyakṣādīni pramāṇāni śāstrāṇi ca—BSūB* 1.1.1, Introd., 42.1). He also makes an opponent say, "How is the apprehension of the real identity of Brahman and the Self by a false sentence of the Upaniṣads possible?" (*kathaṃ tv asatyena vedāntavākyena satyasya brahmātmatvasya pratipattir upapadyeta?—BSūB* 2.1.14, 458.11-12.) In his reply, he does not deny that the Veda is unreal, but merely attempts to answer the opponent's question by examples. But for Maṇḍana the Veda is not in the realm of *avidyā*, whereas *pratyakṣa* and the other *pramāṇas* are: "(The non-existence of phenomenal diversity) is said to be based on Tradition alone, because perception etc. are associated with *avidyā*. For, because they do not take (Brahman) as their object under the form where all difference has disappeared, the disappearance is knowable from Tradition (alone)." (*āmnāyaikanibandhanatvaṃ tu tasyocyate, pratyakṣādīnām avidyāsaṃbhinnatvāt; pratyastamitanikhilabhedena rūpeṇāviṣayīkaraṇād bhedapratyastamayasyāmnāyāvagamyatvād iti—BS* 157.19-21.) If perception etc. are opposed to *śabda* as being associated with *avidyā*, presumably *śabda* is not associated with *avidyā*. It seems that the Veda has a higher ontological status, as well as a higher authority as a means of knowledge, than perception and the remaining *pramāṇas*. This must be because it is identical with Brahman.

4.36

I have tried to show that Maṇḍana implies that *nirvikalpa jñāna* involves a rudimentary sort of verbal knowledge, that the highest knowledge of Brahman, in which all differences and *vikalpas* have disappeared, is still a verbal knowledge, and that the Vedic word has a higher ontological status than the other *pramāṇas*. There are many points in the argument where these conclusions might be attacked. But I can see no other way than by accepting them to fit the defense of *śabdādvaita* in the first *kāṇḍa* into the rest of Maṇḍana's doctrine, so that it will not be an isolated fragment, having no organic relation to his otherwise closely-knit system.

CHAPTER V

ERROR LEADS TO TRUTH

5.1

One of the themes most characteristic of Maṇḍana Miśra is that of the ability of error to lead to truth. This theme is closely bound up with the rest of his theory of error. The place where he expatiates upon it at the greatest length occurs in the first *kāṇḍa* of the *Brahma-siddhi*, where he glosses the *śruti Īśa U* 11: "He who knows both *vidyā* and *avidyā* together, by *avidyā* having crossed over death, reaches immortality by *vidyā*" (*vidyāṃ cāvidyāṃ ca yas tad veda ubhayaṃ saha| avidyayā mṛtyum tīrtvā vidyayāmṛtam aśnute||*). He says:

"Another meaning (of the verse) is that *avidyā* is not devoid of *vidyā*. It is like this: Even the vision of difference is not void of light—if it were absent difference would not appear. Therefore the highest light alone appears in this way or that. As it is said, 'Everything shines after it as it shines, by its light all this shines' (*KaṭhaU* 2.2.15). However, (it shines) as bound up with *avidyā*; as has been said, 'All vision is undeficient and without divisions of mental construction (*avikalpam*), but this interior person conceives it as if it were divided up by mental construction (*vikalpitam iva*).' Therefore, *vidyā*, defined as hearing etc. about the oneness of the Self, cannot be without *avidyā*, because it is bound up with the divisions of hearer, hearing, etc. So, having by *avidyā*, (an *avidyā* which is) near to *vidyā*, crossed over *avidyā*, (namely) the vision of separation, one abides in one's own eternal form, defined as *vidyā*, like water soiled by a reflection upon the cessation of (the reflection).

P: But if (everything) is the one Self, division is unreal (*asatya*); how can hearing etc. based on that (division), which are also unreal, lead to any effect? Besides, the arriving at something real from something unreal is false, as (the inference of fire) from steam wrongly grasped as smoke.

S: There is no invariable rule that something unreal cannot give rise to any effect, because a magic show may be the occasion of delight and fear, and something unreal (may be the occasion) of arriving at something real, as a drawing of a gayal (literally 'a line-gayal') or written syllables.

P: But these things are in their own form (as themselves—*svarūpeṇa*) real and not void, but for him who teaches that (everything) is the one Self these means are unreal even in their own form.

S: Even if they were real in their own form, the form in which they communicate is unreal—a 'reality in their own form' which has no utility for an effect is useless. Besides, the means to the vision of non-difference are not unreal in their own form, because their own form is nothing but Brahman; so it is just Brahman, bound up with *avidyā*, that is the means to attain Brahman, as lines etc. communicate syllables etc. by a form that does not exist—'This is (the syllable) *ka*', 'This is a gayal'.

P: A drawing of a gayal does not inform one about other gayals *as* a gayal, nor do the characters (communicate) as syllables, but rather (in the case of the drawing of a gayal) through similarity—'A gayal is like this', and in the case of the characters by a convention—'When one sees such character one should recall this syllable.'

S: What this person thinks is opposed to ordinary experience. For children are instructed in the characters as if they were syllables, and in ordinary life they are referred to as the same, both by the speaker—'This is a gayal', and by the hearer—'I have seen a gayal'. Similarly, the inference of an unseen cause of a reflection, possessing a particular location and configuration, from its reflection, which is unreal, is not incorrect, and the apprehension of a certain meaning from a word, which is eternal but participates in the unreal divisions of long, (short), etc., is not wrong. Likewise a false snakebite may cause death, and an inference from it to the death, the swooning, or the like (of the person who thinks himself bitten) is not false, any more than (the inference) from a real snakebite in conjunction with particular times and the like (i.e. with certain positions of the stars)." (*BS* 13.11-14.16).[1]

5.2

Some of the examples here used by Maṇḍana appear also in Śaṃkara's commentary on *BSū* 2.1.14, where the opponent asks how the unreal sentences of the Upaniṣads can convey information about the real identity of Brahman and the Self. He answers that a man can die from the venom of an imaginary snakebite, that the consciousness a dreaming person has of unreal objects is real and is not sublated upon waking, that dreams predict real events, and that the 'unreal' written characters lead to the knowledge of the real syllables (*BSūB* 2.1.14, 458.11-450.7). Maṇḍana, although, since he seems to have known Śaṃkara's works, he must have been aware of this passage, does not seem to be dependent on it. His presentation of the example of the written letters is more elaborate than that of Śaṃkara, who merely states it without defending it against objections. The examples of the consciousness a dreamer has of unreal events and of predictive dreams are also missing in the *BS*. The latter example may have been rejected by Maṇḍana on the ground that dreams do not really predict future events, for in the *ViV*, pp. 159-60, he argues against the opinion that they do. The example of the snakebite is found in both Śaṃkara and Maṇḍana, in an equally simple form in both.

5.3

It is more probable that Maṇḍana in the passage under discussion depends on Kumārila's *Śloka-vārttika*, if not for the examples themselves, at least for some of the arguments against them which he combats. In *ŚV Nirālambana*, 128c-129b, Kumārila argues that the Śūnyavādin cannot enter into any arguments because he denies the existence of the means of argument.[2] From 129c through 157, they argue this point on logical grounds, Kumārila calling into question the validity of the distinction between *saṃvṛti-sat* and *paramārtha-sat*. Then he brings in some examples:

"158: We do not observe that hares' horns etc. cause right cognition etc., and the knowledge of, for instance, fire by steam or something else other than smoke is wrong.

159: Therefore the real knowledge from an unreal *hetu* which you uphold is itself unreal; for one cannot arrive at something real from something that merely appears real.

160: Likewise the characters that are observed to convey syllables are not lacking in final reality in their own form.

161: Should you reply that they are not real as syllables, (we reply that) this is the rule in respect to all things. Nothing is thought to be real as some other object".

na dṛṣṭā śaśaśṛṅgādeḥ samyagjñānādihetutā/
bāṣpādināpy adhūmena mithyā vahnyādibodhanam//158//
tasmād asatyahetor yā paramārthe matis tava/
sāpy asatyā na satyaṃ hi satyābhāsena gamyate//159//
ye 'pi rekhādayo dṛṣṭā varṇānāṃ pratipādakāḥ/
na te svenāpi rūpeṇa paramārthatvavarjitāḥ//160//
varṇātmanā na satyāś cet sarvabhāveṣv ayaṃ vidhiḥ/
padārthāntararūpeṇa na satyaṃ kiñcid iṣyate//161//

5.4

Maṇḍana's examples of a valid inference from something false—the inference of a face's location and configuration from its reflection and of death or swoon from an imagined snakebite—are brought in to respond to Kumārila's example of the inference from steam misapprehended as smoke to fire. His insistence that we identify written characters with the syllables they represent, and the additional example of a drawing of a gayal (in which it is perhaps more obvious that we identify the thing communicating and the object communicated), are brought in to answer Kumārila's contention that it is not in so far as they are unreal that written characters communicate, but in so far as they are real. Since they are not found in Kumārila, who did not live long before Maṇḍana, and since they seem to be made to respond to his arguments, it is quite likely that the examples of the inference from a reflection, the inference from an imagined snakebite, and of the drawing of a gayal are all three Maṇḍana's inventions

5.5

Because it is certain, from Kumārila's citation of the example of the characters representing syllables, that this example was in use before Śaṃkara, there is no reason to assume, on the ground that Śaṃkara uses it, that Maṇḍana got it from him. This example, if not the others, was probably in use as a standard illustration for some time even before Kumārila. I am not aware of any Buddhist text where the examples in these texts of Maṇḍana and Kumārila are used. The example of the written syllables (as also of the imagined snakebite) could be used by either a Vedāntin or a Buddhist, by anyone who held a two-truths theory. Therefore it would be risky to attribute it to the Buddhists as its inventors on the grounds that it is found in a section of the *ŚV* directed against the Buddhists. Interestingly enough, Umbeka, in his commentary on *ŚV*, *Nirālambana*, 128c-129b, which, as noted above, introduces this discussion, attributes this theory that unreal means can lead to a real knowledge to the *Vijñānādvaitins*, the 'non-dualists of knowledge', in spite of the fact that the verse itself attributes it to the Śūnyavādins.[3] Does this merely reflect the fact that this chapter of the *ŚV* as a whole is directed against the Vijñānavāda, or does it show that Umbeka saw that the arguments would be equally appropriate to any Buddhist school who held a theory of two truths? If the latter, the examples used may have been common to both the Vijñānavāda and the Śūnyavāda. In glossing the next verse he attributes the doctrine to 'the Advaitavādin',[4] and in glossing the rest of the passage he refers to Advaita, to 'the Advaitavādin' (which he opposes to Kumārila as a Dvaitavādin), and to *vijñānamātra*.[5] It is possible that the use of the word 'Advaitavādin' indicates that Umbeka wishes to include in Kumārila's opponents not only both schools of Mahāyāna Buddhism, but also certain Vedāntins who adhered to the two-truths theory. If this is so, the examples occurring in Kumārila may have been common to Vijñānavāda, Śūnyavāda, and Advaita Vedānta, so that we would not be able to tell who used them first.

5.6

To turn from the examples to the theory which they illustrate, it can be said that Maṇḍana's great originality lies in the manner in which he explains how error can lead to truth. Śaṃkara, and apparently Kumārila's opponent, do not explain the phenomenon so much as give examples to show that it is in fact possible. Maṇḍana, on the other hand, says that the power of *avidyā* to lead to *vidyā* is from the presence in it of *vidyā*, of the supreme light that is Brahman. This is consistent with the rest of his system—for example, with his insistence, as part of his theory of *anyathā-khyāti*, that error always has an objective substrate (*ālambana*), with which the sense is in contact even when it is perceived incorrectly, and with his doctrine that Brahman is given in perception. This, however, is approaching things from the side of the object rather than of the knower. He also insists, as we saw above (§1.52-53), that some knowledge, that is, the presence of consciousness in addition to a substrate, is necessary even for error. Of course, in the final knowledge that is identical with Brahman, the consciousness and its substrate are one and the same, namely Brahman. (Cf. the remarks in the chapter on *vivarta*, §2.2-3). Just as he says, in the passage under discussion that Brahman is the proper form of the means to obtaining it, so he says elsewhere: "Brahman does not have everything for its self, but everything has Brahman for its self; it has positive existence, through the positive existence of Brahman" (*BS* 20.11-12, cf. A/A, 15). Although Maṇḍana does not link up this doctrine with that of *anirvacanīyatva*, it harmonizes with it. The different things that appear, because of *avidyā*, to exist, are not totally different from Brahman. In so far as they have any existence, it is that of Brahman, and this is what enables them to be useful in attaining Brahman.

5.7

There is one other important passage on this theme in the *BS*, 41.4-16. Maṇḍana has been discussing the objection that *pratyakṣa* is stronger than *śabda* as a means of proof because it precedes it (we hear the words of the Veda before we understand its meaning, and our original learning of the meanings of words depends on sensory observation). Maṇḍana replies:

"Besides, it is observed that a later apprehension can be stronger than an earlier one, even if the earlier one is required by the later one as a cause. For instance, the apprehension of trees in far-off trees is stronger than the apprehension of elephants in them. For the clear apprehension of the trees demands the apprehensions of the elephants as a cause; it is not produced from the contact of the sense and the object alone, because it does not exist upon first seeing (the object). Nor is it because of a particular location, because it arises in a person continuing to stand in the same place. Therefore (the correct perception) in regard to the far-off trees must be thought to be produced, in one whose mind is attentive, by the contact of the senses etc., accompanied by the mental impressions that follow the previous error. Similarly, the ideas of the numbers one etc., which are means to the ideas of such (numbers) as twenty, can be given as examples. And so is discarded what some set forth, that the apprehension of the meaning of the Vedānta-texts is self-contradictory, because it is impossible to find out about non-difference without difference, since difference is a means to its apprehension, and thus non-difference, as it is learned about, presupposes difference, so that there is a contradiction. For the apprehension presupposes a means, not the final reality of the means, because the truth may be apprehended even from a false cognition. And we agree that difference is real as regards practical life".[6]

5.8

The passage confirms some of the points just made about the grounding of Maṇḍana's doctrine that error leads to truth in the rest of his epistemology. He explicitly states that, in the example of the trees mistaken for elephants, the sense is in contact with the same external object from the first mistaken cognition to the final clear and correct cognition. He does not explicitly make the application of the analogy to the case of Brahman, but it is not unsafe for us to make it. Brahman is present in every cognition, including perception. Perception, along with those *pramāṇas* which are dependent on it, that is, all except *śabda*, apprehends Brahman, but apprehends it incorrectly.

5.9

This passage is largely dependent on the *Vākyapadīya* and the *Vākyapadīya-vṛtti*. Maṇḍana himself testifies to this by using the example of the trees and the elephants in the prose to *Sphoṭa-siddhi* 19. This is in reply to the objection that it must be the phonemes which are the word rather than the *sphoṭa*, because it is the syllables that we actually hear, and, since it is impossible to apprehend one thing as another, it cannot be that we mis-apprehend the *sphoṭa* as the phonemes. The fact that the opponent denies *anyathā-khyāti* gives a clear illustration of the connection of Maṇḍana's theory of the *sphoṭa* and of errors leading to truth with his doctrine of error. Maṇḍana replies in the *kārikā* of *SS* 19:

"But things vaguely apprehended do indeed appear as otherwise than they are, and through the succession of the impressions of those (errors) the reality appears clearly".

ārūpālociteṣv asti hy anyathāprakāśanam/
tatsaṃskārakramāc cāpi vyaktaṃ tattvam prakāśate//

In the prose (*SS* 90.13-91.2), Maṇḍana insists that it is the *sphoṭa* that is from the first in contact with the sense, just as in the case of trees mistaken for elephants. And just as the misapprehensions finally give rise to a correct cognition, so the cognitions of the phonemes, misconceived as separate from the *sphoṭa*, finally give rise to the cognition of the real word, the *sphoṭa*.

5.10

Then he quotes *VP* 1.89-90:

"89: Just as, having changed an object at a distance or in darkness by the previous perceptions, one determines it as other than it is.

90: So, when a sentence is being manifested by the causes of its manifestation, at first a cognition comes into play having the form of the apprehension of parts (in the sentence that in reality is without parts)".

yathaiva darśanaiḥ pūrvair dūrād santamase 'pi vā/
anyathākṛtya viṣayam anyathaivādhyavasyati//89//
vyajyamāne tathā vākye vākyābhivyaktihetubhiḥ/
bhāgāavagraharūpeṇa pūrvaṃ buddhiḥ pravartate//90//

The example of the elephant and the trees is given by Harivṛṣabha in his commentary on *VP* 1.89: "As it is the characteristic of the senses and their objects that when people of ordinary vision perceive from afar off merely a form they apprehend, for instance, trees as elephants, but in due course, from repeated attention. they perceive (the object) in detail" (*yathā viṣayendriyadharma evāyaṃ prākṛtacakṣuṣāṃ dūrād ākṛtimātropalabdhau vṛkṣādīn hastyādivat pratipadyante. taddeśāvasthitā eva praṇidhānābhyāsāt krameṇa punar yathāvayavam upalabhante.—VPv* 155.5-7). Harivṛṣabha also adds the example of a rope mistaken in a dark place for a snake, so as to illustrate both the circumstances. distance and darkness, mentioned in the *kārikā*.

5.11

The connection with the theory of *anyathā-khyāti* of the theory that error leads to truth by means of the truth—the contact with a real object—that is present even in error, may go back to Bhartṛhari himself. As Biardeau notes,[7] his use in *VP* 1.89 of the words *anyathākṛtya* and *anyathādhyavasyati* may well indicate that he adhered to the theory of *anyathā-khyāti*.

5.12

In closing, it should be mentioned that the example of the ideas of lower numbers leading up to those of higher numbers in the *BS* passage is also borrowed from the *VPv*, from 1.87, where it says that as the numbers one etc. are understood as parts of the numbers one hundred or one thousand, so words are understood (wrongly) as parts of the sentence (which is really a partless whole). This is based on the Vaiśeṣika that the numbers above one are cognized by an *apekṣā-buddhi*, a 'relative cognition', in which the lower numbers figure.[8] However, the Vaiśeṣikas would not regard the lower numbers as unreal.

APPENDIX A

MAṆḌANA'S DATE

A-1

There seems to be a consensus among scholars that Maṇḍana Miśra should be placed in the latter half of the seventh century or very early in the eighth. Various dates within this period have been suggested.[1] Only a few give a later date.[2] I do not wish to give much space to fixing Maṇḍana's date exactly, which could involve us in long discussions of a number of debated questions in the dating of other writers. But a relatively brief discussion can, I think, arrive at a date sufficiently precise for our purposes. What is more important than fixing a particular year for his birth or death is determining his relative chronology, which can help to determine his place in the development of Indian philosophy. Luckily, this is fairly clear, or so it seems to me. To put it briefly, he follows Dharmakīrti, Kumārila, and Prābhākara; he is contemporary with Śaṃkara and presupposes him; and he is criticized by Śaṃkara's disciple Sureśvara. To establish each of these points, I will give only the minimum of proof necessary, without attempting an exhaustive treatment of every indication that Maṇḍana knows another author. After establishing his place relative to other philosophers, we will return to the problem of his calendar date.

A-2

It is clear that Maṇḍana is posterior to Dharmakīrti. In the *Sphoṭa-siddhi*, he quotes a line from the *Pramāṇavārttika* and closely paraphrases a passage from Dharmakīrti's auto-commentary on the work.[3] He does not, so far as I know, quote the Buddhist in the *Brahma-siddhi*, but he does deal there[4] with the notion that the definition of existence is the fulfilling of a purposeful action (*artha-kriyākāritva*), which seems to be an invention of Dharmakīrti.[5]

A-3

He also comes after Kumārila, whose *Ślokavārttika* he

quotes fifteen times in the *BS*, and *Tantravārttika* once.[6] He was traditionally supposed to be both the pupil and the brother-in-law of Kumārila.[7] This however, appears doubtful, since his treatment of the problem of *bhāvanā* seems to presuppose a development of the problem between Kumārila and the *Bhāvanā-viveka*.[8]

A-4

He must follow Prābhākara as well, because in the *BS* and *ViV*, he quotes the *Bṛhatī*,[9] and in the same works, he argues at length against Prābhākara's theory of injunction,[10] and in the *BS* and *VV* against his theory of error.[11] Since certain features of the Prābhākara theory of error as described in the *VV* do not appear in what we have of Prābhākara's works, it is possible that he implies some development within the Prābhākara school after Prābhākara himself. However, it is not impossible that Maṇḍana had access to a lost work of the school's founder.[12] Since Prābhākara and Kumārila must have been roughly contemporary, because if there had been any substantial length of time between them it would be hard to see why they show no knowledge of each other's positions,[13] it would be reasonable to expect that some elaboration of his school's arguments would have occurred between him and Maṇḍana, as between Kumārila and Maṇḍana.

A-5

Perhaps the thinker whose date in relation to Maṇḍana's is most important is Śaṃkara. If the *Brahma-siddhi* was written in ignorance of Śaṃkara's works, and represents a current in pre-Śaṃkara Advaita, we must drastically reduce the usual estimate of Śaṃkara's originality. We must say that the commanding importance he has in the history of Vedānta, so great that all works before him except the *Brahma-sūtras* themselves, the *Gauḍapāda-kārikās*, and possibly the *BS*, have disappeared, was due not to any newness in his ideas or his combination of ideas into a system, but to some other cause—perhaps to his zealous activity as an 'evangelist' of Advaita Vedānta against the Buddhists and the adherents of other systems within Hinduism, or to his activity in setting up *maṭhas* to carry on the tradition he followed. Many of Śaṃkara's themes appear in

Maṇḍana—e.g., that the universe and its divisions have only a practical reality, not a final one, but that the practical reality lasts until liberation; that liberation is the manifestation of the soul's own form; that something unreal can lead to a real result; that the Upaniṣads deny all difference; that to allow any *pariṇāma* in Brahman would be to give it parts, and that reality must be free from all change whatever; that the *jīva* really is Brahman, but appears to be divided from it by false knowledge and by limited adjuncts. These common themes are so numerous that if Maṇḍana did write before Śaṃkara, Śaṃkara's intellectual contribution would shrink to the vanishing point. *Prima facie*, I do not find this very plausible. To attribute the importance of Śaṃkara's influence solely to his activities in debate and organization does not explain how he was able to attract the passionate devotion of a thinker as acute as Sureśvara,[14] nor why he and other Advaitins, both contemporary and later, considered themselves as belonging to Śaṃkara's school, rather than that of some earlier teacher. Nor does it explain Śaṃkara's curious use in some places in the *BSuB* of *bhedābheda* doctrines which he rejects elsewhere. The presence of these places has been attributed to his following an older prestigious commentary by the 'Vṛttikāra'.[15] But if the *Kevalādvaita* were a doctrine with a long history behind it, one would have expected commentaries on the *Brahma-sūtras* according to it to have been written already, and for a smoother and more consistent interpretation to have been worked out, in spite of the intractability of Bādarāyaṇa's sentences to a *Kevalādvaita* interpretation. It should be remembered that Bhāskara accused Śaṃkara and his followers of breaking the established tradition in the interpretation of the *Sūtras*. Therefore it is of great importance that we see if it can be proven that Maṇḍana was influenced by Śaṃkara.

A-6

Some modern scholars who have written on the problem of Maṇḍana's date, as well as the traditional biographies of Śaṃkara,[16] have made him a contemporary of Śaṃkara. Some think he may have been an older contemporary.[17] This would, of course, be no bar to Maṇḍana Miśra being influenced by him, especially since, if the traditional belief that Śaṃkara had a very short life is true (I see no reason to doubt it and am not aware of anyone who has), he must have begun his literary activity at an early age. Thus Maṇḍana could have become aware of Śaṃkara's work in his middle age, and still have had time to write the *Brahma-siddhi*, which is one of his later books,[18] incorporating ideas from him. For instance, if he were twenty years older than Śaṃkara, and the latter wrote the *BSūB* at the age of twenty-five, and the *BSūB* took five years to get to Maṇḍana, Maṇḍana would still be only fifty. I do not, of course, say that this schema is necessarily true. I do not think we are able at present to fix the date of either of the two with such precision that we could tell the exact difference in age between them. I merely wish to show that there is no chronological objection to Maṇḍana's being influenced by Śaṃkara, while being older than he.

A-7

I think the *BS* shows clear evidence of its dependence on Śaṃkara. Here I wish to bring forward only those passages which seem to give the clearest indication of Maṇḍana's knowledge of Śaṃkara.

A-8

The passage which is the most persuasive is *BS* 32.13-34.23, a long *pūrvapakṣa* in which all connection between works and knowledge is denied, on the grounds that knowledge deals with non-duality and works with duality, and that, Brahman not being something to be effected (*sādhya*), it cannot be reached by works.[19] This passage seems to represent Śaṃkara's position in *BSūB* 1.1.4, as Kuppuswami Sastri and Vetter have observed.[20] However, it should at once be observed that the details of the argument do not follow Śaṃkara's passage. An opponent to the *pūrvapakṣa*, who does not completely represent Maṇḍana's ideas,[21] raises new objections, based on the distinction between *avidyā* as non-apprehension and *avidyā* as wrong apprehension, and offers several possibilities for what one might want to gain by some further activity after having gotten knowledge of the unity of Brahman and the Self from scripture. All of this is missing in the *BSūB*. These advances in the argument have led Vetter to speculate that Maṇḍana is dealing with a lost text between him and Śaṃkara.[22] While this is possible, it is equally possible that they reflect contemporary verbal debates, or objections raised by Maṇḍana so as to exhaust all the possibilities of the argument. On the assumption that either of these possibilities is true, we might possibly, though not by any means necessarily, say that there was a smaller gap between Śaṃkara's literary activity and the composition of the *BS* than if we assumed an intermediate written text.

A-9

It should also be observed that this passage represents a more radical position than Śaṃkara's, in that at 32.15 it denies any usefulness of works in the production of knowledge, in addition to any usefulness in cooperation with knowledge once arisen, whereas in *BSūB* 3.4.26, 27 and 33, Śaṃkara says that works help to produce knowledge, which he does not in so many words deny at *BSūB* 1.1.4.[23] This may reflect post-Śaṃkara developments of which we have no literary remains,[24] or it may be merely that Maṇḍana pulled out one thread from the fabric of Śaṃkara's complex and possibly not totally consistent doctrine on works and knowledge, and state it in its most radical form for the sake of argument.

A-10

However this may be, the end of the passage, i.e. 34.13-23, shows a close verbal similarity to part of *BSūB* 1.1.4, pp. 150-52, as Kuppuswami Sastri, S. S. Suryanarayana Sastri, and Vetter have observed.[25] I think the similarity is so close as to prove that Maṇḍana had the *BSūB* before him. Since the passage, which asserts that *saṃsāra* ceases as soon as one has understood from *śruti* that the Self is Brahman, does not occur in Bhāskara's commentary on the *BSū*, and indeed is irreconcilable with his *bhedābheda*, it cannot be attributed to the *Vṛttikāra*, whom Bhāskara seems to follow. And since, as noted in A-5, it is unlikely that there was a *Kevalādvaita* commentary on the *BSū* before Śaṃkara, there is no reason to accept the possibility of a source—which to account for this close verbal similarity would have to be a written text—common to Maṇḍana Miśra and Śaṃkara. I give the passages from the *BS* and the *BSūB* below, leaving a blank space where either has material the other does not, and marking a substantial omission in the *BSūB*.

A-11

BS 34.13-24	*BSūB* 150.1-11 (1.1.4)
nanv avagate 'pi 'tat tvam asi' (*CU* 6.8.7) iti śabdād brahmātmabhāve prāg iva saṃsārikadharmadarśanāt tannivṛttaye bhavaty anyāpekṣā	nanu śrutabrahmaṇo 'pi yathāpūrvaṃ saṃsāritvadarśanān na rajjusvarūpakathanavad arthavattvam ity uktam
naitat sāram; kathaṃ khalv avagatabrahmātmabhāvo viditātmayāthātathyo mithyādarśananimittair dharmair yujyate.	atrocyate—nāvagatabrahmātmabhāvasya yathāpūrvaṃ saṃsāritvaṃ śakyaṃ darśayitum, vedaprāmaṇajanitabrahmātmabhāvavirodhāt. na hi śarīrādyātmābhimānanivṛttau tad eva mithyājñānanimittaṃ duḥkhabhayādimattvaṃ bhavatīti śakyaṃ kalpayitum. na hi dhanino gṛhasthasya dhanābhimānino dhanāpahāranimittaṃ duḥkham dṛṣṭam iti tasyaiva pravrajitasya dhanābhimānarahitasya tad eva dhanāpahāranimittam duḥkhaṃ bhavati. na ca kuṇḍalinaḥ kuṇḍalitvābhimānanimittam sukhaṃ dṛṣṭam iti tasyaiva kuṇḍalaviyuktasya kuṇḍalitvābhimānarahitasya tad eva kuṇḍalitvābhimānanimittaṃ sukham bhavati.
śrūyate ca—'brahma veda brahmaiva bhavati' (*MuṇḍU* 3.2.9) iti. na ca brahmaṇy apahatapāpmani teṣām avakāśaḥ; tathā—ātmānaṃ ced vijānīyād ayam asmīti pūruṣaḥ/kim icchan kasya kāmāya śarīram anusaṃjvaret// (*BU* 4.4.12)	

tathā 'aśarīraṃ vāva santaṃ na priyāpriye spṛśataḥ'	tad uktam śrutyā—'aśarīraṃ vāva santaṃ na priyāpriye spṛśataḥ'
(*CU* 8.12.1) iti	(*CU* 8.12.1) iti
	śarīre patite 'sarīratvaṃ syāt na jīvata iti cen; na
mithyābhimānanimittaḥ śarīrasaṃbandhaḥ	saśarīratvasya mithyājñānanimittatvāt
tasmin yāthātathyadarśanān nivṛtte 'śarīratvam;	na hy ātmanaḥ śarīrātmābhimānalakṣaṇaṃ mithyājñānaṃ muktvānyataḥ saśarīratvam śakyaṃ kalpayitum.
tatra priyāpriyayor asaṃbandha ākhyāyate.	
	(Omission of *BSūB* 150.11-152.8) *BSūB* 152.8-153.1
tasmān nāvagatabrahmātmabhāvaḥ prāg iva saṃsārikadharmabhāk; yas tu tathā, nāsāv avagatabrahmātmabhāva iti.	tasmān nāvagatabrahmātmabhāvasya yathāpūrvaṃ saṃsāritvam. yas tu saṃsāritvaṃ nāsāv avagatabrahmātmabhāva ity anavadyam.

A-12

Although Śaṃkara in the passage just quoted talks of *saṃsāritva* rather than *sāṃsārika* or *mithyājñānanimitta dharmas* (*BS* 34.24, 16), compare *BSūB* 113.7: *śrutabrahmaṇo 'pi sukhaduḥkhādisaṃsāridharmadarśanāt.* In addition, *MuṇḍU* 3.2.9, *brahma veda brahmaiva bhavati*, which Maṇḍana's *Pūrvapakṣin* (*BS* 34.16-17) quotes in support of his position that no activity, nothing but knowledge gained from the scriptures, is necessary for liberation, though it is not used in the passage of Śaṃkara just quoted, is used by him to prove the same point at *BSūB* 121.6-11, in his commentary on the same *sūtra*, 1.1.4.

A-13

In the passage *BS* 19.22-20.21 Maṇḍana attempts to avoid the opposite dangers of, on the one hand, attributing diversity, and with it the fault of the phenomenal world, to Brahman, and, on the other, of making Brahman nothing but the absence of phenomenal diversity, and thus a mere void. In the crucial sentence of the passage (20.11-12), he accomplishes this by saying that the relation of Brahman to the universe is a non-reciprocal one: "Brahman does not have everything for its self, but everything has Brahman for its self; it has positive existence through the positive existence of Brahman." This is a doctrine found in all but identical words at several places in Śaṃkara's works, as the following quotes will show:

Texts from the BS

A. *BS* 20.11-12: *brahmaṇo na sarvātmatā; sarvaṃ tu brahmātmakam; brahmarūpeṇa rūpavat.*

B. *BS* 20.7: *tasmān na prapañcātmakaṃ brahma, avidyāvikrīḍitam eva prapañca iti sāṃpratam.*

Texts from Śaṃkara

1. *BSūB* 2.1.9 (446.20-22): *ananyatve 'pi kāryakāraṇayoḥ kāryasya kāraṇātmatvaṃ na tu kāraṇasya kāryātmatvam 'ārambhaṇaśabdādibhyaḥ'* (*BSū* 2.1.14) *iti vakṣyāmaḥ.*[26]
2. *BSūB* 3.2.21 (712.19): *brahmasvabhāvo hi prapañco na prapañcasvabhāvaṃ brahma.*[27]
3. *BSūB* 4.1.3 (938.15-16): *na hīśvarasya saṃsāryātmatvaṃ pratipādyata ity abhyupagacchāmaḥ. kiṃ tarhi? saṃsāriṇaḥ saṃsāritvāpoheneśvarātmatvaṃ pratipipādayiṣitam iti.*
4. *TUB* 2.6 (74.15-16): *ato nāmarūpe sarvāvasthe brahmaṇaiva ātmavatī, na brahma tadātmakam.*

A-14

Texts 1 and 3 provide particularly close parallels to the *BS*, because they are employed to resolve similar difficulties. Śaṃkara uses Text 1, alongside examples drawn from ordinary life, to show that Brahman is not touched by the qualities of the universe when it dissolves back into it. Text 3 forms part of the reply to the objection that if the Lord is the Self or the transmigrant soul, He will participate in His qualities and cease to be Lord.

A-15

The similarity is somewhat less clear in Text 4, and the second part of the sentence—*na brahma tadātmakam*—could be taken as an *obiter dictum.* However, Śaṃkara does say, immediately before this text: "The differentiation of name and form is Brahman's becoming many. Otherwise there is no coming to be many or limitation of Brahman, it being without parts, as the limitation and manifoldness of the ether is caused only by other things (i.e. *upādhis*)."[28] Therefore it seems that it is again for the sake of protecting Brahman from the world's imperfections that Śaṃkara denies that Brahman has the world as its self.

A-16

Text 2 demands special discussion, and therefore it has been kept till last. Unfortunately, it somewhat weakens the strength of the four texts as evidence that Maṇḍana Miśra was aware of Śaṃkara. The words are put into the mouth of a *pūrvapakṣin*, to be precise, a *Prapañcavilaya-vādin*, one who taught that the Vedas contain injunctions to dissolve, i.e. to see as unreal, the *prapañca*, and thereby to come to know the Ātman.[29] Now it seems that the adherents of this doctrine adhered to the doctrine that the universe is a figment of *avidyā* or *māyā*,[30] as did Śaṃkara and Maṇḍana. Therefore, it may be that statements of the kind we have quoted were standard with all illusionistic Vedāntins. The *pūrvapakṣin* obviously expects that Śaṃkara will agree that Brahman does not have for its self the world, since he concludes his argument by stating that fact, without giving any argument for it, and says that therefore one must, to know Brahman, dissolve the world of names and forms. But this does not allow us to see whether the doctrine we are discussing was common to them both, or peculiar to Śaṃkara, and quoted by the *pūrvapakṣin* for the sake of the argument. Failing further evidence, we cannot be certain whether the doctrine is Śaṃkaran or pre-Śaṃkaran, and so we cannot claim it as decisive evidence of Maṇḍana's knowledge of Śaṃkara. However, it is not mentioned by any of the other authors whom Hiriyanna names as sources for our information on *Prapañca-vilaya-vāda*.[31]

A-17

As Kuppuswami Sastri notes,[32] Śaṅkhapāṇi (264.13-14) tells us that Maṇḍana's position at *BS* 132.21-133.3 is directed against Śaṃkara's at *BSūB* 4.1.19. Śaṅkhapāṇi says: *ato bhogena teṣāṃkṣayapratīkṣeti sūktam 'bhogena tv itare kṣapayitvā'* (*BSū* 4.1.19) *iti bhagavatpādīyamatam upanyasyati—ye tv iti.* Although Śaṅkhapāṇī seems to have lived after Vācaspati Miśra,[33] and therefore is too far removed from Maṇḍana to be taken as a strong authority on his chronological relationship with Śaṃkara, he may well be right. Maṇḍana's opponent says that it is impossible to stop works whose fruits have already begun, just as it is impossible to stop an arrow or a potter's wheel whose motion has already begun. (*pravṛttabhogānāṃ karmaṇāṃ pravṛttavegasyeṣor iva cakrasyeva vā na śakyaḥ pratibandhaḥ, ato bhogena kṣayapratīkṣeti, BS* 132.20-21). The two examples given by the opponent are exactly those used by Śaṃkara, although under different *sūtras* from that mentioned by Śaṅkhapāṇi. In commenting on *BSū* 3.3.32 (818.8-10), Śaṃkara says: *pravṛttaphalasya tu karmāśayasya mukteṣor iva vegakṣayān nivṛttiḥ 'tasya tāvad eva ciram'* (*CU* 6.14.2) *iti śarīrapātāvadhikṣepakaraṇāt.* On *BSū* 4.1.15 (958.10-12): *na tāvad anāśrityārabdhakāryaṃ karmāśayaṃ jñānotpattir upapadyate. āśrite ca tasmin kulālacakravat pravṛttavegasyāntarāle pratibandhāsaṃbhavād vegakṣayapratipālanam.* The similarity is striking. The order in which the examples occur in the *BS* is the same as that in which they occur in the *Bhāṣya*, as if Maṇḍana were leafing through his copy of the latter while composing this passage. Like Śaṃkara, Maṇḍana uses *pravṛtta-* in the beginnings of compounds to mean 'begun', in place of *ārabdha-* used by *BSū* 4.1.15. Bhāskara, in commenting on *BSū* 3.3.32, 4.1.15 and 4.1.18, follows the *sūtra* in using *ārabdha-*, which lessens the possibility that the coincidence of Maṇḍana and Śaṃkara in vocabulary might come from both working from an older commentary on the *BSū*, the *Vṛttikāra*'s.[34] Maṇḍana replies, quite reasonably, that it is possible to stop or destroy a flying arrow, and that therefore his position must be accepted, that all works, those whose fruition has not yet begun and those whose fruition has, are destroyed by knowledge, and that after knowledge only a *saṃskāra* of works remains (133.1-3).

A-18

I have been able to find no other places where Maṇḍana gives an equally distinct impression of being aware of Śaṃkara. Although Kuppuswami Sastri gives a long list of divergences between Maṇḍana and Śaṃkara,[35] in his treatment of none of these does Maṇḍana seem clearly to reflect Śaṃkara's views or wording, and not just what might have been part of the Vedānta tradition available to both of them. But I think that the parallelism of the passages given in A-13 is by itself sufficient for us to conclude that Śaṃkara's work was available to Maṇḍana.

A-19

I do not wish here to reopen the debate on Maṇḍana's identity with Sureśvara, which I consider to have been settled once for all against their identity by Kuppuswami Sastri in his introduction to the *BS.*[36] Any further comments on the problem can be relegated to the notes,[37] and their difference taken for granted in our discussion.

A-20

There is much evidence that Sureśvara knew Maṇḍana's work, In *BS*, pp. x-xiii, a list is given of places in the *Sambandhavārttika* where Sureśvara reproduces material from Maṇḍana with only slight rewording, including one verse found in identical form in both (*BS* III.81=*SV* 737).[38] The similarity is so clear that it is not necessary to discuss the passages or give examples here. They include no doctrines peculiar to Maṇḍana which Sureśvara or any other Advaita Vedāntin could not have accepted;[39] they deny the existence of difference and of an injunction of knowledge of Brahman. A supplementary list is given by Anantakrishna Sastri, *Two Commentaries on Brahma-siddhi*, pp. 541-60. Of these latter I consider the examples numbered 1 through 4 (1) thoroughly convincing by the similarity of wording and sequence of ideas, 4(2-5) slightly less so, and 5 through 8 dubious. The borrowing could not have been the other way, by Maṇḍana from Sureśvara, since as we shall see. Sureśvara attacks Maṇḍana on several occasions, and sometimes seems to presuppose extension or criticisms of his arguments.

A-21

The *SV* develops further Maṇḍana's arguments against Prābhākara, and it has been suggested that what is new in Sureśvara in this context is directed against Śālikanātha's criticisms of Maṇḍana.[40] If this is so, and Śālikanātha intervenes between Maṇḍana and Sureśvara, the interval between them would have to be slightly larger than if no development of the debate was noticeable between them. But there is some doubt about Śālikanātha's date; some would place him later, around the time of Vācaspati Miśra,[41] in which case it would be impossible for Sureśvara to be responding to his attacks. Even if he does come just after Maṇḍana, we are not required to add an extra generation between Maṇḍana and Sureśvara, to which we would assign Śālikanātha, because his writings come between theirs, and also Śaṃkara's, because, being Sureśvara's teacher, he precedes him, and thus to make Maṇḍana come not one generation before Sureśvara, but two, thereby making him not Śaṃkara's approximate contemporary, but his predecessor. There is no justification for the tendency sometimes visible in discussing dates in Indian philosophy automatically to put a full generation of twenty or thirty years between two writers when one of them quotes the other. Especially when they were active in the same region, knowledge of one philosopher's works could spread and reach another philosopher quite rapidly. For instance, it appears from a fragment of Kumārila Bhaṭṭa's lost *Bṛhaṭṭīkā*, that Kumārila may have modified his theory of logical connection, after writing the *Śloka-vārttika*, in response to Dharmakīrti's new theory.[42] Thus Maṇḍana, Śālikanātha, and Sureśvara could have been more or less contemporaries, yet this would not have prevented Sureśvara from knowing and criticizing Śālikanātha's attacks on Maṇḍana.

A-22

In the *Naiṣkarmya-siddhi* Sureśvara reproduces as a *pūrvapakṣa* Maṇḍana's position on the need of repetition in meditation of the verbal knowledge gained from the *Upaniṣads*. He does not follow Maṇḍana's words as closely as in the *SV*, but the similarity of ideas is close. He speaks as if there were two groups of opponents, but it is clear that that is merely a literary device, unless he is referring to others who held the same opinions as Maṇḍana. He merely wishes to sort out two ideas, both of which can be found in Maṇḍana. That they are closely related in his mind is visible from the fact that they are presented together in the prose introduction to *NS* I, V. 67, and answered together in that one verse. In quoting the prose, I will introduce the two positions by 'A' and 'B' for convenience:

NS. I. V. 67, Introd.: *evam upasaṃhṛte* (A) *ke cit svasaṃpradāyabalāvaṣṭambhād āhuḥ*; *yad etad vedāntavākyād ahaṃ brahmeti vijñānaṃ samutpadyate tan naiva svotpattimātreṇājñānaṃ nirasyati. kim tarhi? ahany ahani drāghīyasā kālenopāsīnasya sato bhāvanopacayān niḥśeṣam ajñānam apagacchati, 'devo bhūtvā devān apyeti'* (*BU* 4.1.12) *iti śruteḥ.* (B) *apare tu bruvate: vedāntavākyajanitam ahaṃ brahmeti vijñānaṃ saṃsargātmakatvād ātmavastuyāthātmāvagāhy eva na bhavati. kiṃ tarhi? etad eva gaṅgāsrotovat satatam abhyasyato anyad evāvākyārthātmakaṃ vijñānāntaram utpadyate tad evāśeṣājñānatimirotsārīti, 'vijñāya prajñāṃ kurvīta'* (*BU* 4.4.21) *iti śruteḥ. ity asya pakṣadvayasya nivṛttaye idam abhidhīyate...*

A-23

The first opinion (A), that nescience does not completely cease upon the arising of verbal knowledge, is paralleled in these two passages of the *BS*:

BS 35.11-16: *jāte 'pi tattvadarśane, anāhite ca paṭau saṃskāre, draḍhīyasi ca mithyādarśanaje saṃskāre niścayā api mithyārthā bhavantī; yathā diṅmūḍhasyānanusaṃhitāptavacasaḥ, prāg iva pravṛttidarśanāt; tathā pramitarajjubhāvāyā api rajjvāḥ pramāṇānanusandhāne sarpabhrāntyā bhayadarśanam. tasmāj jāte 'pi pramāṇāt tattvadarśane anādimithyādarśanābhyāsapariniṣpannasya draḍhīyasaḥ saṃskārasyābhibhavāyocchedāya vā tattvadarśanābhyāsaṃ manyate.*

BS 134.11-13: *śābdaṃ tu pramāṇādhīnaṃ kṣaṇikaṃ jñanam, tatra punar api viparyayāvakāśaḥ; dṛṣṭaṃ hi pramāṇānusandhāne punaḥ sarpabhrāntyā rajjor bhayam.* P: *athātrāpi saṃtataṃ jñānam anusaṃdadhīta.* S: *kim anyad upāsanam asmād?*

The verbal similarity is not close. Sureśvara does not use Maṇḍana's example of the return of fear of a snake even after one has been told that it is a rope. Neither does he use the word *saṃskāra*, a favourite with Maṇḍana. But the thought is similar enough to justify Kuppuswami Sastri in giving it as an example of Sureśvara quoting Maṇḍana.[43]

A-24

On the second position (B), that verbal knowledge is insufficient for knowing Brahman because it is acquired from sentences, which are the conjunction (*saṃsarga*) of several words, and therefore involves multiplicity, and has to be supplemented by continuous meditation which will result in a direct knowledge without words or multiplicity. Compare the following:

BS 115.16-20: *na śābdajñānaviṣaya ātmatattvam. vākyalakṣaṇo hi śabdaḥ pramāṇam. tasya ca viṣayo nānāpadārthasaṃsargātmā, tadanugamena pratīteḥ. tajjñānasya ca vividhārthamātrasaṃbhedāvabhāsasyātmatattvaṃ niṣprapañcaṃ dvaitaleśenāpy anavamṛṣṭaṃ katham gocaraḥ syād iti.*

This is in the *siddhānta*, but is not rejected in Maṇḍana's *pūrvapakṣa*. Cf. also these two passages:

BS 74.10-14: *tisraś ca pratipattayo brahmaṇi*; *prathamā tāvac chabdāt, anyā śabdāt pratipadya tatsantānavatī dhyānabhāvanopāsanādiśabdavācyā, anyā tato labdhniṣpattir vigalitanikhilavikalpā sākṣātkaraṇarūpā.*

BS 154.2-5: *atha tu vākyāntarāt tattvaniṣṭhād adhigate tadviṣayapratyayapravāhavidhānam iṣyate*; *bhavatu, na kaścid doṣaḥ*; *tathā ca 'vijñāya prajñāṃ kurvīta'* (*BU* 4.4.21) *ity ātmatattvavijñānasya siddhatāṃ darśayati. tad api vā vyartham eva, prāptārthatvāt*; *sākṣātkaraṇaphalaṃ hi tatadanucintanaṃ dṛṣṭārtham*; *na tato 'nyat phalam ākāṅkṣate.*

Although in the last passage the idea that verbal knowledge involves multiplicity is lacking, note that it quotes the same *śruti* as (B) (*BU* 4.4.22). Maṇḍana's *tatsantānavatī pratipatti*, 'an apprehension involving a continuous succession of that (of verbal knowledge)', and his *pratyayapravāha*, 'a continuous flow of cognitions', resemble Sureśvara's *gaṅgāsrotovat*, 'like the (continuous) flow of the Ganges'. Although it could easily be a coincidence, and has little value as proof, it is worth observing that the order in which Sureśvara reports the two positions is the same as that in which they occur in the *BS*: A first comes up on p. 35, and B afterwards on p. 74. I think that the weight of the evidence is that Sureśvara's opponent here is Maṇḍana.[44]

A-25

Sureśvara presents a similar *Pūrvapakṣa* in the *Bṛhadāraṇyakopaniṣad-bhāṣya-vārttika* 4.3.796-810 (pp. 1852-54). Kuppuswami Sastri thinks that it is Maṇḍana whose views are presented,[45] as does Ānandagiri in his gloss.[46] Again, as in *BS* 154.2-5, the *śruti BU* 4.4.21, *vijñāya prajñāṃ kurvīta*, is discussed, and 'the conjunction of word-meanings' (*padārthasaṃsarga*) involved in knowledge arising from a sentence is mentioned (*passim*), as at *BS* 115.16-20. By repetition (*abhyāsa*, a favourite word of Maṇḍana), one obtains direct vision (*sākṣātdarśana*, V. 809, cf. *BS* 74.10-14). Sureśvara shows much animosity to his opponent or opponents here, sarcastically calling him or them 'thinking themselves learned' (*paṇḍitaṃmanyāḥ*, V. 796) and 'versed in deep reasonings' (*gambhīranyāyavedinaḥ*, V. 810). (We cannot tell from the plural whether he is referring to one opponent or many. It could be a sarcastic plural of honor). This violence of feeling could be attributed to Maṇḍana's refusal to follow Śaṃkara all the way. This gains some confirmation from what was said in the passage quoted above from the *NS*, where Sureśvara attributed the opponents' doctrines to 'pride in the strength of their own tradition'. (*svasaṃpradāyabalāvaṣṭambhāt*) as here he says the opponents explain *BU* 4.4.22 'in accordance with a tradition' (*saṃpradāyānusārataḥ*). It would appear that Maṇḍana, in his ideas on the interpretation of that scriptural sentence, and his doctrine that verbal knowledge must be repeated, belonged to a separate established tradition, that he was not the first to propound them. This is hardly surprising, since it would be natural for debate to arise early on this point. I do not, however, think it likely that Maṇḍana's *system* goes back before him. It is composed of ideas from too many disparate sources for that to be possible.

A-26

In *BUBV* 4.4.876-891, Sureśvara presents another opinion that somewhat resembles Maṇḍana's. Again the topic is *BU* 4.4.12: *vijñāya prajñāṃ kurvīta*. The opponent says that the knowledge produced from the sentences of the Upaniṣads destroys all ignorance, but that since ignorance has been in existence since beginningless time, it may return. We observe that desire and the like persist even after right knowledge. Therefore, one must repeat knowledge until all ignorance is destroyed. This is much the same as what Maṇḍana says in *BS* 35.11-16 and 134.11-13, already quoted (A-23). As in the passage of the *NS*, Sureśvara does not mention Maṇḍana's example of the continuing fear of a snake after one has ascertained it is a rope, nor the word *saṃskāra*. He does mention *abhyāsa* (V. 885), another favourite word of Maṇḍana. Maṇḍana neither in the two passages mentioned here nor elsewhere says explicitly that desire (*rāga*) persists in one who has had right knowledge. This might, however, be implied by his rejection in *BS* 35.1-36.3 of Śaṃkara's extreme position, quoted above (A.11), that "the qualities of a transmigrant' (*sāṃsārikadharmāḥ*), which could easily include *rāga*, cease in one who has realized his identity with Brahman. However, Sureśvara's opponent has a doctrine not found in Maṇḍana. He divides *ajñāna* or *avidyā* into two sorts, innate (*naisargika*) and accidental (*āgantuka*), and says that the accidental is destroyed at once by knowledge, but the innate can be destroyed only by knowledge repeated energetically (Vs. 881-85). He then goes on to quote two *ślokas* from Gauḍapāda and two attributed by Ānandagiri to the *Mahābhārata* which are nowhere quoted by Maṇḍana.[47] This might be the reason to doubt that he was referring to Maṇḍana, were it not that he refers to his opponents as 'great and wise Mīmāṃsakas', (*mahāmīmāṃsakā dhīrāḥ*, V. 891), which fits Maṇḍana very well.[48] This, combined with the other similarities, leads me to suspect that Maṇḍana is here the opponent, or one of the opponents, and that what is additional to his doctrine is from followers of his.[49] This again does not make it necessary to push Maṇḍana back before Śaṃkara. If Maṇḍana were a contemporary or an older contemporary of Śaṃkara and Sureśvara had an ordinarily long life, there would have been plenty of time for Maṇḍana's students or others to develop Maṇḍana's ideas before Sureśvara reported them. When introducing this *pūrvapakṣa*, Sureśvara says: "Others, fault-finding and set in their own notion of the meaning of the Veda, have explained this (*śruti*, *BU* 4.4.22: *vijñāya prajñāṃ kurvīta*) in a different way than this explanation, out of malcontent".[50] This leads me to think that Maṇḍana taught his interpretation of the text even though he knew about Śaṃkara's, thus contributing to Sureśvara's indignation at him. I have not been able to find any additional passages where Sureśvara seems to display an awareness of Maṇḍana's writings.[51]

A-27

We are now in a position to come to some conclusion on Maṇḍana's dates. We know that Maṇḍana comes after both Dharmakīrti and Kumārila. Now, Kumārila seems to have written the *Bṛhaṭṭīkā* between A.D. 630 and 640, after having read the *Hetuprakaraṇa* of the *Pramāṇavārttika* of Dharmakīrti; it seems to have been written after the *Śloka-vārttika* and to have been a work of his old age.[52] Dharmakīrti rose to fame between the visits to India of Hsüan Tsang and I Tsing, but he complains that for many years he failed to achieve recognition. Hsüan Tsang left India in 644, and I Tsing's stay at Nālandā was from 675 to 685. Dharmakīrti died, it would seem, before I Tsing's arrival, for I Tsing does not refer to him as a contemporary. Taking all this into account, we can, with Frauwallner, assign him the approximate dates of 600-60.[53] Kumārila was presumably somewhat older. Prābhākara must have been contemporary to Kumārila, for the two of them seem unaware of each other's theories, and if they were much separated in time, it would be hard to see how the knowledge of one did not spread to the other.[54] It should be noticed that also in setting the early limit for Śaṃkara the most important facts are his quotation of Dharmakīrti and his apparent reference to Kumārila.[55] For fixing Maṇḍana's later date on the calendar, the crucial fact is that Umbeka comments upon Maṇḍana's *Bhāvanā-viveka* and must come some time after him, because he gives variant readings of the text.[56] Umbeka's date can be fixed fairly precisely. He is not mentioned in Śāntarakṣita's *Tattvasaṃgraha*, but is mentioned by name in Kamalaśīla's *Pañjikā* on it.[57] Now according to Paul Demiéville's studies of the Council of Lhasa, in which Kamalaśīla took the leading role, Kamalaśīla arrived in Tibet in 792.[58] The *TSP* must have been written before his leaving India. Likewise, Śāntarakṣita must have written the *TS* before he left for Tibet around 763.[59] Therefore, it is probable that Umbeka's activity, or at least the publication of the *Śloka-vārttika-vyākhyā*, the work of his which Kamalaśīla quotes, lies between 760 and 790. Although the argument from Śāntarakṣita's silence may not be a strong one for his early limit, the later limit is firm. If we give as an early limit for Maṇḍana's literary activity about 660, we will have left plenty of time for the fact that the theories of the Bhāṭṭa and Prābhākara schools, as they appear in Maṇḍana, seem to have undergone some development after Kumārila and Prābhākara. If we give as a later limit 720 or thereabouts, sufficient time will be left for variant readings to have crept into Umbeka's text of the *Bhāvanā-viveka*, especially in view of the fact that it appears that it was an early work, written before both the *Vidhi-viveka* and the *Brahma-siddhi*, as said in Appendix B-2 and B-3.

APPENDIX B

THE ORDER OF MAṆḌANA'S WORKS

B-1

The fact that an author writing in Sanskrit cites another of his own books is not an infallible indication that the book mentioned is earlier than the book in which it is mentioned; for such a reference could be inserted in a book long after its original composition. This is demonstrated by the fact that two of Abhinavagupta's works, the *Īśvarapratyabhijñāvivṛtivimarśinī* and the *Abhinavabhāratī*, quote each other.[1] Cross-quoting was all the easier because Indian books were neither printed nor bound; to make an insertion all that would be necessary would be to untie the manuscript, remove one leaf, and rewrite it. Therefore speculations on the order of a writer's works solely on the basis of which mention which are inconclusive. In the following discussion we will therefore try to supplement the evidence of the citations with other evidence, when possible.

B-2

On the basis of explicit citations we can say that the *Bhāvanā-viveka* precedes the *Vidhi-viveka*, which in turn precedes the *Brahma-siddhi*. The *ViV* refers to the *BV* in two places: *ViV* 102.1-103.2 and 368.1-3. The first is worth reproducing here: (P) *nanv iṣṭasiddhyupādhau bhāvārthe niyogāt phalasiddhiḥ syāt*? (S) *syād yadīdṛśo bhāvārthaḥ. na tv ayam evety uktaṃ bhāvanāviveke. naimittike ca phalaprasaṅgaḥ. yathā cāsmin darśane na karmaphalasaṃbandhas tathoktaṃ bhāvanāviveke.* This is more than a sort of footnote, an incidental reference in the middle of a long argument referring to a similar argument elsewhere; instead it dismisses with the need for argument in the *ViV* on the point in question by referring to the prolonged argument in the *BV*. Therefore, the reference is not a later insertion, but an integral part of the original version of the *ViV*. which must therefore follow the *BV*.

B-3

The *BS* cites the *ViV* in three places (11.19-20, 117.7-9, 118.13-14), quotes it directly without naming it in one place (116.9-10, cf. *ViV* 460.1), and refers to the *BV* in one place (111.19-20 again). Of these all but the reference to the *ViV* at 117.7-9 could be insertions. That passage, however, seems to be tightly tied into the rest of the *BS* text. In *BS* 117.3-20 Maṇḍana gives three alternative explanations of Vs. III.105ab. In two out of the three the *pūrvapakṣa* is refuted with a few words and a reference to the proof of Maṇḍana's point in the *ViV*. Therefore it seems reasonably certain that the *BS* follows the *ViV*, as the latter follows the *BV*.

B-4

As already mentioned in paragraphs 1.71, 1.72, 1.73 and 1.75 the failure of the *Vibhrama-viveka* to mention the form of the *anirvacanīya-khyāti-vāda* that the *BS* defends, in which it is combined with the *anyathā-khyāti-vāda*, indicates that the *BS* is later than the *VV*. There is additional evidence for this same conclusion. It appears that the *BS* refers to a lost prose commentary to the *VV*. At *BS* 139.21-23, Maṇḍana says: *darśitam cedam—sāmānyadarśane 'pi kadācid ekāṃ koṭiṃ smarato na saṃśayo na viparyayaḥ, doṣāṇām apuṣṭeḥ.* Commenting on this, Śaṅkhapāṇi says (273.27-274.1):

...*yato darśitam idaṃ vibhramaviveke—"yad ūrdhvatādisāmānyadarśane 'pi sthāṇuṃ vā puruṣaṃ vā ekāṃ koṭiṃ smarataḥ ubhayakoṭismaraṇābhāvāt na saṃśayaḥ, doṣāṇām adṛṣṭatvāc ca na viparyaya" iti.*

The words in ŚP within quotation marks are in prose, and the point made by them and by Maṇḍana is not found in the *kārikās* of the *VV* as we have them, nor elsewhere in the *BS*. Therefore, as L. Schmithausen observes,[2] there must originally have been an autocommentary in prose to the *VV* which is now lost. This would hardly be surprising, since all the rest of Maṇḍana's works are mixed prose and verse (*miśraka*), except for the *Mīmāṃsānukramaṇikā*, which would not need a commentary, being a verse summary for mnemonic purposes of the *Śabara-bhāṣya*. The fact that Maṇḍana does not mention the *VV* by name does not prove that he is not quoting from it, because at *BS* 116.9-10, he concludes a direct quote from the *ViV* with the words *ity uktam* and no mention of the book he is quoting.

B-5

Schmithausen[3] argues convincingly that the fact that Maṇḍana's argumentation is tighter in the section on error in the *BS* than in the *VV*, and that the *BS* gives a number of new arguments not in the *VV*, shows that the *BS* is later. He gives a persuasive analysis of two passages from the *BS* where the order of the argument can best be explained by saying that the argument of the *VV* has been reworked leaving traces of itself in the *BS*. The weight of the evidence is sufficient to show that the *BS* comes after the *VV*.[4]

B-6

Although none of Maṇḍana's other works quote the *VV*, I am inclined to regard it as his first book. It is the only one whose doctrine is clearly radically modified in his other works. It confines itself to one topic and to defending Kumārila's ideas on that topic, adding to it certain innovative features, but not modifying what Kumārila had said. This might indicate that it was the exploratory first attempt at writing by someone just out of studentship. However, it is also true that if the book included a prose commentary, and the ratio of prose to verse was similar to that in his other works (which seems likely if one considers that our one citation from it brings up an interesting point mentioned nowhere in the *kārikās*), it was a fairly sizeable book. Therefore it cannot be said with confidence that it was his first book.

B-7

The *Sphoṭa-siddhi* stands apart from the rest of Maṇḍana's works, neither mentioning them nor being mentioned by them. However, the penultimate verse (36) may refer to the *BS*. Let us first give the verse and a translation:

nirastabhedaṃ padatattvam etad vyādarśi yuktyāgamasaṃśrayeṇa |
vidhūtabhedagraham etayaiva diśāparaṃ sampratiyanty abhedam ||

"The essence of the word, from which difference is removed, has been shown on the basis of reason and tradition. Let them also understand the other non-difference, from which the apprehension of difference has been removed, in the same manner".

As M. Biardeau[5] remarks, the *Gopālikā* on this verse suggests that the *aparam abhedam* may refer to the passage on *akṣara* in the *BS*, that is, to *śabdādvaita*, although it also suggests that it refers to the *vākya-sphoṭa*, Maṇḍana's previous arguments having dealt mainly with the *pada-sphoṭa*. This verse is not absolutely necessary to point out that Maṇḍana's arguments apply equally well to the *vākya-sphoṭa*, since the *vākya-sphoṭa* has already been mentioned several times.[6] The use of Advaita terminology (*nirastabheda, vidhūtabhedagraham*) would be pointless if Maṇḍana's intent had been merely to say that the arguments should be applied to the *sphoṭa* of the sentence. If that had been his intent, he would have said so clearly, or at least added a commentary to the verse and explained it there. Also, putting this verse into a different metre than all the preceding verses takes it out of the argumentative part of the work and associates it with the last verse in stating the wider context and aim of the book. Finally, the first verse of the *SS* invokes the *Ātman*. All these considerations point to the conclusion that the *abheda* of V. 36 is that of Brahman, and that Maṇḍana accepted a form of Advaita when he wrote the *SS*. However, this does not justify us in taking the verse as a reference to a particular book, to the *BS*, and drawing any conclusions about the chronological relation of the two books.[7] No book is mentioned, and even if one thinks that the *BS* is hinted at, the verse fits loosely into the other verses, and could easily be an insertion.

B-8

It is interesting that the *SS* and the *BS* are the only two of Maṇḍana's books to have invocations. This fact might lead us to wonder if when he wrote his other works, which are all on *Pūrva-mīmāṃsā*, he were an atheistic Mīmāṃsaka, though the *ViV*, which has no invocation, contains a long defense of the meaningfulness of the statements of the Upaniṣads which differs not at all from the doctrine of the *BS* on the point.[8] So we cannot deduce anything from the presence or absence of invocations in his various works.

B-9

The *Mīmāṃsānukramaṇikā* neither mentions any of Maṇḍana's other works nor is mentioned by them, and we can say nothing on its place in the order of his works.

B-10

The conclusions we have arrived at, then, are these: The *BV*, *ViV* and *BS* were written in that order. The *VV* was written before the *BS*, and is possibly Maṇḍana's first book. We do not know when the *SS* was written in relation to the *BS* or the other books, nor do we know anything about the place of the *Mīmāṃsānukramaṇikā.*

REFERENCES

CHAPTER I

1. See Hacker, "Eigentümlichkeiten", pp. 261-64.

2. nāvidyā brahmaṇaḥ svabhāvaḥ, nārthāntaram, nātyantam asatī, nāpi satī; evam eveyam avidyā māyā mithyāvabhāsa ity ucyate. svabhāvaś cet kasyacit, anyo 'nanyo vā paramārtha eveti nāvidyā; atyantāsattve khapuṣpasadṛśī na vyavahārāṅgam; tasmād anirvacanīyā. sarvapravādibhiś cettham iyam āstheyā. tathā hi—śūnyavādināṃ sattve yathādarśanam, nāvidyā; khapuṣpatulyatve na vyavahārāṅgam. vijñānamātravādino 'pi yathāvabhāsaṃ jñānasadbhāve nārthāpahnavaḥ, nīlapītāder jñeyākārasya bahiravabhāsānapahnavāt, atyantāsattve bahiravabhāsāyogaḥ (With TV, *MBS*, p. 61, n. 74, I read *-yogaḥ* in place of KS's *-yogāt.*), khapuṣpavat. Bāhyārthavādinām api anityādiṣu nityādikhyātayo rajatādivibhrāntayaś cāvabhāsamānarūpasadbhāve nāvidyātvam aśnuvīran; nātyantāsattve tannibandhanaḥ kaścana vyavahāraḥ syāt. P: syād etat—avabhāsamānaṃ rūpaṃ mā bhūt, avabhāsas tu sann eva, sa cāvidyeti gīyate. S: naitat sāram; avabhāsamāne 'sati tadavabhāso 'pi satyato durnirūpaḥ; avabhāsamātraṃ tu syāt; tadavabhāsa ity api bhrāntir eva. tasmān nāvidyā satī, nāpy asatī. ata eva cāsya nivṛttir adṛḍhasvabhāvāyāḥ, māyāmātratvāt, anyathā svabhāve (With TV, *MBS*, p. 62, I prefer this reading to KS's *anyathāsvabhāve.*) dṛḍham vyavasthitāyaḥ katham anyathātvam? svabhāvahānāt; śūnyatve svayaṃ nivṛttatvāt. evaṃ ca nādvaitahānam, na nivartanīyasyābhāvo vā.

3. It is debated whether the *Vākyapadīya-vṛtti* is by the same writer as the *kārikās* of the *VP*. Some MSS attribute it in their colophons to 'Harivṛṣabha', which they may or may not intend to be the same man as Bhartṛhari. M. Biardeau, *VPBK*, pp. 1-20, maintains that the two authors are different. K. A. S. Iyer, *VPBH*, Introd., pp. xxvi-xxxvi, and *Bhartṛhari*, pp. 16-36, decided tentatively that they are the same. A. Aklujkar, "Authorship of the *Vākyapadīya-vṛtti*", to be published in *WZKSO*, defends their identity. I do not wish to enter this involved argument here. However, I do not think that the two works are by one man. In addition to the apparent differences in doctrine between the *VP* and the *Vṛtti* noted by Biardeau, the difference in style between the *VPv* and Bhartṛhari's *Mahābhāṣyadīpikā* persuades me that Harivṛṣabha and Bhartṛhari are two men. The style of the *Vṛtti* is obscure and overloaded, and uses many long compounds (although it does not use the long compounds ending in abstract suffixes in the instrumental or ablative, that seem to be a feature that enters philosophical Sanskrit at a later time, around that of Śaṃkara). The style of the *Mahābhāṣyadīpikā* is limpidly simple, without long compounds. The similarities between the *VPv* and the *Mahābhāṣyadīpikā* noted by Iyer (*Bhartṛhari*, pp. 27-29) can easily be explained by assuming that the author of the *Vṛtti* knew the *Mahābhāṣyadīpikā*. On the other hand, it is probable that the *Vṛtti* was written not long after the *VP*, for the last two verses of Dignāga's *Traikālyaparīkṣā*, the rest of which consists in verses from the *Saṃbandha-samuddeśa* of the third *kāṇḍa* of the *VP*, with a few modifications, are found not in the *kārikās* of the *VP*, but in the *Vṛtti*

on *VP* 1.1 (13.5-14.2). (See Frauwallner, 'Dignāga', pp. 107, 113.) There is nothing in the *Vṛtti* introducing these verses to indicate that they are Bhartṛhari's; they are introduced by the words *tathā hy uktam*, whereas in one place the *Vṛtti* introduces what is apparently a loose quote from the *kārikās* with *evaṃ hy āha* (see N. 2.8), and the *Vṛtti* on 2.42 introduces a quote, which may be of Bhartṛhari, with the words *ataś ca tatrabhavān āha* (Iyer, *Bhartṛhari*, pp. 31-32). (However, the *Vṛtti* does at places introduce quotes for which there is no reason to believe that they are from Bhartṛhari, e.g. on 1.86.) Frauwallner's suggestion that they may be from a lost work of Bhartṛhari, the *Śabdadhātusamikṣā* ('Dignāga', p. 113, n. 47) is based on the assumption that the *Vṛtti* is by Bhartṛhari himself. There is nothing in M's use of material from the *Vṛtti* to indicate that he thought that the *VPv* was by Bhartṛhari. (To the contrary, see Iyer, *VPBH*, Introd., pp. xix-xx, and *Bhartṛhari*, pp. 19-21, and Aklujkar, op. cit.) All his citations prove is that he was acquainted with the *VPv*; he nowhere explicitly ascribes quotations from the *Vṛtti* to Bhartṛhari or the *VP*. On the other hand, there is no evidence that he thought the *VP* and the *VPv* to be by different hands. In any case, if the *VPv* was written before Dignāga, there would have been sufficient time between it and M for its real authorship to have been forgotten, and so whether or not M thought it was by Bhartṛhari has little importance as evidence. Biardeau, *PMM*, p. 26n., raises the possibility that it may be the *VPv* that follows M, rather than vice versa. This is unlikely, if the *VPv* was already known to Dignāga.

4. Cf. Par. 1.35, 2.5, 3.32, 4.12, 4.19-24, 4.27, 5.9-10.

5. Cf. *VPv* 1.1 (13.1-2): *śāntavidyātmako yo 'ṃśaḥ tad u haitad avidyayā/ tayā grastam ivājasraṃ yā nirvaktuṃ na śakyate//*

5a. There is at least one place where Śaṃkara seems to display the two concepts of existence and identity, though without using the concept of indescribability. At the beginning of his commentary on *BSū* 2.1.18 (467.14), he says; "And that the effect before its production exists and is not different from its cause follows from reasoning" (*yukteś ca prāg utpatteḥ kāryasya sattvam ananyatvaṃ ca kāraṇād avagamyate*). But Saṃkara says that the effect as anything over and above its cause does not exist (*BSūB* 2.1.14, 454.12: *brahmavyatirekeṇa kāryajātasyābhāva iti gamyate*), not that it is *anirvacanīya*. Still, this shows how logically the two pairs *tattvānyatva* and *sadasat* go together when Brahman is the only real existent.

5b. With the older eds., e.g., MB, *VPBK*, p. 30, I read *abahistattvāḥ* instead of the *bahistattvāḥ* of the crit. ed.

6. Cf. *VPv* 1.120 (184.1): *śaktisamūham avidyākāraṇam.*

7. Cf. Par. 3.27-34.

8. M argues against the Vedāntic *bhedābhedavāda* at *BS* 125.13-18, and against the *bhedābheda* of particular and universal held by Kumārila and the Jains in *BS* 54.12-14 and 59.20-70.5. This last section is also perhaps implicitly directed against Vedāntic *bhedābheda.*

9. Hacker, *Vivarta*, pp. 226, 236.

10. Ingalls, "Śaṁkara on the question", p. 72.

11. Cf. Par. 3.29.

12. Hacker, 'Eigentümlichkeiten', p. 275.

13. Hacker, *Vivarta*, p. 213.

14. *TS* text, I, 74.

15. *TS*, trans., pp. 130-31. I have modified it by translating *avidyā* throughout by 'Ignorance.' Jha occasionally translates it by "Illusion."

16. na cāpi bhavatāṃ tadvyatirekiṇy avidyāsti yadvaśāt tat tathā pratibhāsata iti syāt—*TS* 75.23-24.

17. athāvidyā na brahmaṇaḥ svabhāvaḥ, arthāntaraṃ brahmaṇa āpadyeta.

18. P: athāpi syād avidyāvaśāt khyātīty anenāvidyātmakatvam eva khyāpyata iti. S: yady evaṃ sutarāṃ mokṣābhāvaprasaṅga eva khyāpito bhavati. na hi nityaikarūpe brahmaṇy avidyātmake sthite sati tadātmikāyā vyapagamaḥ saṃbhavati yenāvidyāvyapagamān muktir bhavati—*TS* 74.25-27.

19. ...tadarthāni śāstrāṇi tadarthāś ca pravṛttayo vyarthāḥ syuḥ...avidyāsvabhāvaṃ cet, tasya nityatve pūrvasvabhāvātyāgāt svabhāvāntarānāpatteś ca.

20. ...brahmaṇaḥ svabhāvaś cet sa nityaḥ kathaṃ nivartyeta?

21. *Tattvānyatvābhyām*. I have corrected Jha's translation, "neither real nor unreal".

22. atha vyatiriktāvidyāṅgīkriyate, evam api nityatvād anādheyātiśayasya brahmaṇaḥ sā na tat kiṃcit karotīti, na yuktam avidyāvaśāt tathā pratibhāsanam. tataś cāvidyayā saha tasya sambandhābhāvāt saṃsārābhāvaprasaṅgaḥ. na cāpi sā tatvānyatvābhyāṃ [sic] nirvaktuṃ śakyata iti yuktaṃ vaktum, vastudharmasya gatyantarābhāvāt. anyathā vastutvam eva na syāt. na cāvastuvaśāt tathā tasya khyātir yuktātiprasaṅgāt—*TS* 74.23-75.4.

23. yady evaṃ prāgayogitvāvasthāyāṃ [sic—correct to *prag yogitvāvasthāyāṃ*?] kiṃ tasya rūpam iti vācyam. yadi sadaiva jyotīrūpaṃ tadā tarhi na kadācid ayogitvāvasthāsti, sadaivātmajyotīrūpatvād brahmaṇaḥ. tataś cāyatnataḥ sarveṣāṃ mokṣaprasaṅgaḥ. athāpi syād yathā bhavatāṃ svapnādyavasthāsu jñānam advayam api vicitrākāraparigraheṇa pratibhāsate tathā tad advayam apy avidyāvaśād aviśuddhasantatīnāṃ tathā prakāśata iti. tad asamyak. na hi tadvyatirekeṇānye kecid aviśuddhasantatayaḥ santi yeṣāṃ tat tathā pratibhāsate...asmākaṃ tu viśuddhajñānāntarodayān muktir yujyata eva—*TS* 74.16-23.

24. anye tu...vidhūtaviṣayākāropaplavaviśuddhavi-jñānotpādalakṣaṇāṃ (brahmaprāptim āhuḥ).

25. vidyāsvabhāvaṃ cet, na kiṃcin nivartyam avāptavyaṃ vā syāt, avidyāyā abhāvād vidyāyāś ca bhāvāt...

26. sā ca nityā brahmaṇi na ca brahmaṇo 'nyo 'sti, yasya tattvāgrahaṇaṃ brahmaṇi prayatnalabhyayā vidyayā nivartyeta.

27. See Appendix A-27.

28. *BS* 16.23-19.13. Cf. Paragraphs 2.4-9, 3.32.

29. *TS*, V. 151: viśuddhajñānasantānā yogino 'pi tato na tat/ vidanti brahmaṇo rūpaṃ jñāne vyāpṛtya saṅgateḥ// (p. 74, ll. 10-11); *TSP* thereon: yadi hi jñāne yogaje tasya vyāpāraḥ syāt tadā yoginas tasya rūpaṃ paśyantīti syāt (74.12), etc.

30. I am not aware of an occurrence of the word *yogin* in the *VP* or *VPv*. However, the expression *śabdapūrva yoga* or variants of it occur in *VP* 1.20 and *VPv* 1.26 (72.1), 1.14 (47.6), 1.130 (201.2) and 1.131 (202.1). *Ṛṣis* are mentioned in *VP* 1.5 and *Vṛtti*, *VP* 1.30 and *Vṛtti* and *VPv* 1.145, and, as Biardeau says (Théorie, p. 309, n. 2) the *ṛṣi* is conceived here on the model of

the *yogin*. Maṇḍana mentions the *ṛṣis* in the prose to *SS* 21, but this is based in *VPv* 1.5 and 1.85 (M quotes *VP* 1.85); the *ṛṣis* are not important in his own doctrine.

31. Cf. Paragraph 1.40.

32. Hacker, *Vivarta*, p. 217, etc.

33. MB, *VPBK*, pp. 10-11.

34. S: kartā bhoktā ca saṃsārī; na ca saṃtatir avastutvāt kartrī bhoktrī vā. kathaṃ vāsato muktibandhau? P: atha matam—nātyantam asatī saṃtatiḥ, nāpi satī, kalpanayā tu satī, tadvimokṣāya śāstrāṇi pravṛttayaś ceti; S: kalpitas tarhi saṃsarati vimucyate ca; kalpitaviṣayau ca saṃsāravimokṣāv api kalpitāv eva; tad etad asmābhir ucyamānaṃ kiṃ na bhavato 'bhimatam? uktam etat—kalpitaviṣayāv eva saṃsāramokṣau, na parasmin paramārthe.

35. tasmād avidyayā jīvāḥ saṃsāriṇaḥ, vidyayā mucyante.

36. anyā vyākhyā dvitīyārdhasya—P: vyatirekāvyatirekavikalpe pratyavatiṣṭhate: vastugata eṣa vibhāgaḥ—tatsvabhāvatvam anyatvaṃ ceti, nāvastuni vikalparacitaśarīre bhede 'vatāram arhati. tathā hi—tattvānyatvābhyām anirvacanīyo 'nādivikalpavāsanopādānavikalpaparidarśitaśarīraḥ "ayam asmād bhinnaḥ, ayam anayor bhedaḥ" iti vyavahāraṃ pravartayati; na bhedo nāma kiṃcid vastu, yasya tattvam anyatvaṃ vā kiṃcid vicāryeta. S: tatredaṃ punar upatiṣṭhate—arūpeṇa ca bhinnatvaṃ vastuno nāvakalpate. yadi tarhy arūpo niḥsvabhāvo bhedaḥ—na hi vastusthityāsti, vikalpair eva kevalam upadarśyate—na tarhi vastuno bhinnatvam, paramārthato bhedābhāvāt; na hi kalpitena svabhāvena pāramārthikī tadvattā yujyate; kalpitaiva syāt. tad etad asmābhir ucyamānaṃ kim iti bhavān nānumanyate? vayam apy etad eva brūmaḥ—na bhedo bhāvato 'sti, anādyavidyāvilasitam etad iti.

37. Stcherbatsky, *Buddhist Logic*, II, 261, n. 8; 270; 293, n. 2; 367, n. 3.

38. See N. 4.11.

39. ...bhedadarśanena brahmaiva saṃsarati, abhedadarśanena ca mucyate ...tasmād avidyayā jīvāḥ saṃsāriṇaḥ, vidyayā mucyante.

40. Stcherbatsky, op. cit., I, 45.

41. The lines of the *TSP* that immediately follow what we have just quoted might, however, be interpreted to be a provisional acceptance of inexpressibility: "If, even in that state, it is called a 'State' or 'Condition', in the sense that its nature is capable of fruitful action—we have nothing to say against that. As for us (Buddhists), Ignorance [*avidyā*]...is only the disposition of wrongful attachment...and this disposition is called a 'Faculty'..." (Jha's trans., p. 130) (*tathābhūtasya cārthakriyākāriṇaḥ svabhāvasyāvasthitināmakaraṇena no 'sti* [I prefer this to *nāsti*, given as an alternative] *vivādaḥ. asmākaṃ tu vitathābhiniveśavāsanaivāvidyā sā ca vāsanā śaktir ucyate.*—*TS* 75.4-6). I am not, however, certain that *tathābhūta svabhāva* means *anirvacanīya avidyā*, rather than merely *avidyā*. In any case, the Buddhist manifestly does not fully embrace the inexpressibility theory as his own.

42. P: atha matam—adṛṣṭasya darśanād iti. S: tad asat, ekasmād api kramavatāṃ kāryāṇāṃ darśanāt. P: syād etat—ekāntato 'bhede kāryadarśanādarśane na yukte, viśeṣābhāvāt. S: na tarhi kāryabhedo 'bhedam apabādhate; tadanupamardena viśeṣamātrānumānaṃ syāt; tac ca kalpanāviṣayaṃ naivāvajānīmahe, vastusatas tasyāyogāt, tattvānyatvayor asaṃbhavāt.

43. See Śaṅkhapāṇi, 147.17-20.

44. sa cāyaṃ virodhidharmayogo bhedahetur anantaram eva nirāsi; yathā khalu dīrghakālāḥ padārthā mitakālair dharmaih saṃbadhyamānās taddharmāṇo 'taddharmāṇaś ca na virodhapadabhājaḥ, tathā parimitadeśair vipuladeśā anantāś ca. P: katham anantasyāntavān dharma iti cet. S: vyatireke 'nirvacanīyatve vā nāsty asaṃbhāvanāvakāśaḥ; avyatireke 'pi dīrghakālasyeva mitakālaḥ.

45. ...viśeṣamātrahetutvāt tasya ca tattvānyatvābhyām anirvācyasya kalpanāviṣayatvāt....

46. P: nanūktena prakāreṇa pramāṇād anyato 'pi bhedajñānasyodayo na saṃbhavati. S: ko vānyathāha? na hi paramārthato bhedāvagamo 'sti: yadi syāt, kathaṃ bhedo 'pahnūyeta? apahnave vā katham tadavagaḥ? nāvagamyam asti, avagamyate ceti durghaṭam. P: kiṃ tarhīdam? S: avidyā vibhramaḥ, yathāvabhāsaṃ ca vedyasadbhāve na vibhramaḥ, kiṃ tu samyagjñānam; asati cāvagamo 'nupapannaḥ. tasmān na paramārthataḥ sattvena nirucyate, nāpy asattvena, loke siddhatvāt sarvapravādeṣv ity uktam.

47. Hacker, *Vivarta*, p. 213.

48. See LS, *VV*, pp. 149-50, 237-39.

49. Cf. Paragraph 3.18.

50. Cf. Paragraph 1.2, and LS, *VV*, p. 101, "die bestimmte Erkenntnis und ihre Bestimmtheit hinsichtlich ihrer Wirklichkeit immer gleich sind."

51. yasyaikam ubhayātmakam vastu, na tasya sāmānyamātraṃ vastuna ātmā, na viśeṣamātram; tanmātratve vastubhedaprasaṅgāt. tasmāt saṃbhinnobhayarūpaḥ śabalo vastvātmā; na ca śabalasyānyatrānugamaḥ; yasya tv anugamaḥ, sa vasturūpo na bhavati. tathā ca śabdāntaram avalambya bhedā eva satyā ity etat pratipādyate, śabdāntareṇa vā hetunā dvyātmakam ekam iti; anugantur avastusvabhāvatve kalpanāviṣayatvāt. P: syād etat—mā bhūt vastu, tadaṃśatvam tu na vāryate; anyathā nirbījā kalpanāpi na bhavet. S: kaḥ punar ayam aṃśo nāma? na tāvad vastv eva; tanmātrarūpatve vastuno bhedaprasaṅga ity uktam; nāpi vastuno 'nyat svayaṃ vastu, sāmānyaviśeṣatadvatāṃ trayāṇāṃ vastūnāṃ prasaṅgāt. atha na vastv eva, nānyat svayaṃ vastu; pariśeṣāt kalpanāviṣayas tattvānyatvābhyām anirvacanīyaḥ.

52. prayatnabhedato bhinnā dhvanayo 'sya prakāśakāḥ/ pratyekam anupākhyeyajñānatadbhāvanākramāt//.

53. *SS* 89.1-14: tathā hi—pūrve dhvanayo 'nupajātabhāvanāviśeṣamanasaḥ pratipattur avyaktarūpopagrāhiṇīr uttaravyaktaparicchedotpādānuguṇabhāvanābījavāpinīḥ prakhyāḥ prādurbhāvayanti; paścimas tu purastanadhvaninibandhanavyaktaparicchedaprabhāvitasakalabhāvanābījasahakārisphuṭataravinivisṭasphoṭabimbam iva pratyayam ativyaktataram udbhāvayati: yathā ratnaparīkṣiṇaḥ parīkṣamāṇasya prathamam asamadhigamānupākhyātam anupākhyeyarūpapratyayopahitasaṃskārarūpāhitaviśeṣāyāṃ buddhau krameṇa carame cetasi cakāsti ratnatattvam; na hy anyathā sphuṭaprakāśa-upapadyate pura iva paścād api, viśeṣābhāvāt. tad idam uktam—"yathānuvākaḥ śloko vā sodhatvam upagacchati/ āvṛttyā na tu sa granthaḥ pratyāvṛtti nirūpyate// pratyayairanupākhyeyair grahaṇānuguṇais tathā/ dhvaniprakāśite śabde svarūpam avadhāryate// nādair āhitabījāyām antyena dhvaninā saha/ āvṛttaparipākāyāṃ buddhau śabdo 'vadhāryate//" anupākhyeyākārasphoṭopalabdhijanmānaś ca tatraiva sphuṭataraparicchedāṃ dhiyam utpādayantīti na varṇavādina ivārthaviṣaye nānātvadoṣaḥ.

54. *VPv* 1.82 (149.2-3): kṛtsnam api śabdarūpam prakāśīkṛtaṃ yāvad asvīkṛtākāram anupagṛhītaviśeṣaṃ buddhāv asaṃniviṣṭaṃ tāvad anupalabdhenaiva tena vyavahāro na kaścid api prakalpate. *VPv* 1.83 (149.6-7): vyaktarūpagrahaṇānuguṇā anupākhyeyākārā bahavaḥ upāyabhūtāḥ pratyayā dhvanibhiḥ prakāśyamāne śabde samutpadyamānāḥ śabdasvarūpāvagrahahetavo bhavanti. *VPV* 1.84 (150.4-5): nādaiḥ śabdātmānam avadyotayadbhir yathottarotkarṣeṇādhīyante vyaktaparicchedānuguṇasaṃkārabhāvanābījāni.

55. asataś cantārale yāñ cchabdān astīti manyate/ pratipattur aśaktiḥ sā, grahaṇopāya eva saḥ / Cf. MB, *Théorie*, p. 377.

56. However, as MB, *SS*, p. 43, notes, the *Gopālikā* glosses *asataḥ* by *paramārthato 'sataḥ*.

57. See Note 1.54.

58. MB, *SS*, p. 43. Compare *SS* 91.16 and 92.6-7 and *VPv* 152.1.

59. *SS* 21 (92.17): jñānasyāsadgrāhyākārānukāraviparyāsopaplavo niyataḥ.

60. MB, *SS*, p. 40.

61. Ibid.

62. As Biardeau herself notes (*Théorie*, pp. 275, 281, 310), BH does not teach metaphysical ignorance or say that the world is an illusion.

63. MB, *SS*, loc. cit.

64. Iyer, *Bhartṛhari*, p. 162.

65. MB, loc. cit. Note that here she says that M says that in false perception there is a real contact of the sight with the serpent. She corrects this statement in *PMM*, p. 44 and n.

66. *SS* 19 (90.14):...bahutarālokāc ca deśān mandatarālokagarbhagṛhādiṣu praviṣṭasya rajjvādiṣu vyaktam aprakāśamāneṣu sarpādyākāraprakāśodayaḥ; (90.19): ...pūrvadarśanāny eva ...vyaktavṛkṣādipratipattinimittam bhavanti.

67. See Chapter 5.

68. *BS* 41.4-10.

69. See *VPv* 1.4, quoted above, Par. 1.4.

70. *Anākhyeya* is also used to describe a subtle form of verbal thought, which is inexpressible. See Par. 4.20.24.

71. See *VPv* 1.1, quoted above, Par. 1.5.

72. Thibaut, *The Vedānta-Sūtras of Bādarāyaṇa with the Commentary by Śaṅkara*, I, 410, translating a use of it by Śaṃkara.

73. yady evaṃ pramāṇābhāvo viṣaya uktaḥ syāt 'nāsti' iti dhīśabdayoḥ, tatra ko 'parādhaḥ syāt prameyābhāvasya, yena tam atilaṅghya pramāṇābhāvo viṣaya ucyate? na hi tayor nirupākhyatve kaścid viśeṣaḥ.

74. nirupākhyavailakṣaṇyena satāṃ tulyarūpatā prakāśate; anyathā nirupākhyavat santo 'py atyantavilakṣaṇāḥ prakāśeran.

75. *PMM*, pp. 268, 272.

76. abhāvagrāhiṇī buddhir bhāvāntaram upāśritā/ 133 // tadanyasmāt pṛthaktvena; nirupākhyo na vidyate/ ato bhāvāntaraṃ muktvā tatrābhāvanirūpaṇāt // 134 // na buddhyā bhāvaśūnyatvaṃ mṛṣā ceti vipaścitaḥ/ na vai śaśaviṣāṇe 'pi khyātasya nirupākhyatā;// 135 // śaśasaṃsargirūpaṃ hi viṣāṇaṃ tatra gamyate;/ avastu tac ca no, yena khuradharmiṇi vīkṣitam;// 136

77. na jñeyaśūnyam vijñānam, svātmahāniprasaṅgataḥ/nirupākhyād.....

78. *BSūB* 2.1.18 (469.11-15), 2.2.22 (533.6-8) and 2.2.24 (532.1-2). VM illuminates the use of the word when he glosses *BSūB* 1.1.1, Introd. (89.1-2):

śūnyam ity apare (ātmānam āhuḥ). VM says, "In the doctrine of Voidness, how can (the Self) be the reference of the words 'that' and 'thou', lacking in all appellations and therefore not the reference of a word (or: "not an object")? (*śūnyapakṣe 'pi sarvopākhyārahitam apadārthaḥ kathaṃ tattvamor gocaraḥ*—*BSūB* 82.12).

79. *VPv* 1.28 (83.1-2) and 1.37 (95.1) *Anupākhya*: *VPv* 1.8 (31.3).

80. Cf. Par. 4.18 and 4.30-36.

81. api ca santy arthā vyāvahārikāḥ, yeṣāṃ na śabdavivartād anyat tattvam; tatsāmānyād itare 'pi tathāvasātavyāḥ; yathā—"kuryāt na kuryāt" iti vidhiniṣedhau, vākyārthaḥ, samūhaḥ, asantaś cālātacakraśaśaviṣāṇādayaḥ.

82. As LS, *VV*, p. 23, n. 14, and p. 25, n. 18, notes, the reading of Vs. 35cd is suspicious, and the MS puts a *daṇḍa* in the middle of the line before *vaiśvarūpyam*, which may show that a half-verse has dropped out here. My translation is based on the possibility that the line as reconstructed by LS is correct.

83. ato 'nirvacanīyatvaṃ varaṃ brahmavido viduḥ;/ avidyāyā avidyātvam anyathā parihīyate //28// sattve na mithyā, śūnyatve durnirūpaṃ prakāśanam;/ sadasadbhyām anirvācyāṃ tām avidyāṃ pracakṣate// 29 // vastuno 'nveṣaṇā tasyāṃ bāhyābhyantaravartinaḥ/ na yujyate, yatra tatra vedyavastuni tatkṣateḥ// 30 // nāmarūpaprapañco 'yam avidyaiva ca varṇyate./ anyasya tu anyathā khyātau na prapañcavyapahnavaḥ.//31// akhyātau śūnyam eva syāt, prapañcaḥ kiṃnibandhanaḥ?/ aprapañcaḥ saprapañcarūpo bhātīti yujyate//32// asphuṭagrahaṇe kāmaṃ mā bhāsi sphuṭam ātmanā./ avidyamāne tv adhyasye vaiśvarūpyaṃ vṛthākṛtam.//33// citau vicitrākārāyāṃ prapañcātmatayaiva hi/ anirmokṣas tathā ca syād athavānityatāpatet. //34// anekākāravibhrāntau gandharvanagarādiṣu/ ākārā vyaktam ekasyā dhiyo 'satyāś cakāsati //35// na bhūtaṃ cetaso rūpaṃ nādhyāropāsphuṭagrahau;/ vibhrameṣu vivartatvam ato brahmavidāṃ matam //36//

84. To the contrary, see Hacker, "Jayantabhaṭṭa und Vācaspatimiśra", pp. 166-67, who says Vimuktātman was the first Vedāntin to use it.

85. Thus LS, *VV*, p. 237.

86. Ibid., p. 101.

87. On the other hand, *avidyā* and *vibhrama* are presented as synonyms at *BS* 60.7, quoted Par. 1.28.

88. Cf. Par. 1.29 and LS, *VV*, pp. 100-1.

89. Cf. Par. 1.6 and LS, *VV*, loc. cit., as well as pp. 149-50, 234 and 238. LS points out that this position is taken by the Mādhyamika.

90. Vs. 1 and 164, which list the theories, do not list *anirvacanīya-khyāti-vāda* separately. V. 37, which begins the reply of the *akhyāti-vādin* (the Prābhākara), begins *asato bhāsanāyogāt*, clearly including *anirvacanīya-khyāti-vāda* under *asat-khyāti-vāda*.

91. Cf. Vs. 79-80 and 141.

92. LS, *VV*, p. 101. Cf. Par. 1.65.

93. LS, *VV*, p. 56.

94. The MS reads *taddhyasye*. Cf. N. 1.82.

95. See LS's 'Analyse,' *VV*, pp. 85-86.

96. tasmād vibhrama evāyam iti yukto viniścayaḥ;/ na saṃvidānusāreṇa nimittaṃ tasya yujyate//. For the translation of *saṃvidānusāreṇa*, see 25c and 26a and LS's trans., *VV*, p. 55, and commentary on 27, p. 100.

97. LS, *VV*, p. 87.
98. Cf. V. 141.
99. 37a: asato bhāsanāyogāt...
100. *na kiṃcid bhāsate ceti viruddham iva dṛśyate;/ bhāsane rūpavattvena nāsat, saṃvidvirodhataḥ//* For *rūpa* as "positive form", "positive existence", cf. *BS* 20.11-12: *sarvaṃ tu brahmātmakam, brahmarūpeṇa rūpavat, na tu śūnyam eva.*
101. Cf. *BS* 18.24: *na cānālambanā jñānasvabhāvatvāt pratibhā yuktā*; 19.2: *na jñeyaśūnyam jñānam.*
102. LS, *VV*, p. 105. The plural (*vṛddhānām*) is honorific.
103. *ekāntasattve kā bhrāntir, asattve kiṃ prakāśatām;/ dvayānuguṇyād vṛddhānāṃ saṃmatā khyātir anyathā//*
104. *abhāvagrāhiṇī buddhir bhāvāntaram upāśritā.*
105. *VV* 130ab: *bhāvāntaram abhāvo hi, kayācit tu vyapekṣayā. VV* 148ab: *khyāti sannihite 'śūnyam sad bhāvāntaraghaṭṭitam.*
106. LS, *VV*, p. 239 and n. 175.
107. Ibid., pp. 203-5, 226-7. To the verses quoted from the *VV*, cf. KB, *ŚV, Nirālambana*, 118cd: *bhāvāntaram abhāvo 'nyo na kaścid anirūpaṇāt.*
108. See *BS* 44.10-45.7 and 48.4-49.12, and Par. 4.
109. *abhāvo bhāvarūpeṇa bhātīti yadi manyate,// anyathā khyātir eveṣṭā.*
110. *śūnyam tad api cen matam.*
111. *naitad; vipratiṣidhyete śūnyatābhāvarūpate.*
112. LS, VV, p. 102.
113. Ibid., loc. cit.
114. Ibid., p. 106 and n. 15.
115. MS (LS, *VV*, p. 40): evam nirvacanīyā ca na vidyā paribhāsyati/ avidyātvaṃ yatonyasya sānyarūpaṃ prakāśati// LS's reconstruction (p. 41): evaṃ nirvacanīyā ca nāvidyā parihāsyate/ avidyātvaṃ yato 'nyasya sānyarūpaṃ prakāśayet// KS's only difference in reconstruction is negligible: *sānyarūpaprakāśikā* in *pāda* d (p. 41, n. 90).
116. Cf. the opponent's use of *avidyā* in V. 28 and *vibhrama* in V. 36.
117. Paragraphs 1.37-38.
118. Antecedent in Vs. 150; see n. 1.115.
119. MS (LS, *VV*, p. 40):....tadabhāvena vai matiḥ/ kubjādāv iva kā bhrāntiḥ kāvidyā yatra no matā. KS's reconstruction (Ibid., p. 41, n. 91): tasyānyathāmatis seyaṃ tadābhave na vai matiḥ/ khābjādāv iva kābhrāntiḥ kāvidyā yatra no matā// Because of the state of the text, LS does not venture upon a reconstruction or translation.
120. na jñeyaśūnyaṃ vijñānam, svātmahāniprasaṅgataḥ...asvātantryāc ca cetasaḥ.
121. na jñeyaśūnyam jñānam.
122. LS, *VV*, p. 40, n. 27: "'*vai*-' undeutlich; der Schreiber hat anscheinend zuerst statt des '*v*' ein '*m*' geschrieben."
123. *khābjādāv* for *kubjādāv*.
124. The scribe of our MS could have thought, seeing the same word *matih* at the end of both lines of the *śloka*, that the previous scribe had miscopied when his eye slipped back to the end of the first line. The scribe of our MS would then have attempted a correction, to *matā*.

125. See LS, *VV*, p. 237: "Als reine Erkenntnis (*avabhāsamātram*, BS 9, 23) ist diese zwar mit der Geistigkeit (*citiḥ*) des Brahman identisch und somit wirklich, als bestimmte Erkenntnis (*tadavabhāsaḥ*, BS 9.22) aber ist sie unbestimmbar, weil die Bestimmung unwirklich (*asatyaḥ*) ist". I do not, however, think this passage clearly makes this point (for the passage, see par. 1.2). More to our point, see *BS* 13.11-12: *nāvidyā vidyārahitāsti. tathā hi—bhedadarśanam api na prakāśaśūnyam*; *tadabhāve na bhedaḥ prakāśeta.*

125a. MS (LS, *VV*, p. 40): svarūpeṇa prabhijñoyanāvidyā ..../ ātmatvena grahastatra vidyāvidyeti varṇyate// KS's reconstruction (Ibid., p. 41, n. 91): svarūpeṇa prabhidyeta nāvidyā vidyayā yataḥ/ atattvena grahas tatra vidyāvidyeti varṇyate// LS does not attempt a reconstruction.

125b. bhrāntijñeye ca bāhyatvaṃ bādhakair na nirasyate/na gamyate 'ntarvartitvam, nānirvācyatayā matiḥ// kiṃ tv ataddeśakālatvaṃ gamyate bāhyavastunaḥ/

126. See Hacker's list, "Eigentümlichkeiten," p. 262, and discussion pp. 262-4.

127. Thibaut, *The Vedānta-Sūtras of Bādarāyaṇa with Commentary by Śaṅkara*, I, 243.

128. Hacker, op. cit., pp. 272, 274-5.

129. Cf. Par. 3.18.

130. See Par. 1.9.

131. Ingalls, "Śaṁkara on the question", p. 72. Before the time of Śaṃkara, the Sāṃkhya and Yoga applied the term *anirvacanīya* to the state of equilibrium of *prakṛti*, in which the *guṇas* are *anirdeśya-svabhāva*, "not having a specifiable nature," and *niḥsadasat*, "neither existent nor non-existent" (Frauwallner, *Geschichte der Indischen Philosophie*, I, 353, and 402, and cf. Vyāsa on *YS* 2.19). Here *sat* clearly refers to phenomenal existence. Since Ś on *BSū* 2.1.14 includes *prakṛti* in a list of synonyms along with *nāmarūpa* and *avidyā*, it is interesting that he should not include the *sadasadbhyām anirvacanīya* formulation as well as that with *tattvānyatvābhyām*. There are two possible reasons for this. First, he would in general reserve the term *sat* to the perfect existence of Brahman. Second, he would be particularly wary in this context, because to use *sadsadbhyām* would be to risk the word being used in that absolute sense, which we would wish to avoid for the reasons given elsewhere. Therefore, since M's works show that both *sadasadbhyām* and *tattvānyatvābhyām* were in use before M's and Ś's time. Ś's failure to take over *sadasadbhyām* from Sāṃkhya-Yoga in the cosmological context in which the latter uses it is perhaps additional confirmation that he consciously chose not to use it.

132. Hacker, op. cit., pp. 268, 271-2.

133. Ibid., p. 269.

134. Ibid., p. 275

135. Hacker, *Vivarta*, pp. 210-13.

135a. tasmād yathā ghaṭakarakādyākāśānāṃ mahākāśānanyatvam, yathā ca mṛgatṛṣṇikodakādīnām ūṣarādibhyo 'nanyatvam...evam asya bhogyabhoktrādiprapañcajātasya brahmavyatirekeṇābhāva iti draṣṭavyam.

136. Ingalls, loc. cit.

137. See especially the introduction to *BSūB* 1.1.1.

138. *BS* 51.8-9: advayaṃ jagat; 67.12: advaitaṃ jagat.
139. *BS* 20.11-12: brahmarūpeṇa rūpavat.
140. See Appendix A.
141. In the third *kāṇḍa*, the *Niyoga-kāṇḍa*.
142. *BS* 35.1-37.3.
143. LS, *VV*, pp. 218-20.
144. Cf. Par. 2.3 and 2.11.
145. Cf. Par. 1.44.
146. See Par. 3.2 and 3.23-26.
147. MB, *PMM*, p. 182n.
148. TV, *MBS*, p. 113, n. 212. Ānandapūrṇa, 232.3, calls the opponent to the *pūrvapakṣa* the *siddhāntin*; Citsukha, 232.22, the *siddhāntaikadeśin*.
149. Thus KS, *BS*, pp. xxvii and lxiii.
150. Par. 1.44-45.
151. Noted by LS, "Parallelstellen", *VV*, pp. 71-84.
152. *VV* 47c: *vṛddhānāṃ*. Cf. n. 1.102.
153. LS, *VV*, pp. 220-23.
154. A summary of the arguments of the *Śabara-bhāṣya* on the *Mīmāṃsā-sūtras*.
155. Cf. Par. 1.42.
156. LS, *VV*, p. 91.
157. Cf. Par. 1.44-45, 1.52.
158. Against the—tentative—conclusions of Hasurkar, "Maṇḍana Miśra's Views on Error", pp. 37-38.
159. See Appendix B.4-6.

CHAPTER II

1. Hacker, *Vivarta*, p. 35, says that the prefix *vi-* added by Maṇḍana to the *pariṇāma* indicates becoming many. But this is not certain, because at *BS* 7.14-15, just a few lines before the first instance of *vipariṇāmād vivartanād vā*, he uses *vi-pari-vart(ante)* in a context in which it is clear that the meaning is simply the ordinary one, "to change", "to undergo modification": *na khalu pratipattuḥ pratyayam anu viparivartante vastūni*, "for things do not change in accordance with the notions of the apprehender".
2. As Hacker, loc. cit., maintains.
3. Ruegg, *JAOS* 78 (1958), p. 140; TV, *MBS*, p. 56, n. 63.
4. Cf. Par. 4.19-24, 4.27.
5. Śaṅkhapāṇi, 52.23; Ānandapūrṇa, 90.16-17.
6. See Par. 3.11 for passages where M says that the original object (*bimba*) is the *upādāna* of its reflections.
7. *Vijñaptimātratāsiddhi*, ed. Sylvain Lévi, Bibliotèque de l'École des Hautes Études, No. 245 (Paris: Honoré Campion, 1925), p. 14. Quoted by Hacker, *Vivarta*, p. 34.
8. *VP* I.18 (50.3-4): *pratyastamitabhedāyā yad vāco rūpam uttamam/ yad asmin neva tamasi jyotiḥ śuddhaṃ vivartate//* "...which is the highest form

of speech where all difference has disappeared from it, the pure light which appears in this very darkness". The *Vṛtti* does not comment on this verse separately. In commenting on *VP II*.5 the *Vṛtti* says: *evaṃ hy āha—"vedābhyāsāt varam āntaraṃ śuklam ajaraṃ jyotis tasmin nevāpāre tamasi vīte vivartate" iti*, "For thus he (or 'it') says: 'Through repetition of the Veda the interior and best light, pure and free from old age, appears, when this boundless darkness has departed'." Since this sentence closely resembles the *VP* verse just quoted, it may be that it is a loose quotation from it, and thus a piece of evidence that the author of the *Vṛtti* is different from Bhartṛhari.

9. A sort of *pratibimba-vāda* of the *sphoṭa* and the *dhvanis* occurs in *VPv* I.99-100 and its *Vṛtti*. Cf. *SS* V. 22. *VPv* I.130 (200.12) says that there are two *śabdātmans*, the *nitya* and the *kārya*, of which the second is the *partibimba* of the first. But neither of these passages brings in *vivarta*.

10. Dasgupta, *History*, I, 475-6.

11. Śaṃkara, *TUB*, 2.6, gives precisely this as a reason for rejecting the *pratibimba-vāda*: "If you should say that (Brahman's) entering (in the *śruti* being glossed, 'Having emitted it, he entered it') is like that of reflection, such as that of the sun in water—No, for it is unlimited and without spatial form. The reflection of something that is limited and possesses spatial form, such as the sun, can arise in something different from it and of a luminous nature, such as water. But this is not possible for the Ātman, because the Ātman, the cause of ether etc., is without spatial form, because (if it did have spatial form) it would not be all-pervasive. Its entering like a reflection is impossible also because there exists no other thing, different from it and spatially separated from it, to be the receptacle of the reflection". (*jalasūryakādipratibimbavat praveśaḥ iti cen na. aparicchinnatvād amūrtatvāc ca. paricchinnasya mūrtasyānyasyānyatra prasādasvabhāvake jalādau sūryakādipratibimbodayaḥ syāt. na tv ātmanaḥ, amūrtatvād ākāśādikāraṇasyātmanaḥ, avyāpakatvāt. tadviprakṛṣṭadeśapratibimbādhāravastvantarābhāvāc ca pratibimbavat praveśo na yuktaḥ.—TUB* 76.28-77.4). On the other hand, Ś accepts the *pratibimbavāda* in *CUB* 6.3.2 (338.1-10), and *BSūB*, 2.3.50 and 3.2.18-20. In the *BSūB*, however, he is required to do so by the text of the *sūtras*.

12. Hacker, *Vivarta*; pp. 15-16; MB, *Théorie*, p. 377, n. 2.

13. M was at least aware of the difference in Dignāga's and Dharmakīrti's definitions of *pratyakṣa*. At *ViV* 184.3 he gives Dignāga's definition: *kalpanāpoḍhatvaṃ pratyakṣalakṣaṇam iti cet*...Then at 192.2-3, he refers to Dharmakīrti's: *atha sāmānyākārapratītir vastuni kalpanā na tat pratyakṣaṃ sāmānye tu bhrāntatvāt. kā punar iyaṃ bhrāntatā*?...(I have inserted a *na* into the text of the second quotation, following Vācaspati Miśra: *śaṅkate—atha sāmānyākārapratītir vastuni kalpanā samāroparūpatvāt na pratyakṣam—ViV* 192.1-14.) VM confirms that M is referring to the difference in the doctrine of the two Buddhists: *na khalu "pratyakṣaṃ kalpanāpoḍham anyanirdiṣṭalakṣaṇam" iti praṇayato dignāgasyaiva kalpanāpoḍhamātraṃ pratyakṣalakṣaṇam api tu tad evābhrāntatvasahitaṃ pratyakṣalakṣaṇam iti manyate sma kīrtiḥ. yathāha "pratyakṣaṃ kalpanāpoḍham abhrāntam" iti.—ViV* 192.16-20.

14. Śāntarakṣita, *Tattvasaṅgraha*, I, 123-5 (Vs. 328-35).

15. Hacker, op. cit., pp. 35-6.

16. Ibid., p. 35, to contrary.

17. LS, *VV*, pp. 102, 150-51, 237-8; Ruegg, "The term *buddhivipariṇāma*", p. 279.

18. TV, *MBS*, p. 56, n. 63.

19. Hacker, op. cit., p. 19.

20. With Iyer, *VPBH*, pp. 107-8, I have taken this sentence to state a number of alternatives. Biardeau, *VPBK*, p. 155, interprets it differently, to contain a long series of words in apposition.

21. Referred to by *VP* I.3 (not named individually in VPv). They are first given in the *Nirukta*, 1-2: *jāyate, asti, vipariṇamate, vardhate, apakṣīyate, vinaśyati.*

22. Cf. the comments on this verse in n. 1.3.

23. MB, *VPBK*, p. 7.

24. The following is a list of places in the *BS* where M uses the analogy of reflection: 7.9-13, 7.18, 8.8-10, 11.10-12, 12.10-11, 13.17-18, 14.13, 60.17, 72.5, 72.13, 72.15-18, 125.19-126.2, 133.9-13.

CHAPTER III

1. See, e.g., *BS* 55.23; 62.24; 67.15; 76.20-21; 77.16-17; 82.6; 87.8; 101.10, 21-22; 157.13-21.

2. See, in *VP* I, Vs. 10b, 13b, 15b, 43b, 59b, 60b, 118b, 125b, 134d, 137d, 141d.

3. Hacker, "Eigentümlichkeiten", pp. 253-4.

4. Ibid., p. 254.

5. Ibid., p. 248. Śaṃkara uses the word *adhyāsa* to define *avidyā* in the introduction to the *BSūB* (40.1), where he is giving a summary of his doctrine in his own words, without being obliged to follow an earlier text. This fact shows the importance of *adhyāsa* in this concept of *avidyā* most clearly.

6. MB, *PMM*, p. 153, and TV, *MBS*, p. 63, therefore beg the question by translating *upādāna* as 'material cause'.

7. Stcherbatsky, *Buddhist Logic*, II, 259, n. 11, and 367, n. 3.

8. Ibid., II, 270 and nn. 6-9.

9. Cf. ibid., II, 312.

10. Hacker, "Eigentümlichkeiten", pp. 249, 254.

11. Hacker, "Eigentümlichkeiten", p. 255; Sengaku Mayeda, "The Authenticity of the *Bhagavadgītābhāṣya* attributed to Śaṅkara", *WZKSO*, 9 (1965), p. 169. *BSūB* 1.1.1 (Introd.), p. 45.2-3: *evam ayam anādir ananto naisargiko 'dhyāso mithyāpratyayarūpaḥ kartṛtvabhoktṛtvapravartakaḥ sarvalokapratyakṣaḥ*. *BGB* 18.6 (Introd.), p. 521.4-5: *kriyākārakaphalabhedabuddhir avidyayātmani nityapravṛttā mama karmāhaṃ kartāmuṣmai phalāyedaṃ karma kariṣyāmītīyam avidyānādikālapravṛttā.*

12. I have omitted the following because they represent a Buddhist opponent whose ideas Maṇḍana clearly rejects: 15.2-5, where it is a question of the beginninglessness of the *saṃtati*, and 73.8-9, where the Buddhist says that the appearance of non-difference (*abhedāvabhāsa*) is *anādivāsanopādāna*. I

have kept in 48.7, because, although it is put into the mouth of a Buddhist, Maṇḍana accepts it in the sequel.

13. Hacker, loc. cit.

14. I have omitted 10.19-20—*na hy avidyā prayojanam apekṣya pravartate*; *na hi gandharvanagarādivibhramāḥ samuddiṣṭaprayojanā bhavanti*—because *vibhrama* occurs in a *dṛṣṭānta*, and so is not clearly equivalent to *avidyā*.

15. See *BS* 32.21, 122.21, 149.22 and MB, *SS*, p. 38.

16. Hacker, *Vivarta*, pp. 213, 236.

17. Hacker, "Eigentümlichkeiten", p. 270.

18. Ibid., p. 268.

19. Ibid., p. 279.

20. Ibid., p. 271.

21. LS, *VV*, p. 152.

22. Hacker, "Śaṃkara der Yogin", p. 141.

23. Cf. MB, *PMM*, pp. 54-5.

24. In 3.26-4.15 the metaphor of the lamp, referred to in 7.22-23, does not occur. It is for this reason that I have translated 7.22-23 as I have, instead of thus: "It is like a lamp, or like the fruit of a means of valid knowledge, as has already been said". Obviously, the point of the metaphor is that a lamp does not need another lamp to illumine it.

25. In the *Yoga-Sūtras* themselves, *dṛkśakti* appears in 2.6 (*dṛgdarśanaśaktyor ekātmatevāsmitā*), and *citiśakti* in 4.34 (*puruṣārthaśūnyānāṃ guṇānāṃ pratiprasavaḥ kaivalyaṃ svarūpapratiṣṭhā vā citiśaktir iti.*). Vyāsa glosses *draṣṭṛ* in *YS* 1.3 with *citiśakti*, and with *dṛkśakti* when it occurs in 2.20. Cf. *bhoktṛśakti* in *YSB* 4.22.

26. For *mokṣa* or *kaivalya* as the 'abiding in its own form' (*svarūpapratiṣṭhā* or *svarūpāvasthāna*) of *citiśakti*—*puruṣa*, see *YS* 1.3 (*tadā draṣṭuḥ svarūpe 'vasthānam*), *YS* 4.34, quoted in the preceding note, and *YSB* on both, as well as *YSB* 2.6 and 3.50. "Abiding in one's own form is also M's definition of *mokṣa*. For *mokṣa* as *svarūpāvasthāna* see *BS* 12.19-20; 13.9-11, 18; 78.12-13; and 115.21. Cf. *svātmasthiti* in 115.9 (and *ViV* 277.5). For *mokṣa* as 'manifestation of one's own form' (*svarūpāvirbhāva*), see *BS* 121.13, 18; 126.12, 15; 127.3-4; 128.13; and 154.6. Cf. *svarupābhivyakti*, 37.6. Finally, for *mokṣa* as 'attaining one's own form' (*svarūpaprāpti*), see 120.1.

27. *YSB* 3.55.

28. Koelman, *Pātañjala Yoga*, p. 37.

29. Śaṃkara, in defending in *BSūB* 2.3.18 the Sāṃkhya theory that the Ātman is by its nature eternal consciousness (*nityacaitanyasvarūpa*—603.11-12) against the Vaiśeṣika theory that consciousness is an accident of the Ātman (*āgantukacaitanya*—603.11), says that the absence of actual cognition in sleep is due not to the absence of consciousness, but to the absence of objects, as the fact that the light pervading ether is not manifested is due not to the absence of light, but to the absence of objects to be illuminated (604.15-16).

30. Hacker, "Eigentümlichkeiten", p. 255; Sengaku Mayeda, "The Authenticity of the *Bhagavadgītābhāṣya* attributed to Śaṅkara", *WZKSO*, 9 (1965), pp. 167-8.

31. Unlike M, Ś holds that Brahman is attained in deep sleep, See *BSūB* 3.2.7., 11, and 31.

32. S, *GKB* 1.13 (48.21): *saiva ca (nidrā) viśeṣapratibodhaprasavasya bījam.*

33. *GK* 3.35: *līyate hi suṣupte tan nigṛhītaṃ na līyate/tad eva nirbhayaṃ brahma jñānālokaṃ samantataḥ//. GK* 3.42: *upāyena nigṛhṇīyād vikṣiptaṃ kāmabhogayoḥ/ suprasannaṃ laye caiva yathā kāmo layas tathā//. GK* 3.44: *laye saṃbodhayec cittaṃ vikṣiptaṃ śamayet punaḥ/ sakaṣāyaṃ vijānīyāc samaprāptaṃ na cālayet//. GK* 3.46: *yadā na līyate cittaṃ na ca vikṣipyate punaḥ/ aniṅganam anābhāsaṃ niṣpannaṃ brahma tat tadā//.*

34. Cf. *VV* 117c-118b: *nirodhād yuktakāryasya viparītasya sādhanāt/ doṣāṇāṃ nitarāṃ doṣabhāvo 'bhivyaktim ṛcchati/*

CHAPTER IV

1. Śaṃkara always approaches Brahman from the side of the subject, rather than the side of the object. See *BSūB* 1.1.4 (124.8-9): *na hi śāstram idaṃtayā viṣayabhūtam brahma pratipipādayiṣati. kiṃ tarhi? pratyagātmatvenāviṣayatayā pratipādayad avidyākalpitaṃ vedyaveditṛvedanādibhedam apanayati.*

2. As TV, *MBS*, p. 98, n. 165, thinks.

3. Iyer, *Bhartṛhari*, pp. 246-7, 259-63.

4. At *BS* 56.13-14, *dravya* is the substrate (*āśraya*) of *śaktis*. At 68.5-69.15, *dravya* (e.g., gold) is opposed to *paryāya*, particular variant form (e.g., a bracelet)—a Jaina view. At 81.8-9, *dravyatva* is given along with *sattā* and *guṇatva* as something perceptible by several senses.

5. *VP*, 3, *Dravya* (2).1: *ātmā vastu svabhāvaś ca śarīram tattvam ity api / dravyam ity asya paryāyās tac ca nityam iti smṛtam//.*

6. *BS* 71.3-5: *sa tu bhedaḥ śabdenāsaṃsparśān na tathopalakṣyate, yathā vikalpabuddhau. tad ayuktam, vipratiṣedhāt; na copalakṣyate pratyakṣabuddhau viśeṣaḥ prakāśate ceti vipratiṣiddham; ato 'tisāhasam ity ucyate.*

7. See *BS* 48.4-15, 60.12-18, 70.6-7.

8. See MB, *PMM*, p. 49: "...l'auteur de la *Brahmasiddhi* est...parfaitement conscient de défendre une conception exactement symétrique de celle du bouddhiste".

9. E.G., at *BS* 60.12-18 and 70.6-7, he opposes his idea that *abheda* is the *upādāna* of *bheda* to the Buddhists' that *bheda* is the *upādāna* of *abheda*. At 51.16-18, 52.3-5 and 54.11-12, he says that if the similarity of effects from effects can come from an imagined (*kalpita*) *abheda*, as the Buddhists say, why cannot the difference of effects come from an imagined *bheda*? At 61.8-18, he says that if many things can appear as one, one thing can appear as many.

10. See *BS* 48.16-50.2.

11. Stcherbatsky, *Buddhist Logic*, I, 246-8.

12. See *BS* II.1ab (39.3-4): *āhur vidhātṛ pratyakṣaṃ na niṣeddhṛ vipaścitaḥ/* "The wise say that perception affirms and does not negate".

13. Stcherbatsky, op.cit., I, 192-3 and 363-90, esp. 363-4 and 387.

14. Umbeka, *Ślokavārtikavyākhyā*, p. 148, and Jha, ed., *ŚV*, p. 169.

15. Ingalls, *Materials*, pp. 37-8; Keith, *Indian Logic and Atomism*, pp. 195-6.

16. Bhartṛhari: Iyer, *Bhartṛhari*, p. 246; Kumārila: Jha, *Pūrva-Mīmāṃsā*,

p. 76; Nyāya-Vaiśeṣika, Kuppuswami Sastri, *A Primer of Indian Logic*, pp. 23-5, 32-3.

17. See *BS* 59.17-19.

18. Jha's trans. of 118 (*Ślokavārttika Translated*, p. 88) leaves a certain ambiguity whether there might be an opponent's opinion, a second sort of perception that apprehends particularity: "And without such recognition of these (specific characters), through specification and generalization, there would be no difference between the perception of the *cow* and that of the *horse*".

19. E.G., *ŚV*, *Pratyakṣa*, 120-21: tataḥ paraṃ punar vastudharmair jātyādibhir yayā/ buddhyāvasīyate sāpi pratyakṣatvena saṃmatā// karaṇaṃ cendriyaṃ buddher na tatra jñānam āhitam/ tataḥ smṛtyasamarthatvād vikalpo 'to na vāryate//.

20. Śaṅkhapāṇi, 160.9-10, says this refers back to *BS* II.1. Citsukha, 226.25-26, says it refers to II.5.

21. For discussions of the meaning of the somewhat obscure passage from which this is taken, see MB, *VPBK*, p. 184n., and Iyer, *Bhartṛhari*, pp. 96-7.

22. For a similar instance of a 'substantialist' use of *sāmānya*, cf. Ś, *BSB* 2.3.9: "For particulars are observed to be produced from a universal, as, for instance, pots from clay, but not a universal from particulars" (*sāmānyād dhi viśeṣā utpadyamānā dṛśyante mṛdāder ghaṭādayo na tu viśeṣebhyaḥ sāmānyam*—589.1-2).

23. atha vā na loke 'tyantam aprasiddhaṃ brahma, sarvapratyayavedyatvāt, brahmaṇo vyatirekeṇa pratyetavyasyābhāvāt, viśeṣapratyayānāṃ ca sāmānyarūpānugamāt, bhedopasaṃhārāvaśiṣṭaṃ ca satyaṃ brahma—iti pratipādanāt, "vācārambhaṇaṃ vikāro nāmadheyaṃ mṛttiketyeva satyam" (*CU* 6.1.4) iti dṛṣṭāntāt. kiṃ tarhi śabdena pratipādyate? prapañcābhāvaḥ. tatra prapañcapadārtho 'pi siddhaḥ, niṣedho 'pi siddhaḥ, tayoḥ saṃsargāt tadabhāvapratipattiḥ. āmnyāyaikanibandhanatvaṃ tu tasyocyate, pratyakṣādīnām avidyāsaṃbhinnatvāt; pratyastamitanikhilabhedena rūpeṇāviṣayyikaraṇād bhedapratyastamayasyāmnāyāvagamyatvād iti.

24. Stcherbatsky, *Buddhist Logic*, II, 71, n. 4.

25. This sentence is made somewhat unclear by the cumbrous compound *pūrvaśabdāveśabhāvanāsaṃskārādhānāt*. Iyer, *VPBH*, p. 109, translates the sentence thus: "In children in whom the germs of the word exist according to their kind, because of the existence in them of the residual traces of their use of words in their former births, there arises cognition based on vague words (*anākhyeyaśabda*) in the course of their various purposeful activities". Biardeau, *VPBK*, p. 157, translates thus: "Même chez les bébés ou la parole habite dès leur naissance à cause des impulsions et des dispositions qui restent en eux, produites par la parole (dans leurs vies) antérieures, naît une connaissance relative à chacune des actions (en vue) d'un objet, qui est fondée sur une parole non proférable". Vṛṣabhadeva glosses the long compound thus: *pūrvaśabdāveśa iti. śabdaparicchedī pratyayaḥ anupraviṣṭa iva śabdam. tatra tasya bhāvanā abhyāsaḥ. so 'yaṃ saṃskāram ādhatte.* (Iyer, ed. *VP Kāṇḍa* 1, p. 187, ll.7-8).

26. See previous note.

27. Iyer, ed., *VP Kāṇḍa* 1, p. 190, 11.23-25: nimittānām iti. tato hi prathamopanipātipratyayād uttarakālaṃ grahaṇaṃ yatas teṣāṃ vastusaṃbandhināṃ gotvādīnāṃ viśeṣāṇām.

28. Biardeau, *Théorie*, p. 317: "Elle n'est exprimable d'aucune manière aux autres, mais elle est réalisée par un processus propre à chaque être individuel—*pratyātmā*—et n'est pas explicable même par son auteur". Iyer, *Bhartṛhari*, p. 87 (a close paraphrase rather than a translation): "Everybody experiences it without being able to define it properly to himself, what to say of explaining it to others". The *VPv*'s gloss pays no attention to "*idaṃ tad iti*": *sā copajāyamānā ākhyātum anyasya na śakyate kevalaṃ tu svasaṃvedanasiddhyaivāsau pratipannāpi svasaṃvedanasamaye niyatena rūpeṇa nirūpayitum aśakyaiva sā*. *VP*, ed. G. S. Mānavallī, Benares Skt. Ser., Nos. 11, 19 and 24 (Benares, 1887), p. 141. This verse is numbered 2.146 in this ed.

29. yathāsya saṃhṛtarūpā śabdabhāvanā tathā jñeyeṣv artheṣūtpannenāpy avikalpena jñānena kāryaṃ na kriyate. tadyathā tvaritaṃ gacchatas tṛṇaloṣṭādisaṃsparśāt saty api jñāne kācid eva sā jñānāvasthā yasyām abhimukhībhūtaśabdabhāvanābījāyām āvirbhūtasvārthopagrāhiṇāṃ ākhyeyarūpāṇām anākhyeyarūpāṇāṃ ca śabdānāṃ pratyarthaniyatāsu śaktiṣu śabdānuviddhena śaktyanupātinā jñānenākriyamāṇa upagṛhyamāṇo vastvātmā jñānānugato vyaktarūpapratyavabhāso jñāyata ity abhidhīyate.

30. MB, *VPBK*, pp. 13-15.

31. *VP* 1.123: na so 'sti pratyayo loke yaḥ śabdānugamād ṛte/ anuviddham iva jñānaṃ sarvaṃ śabdena bhāsate//.

32. This is based on *VPv* 1.119 (182.6-183.1): gopālāvipālādayo hi nibandhanapadāni prakalpya gavādiṣu viśeṣaviṣayaṃ vyavahāram ārabhante.

33. Śaṅkhapāṇi, 52.3-8; idānīṃ gānaśāstrānabhijñasya ṣaḍjādiṣu gavādiṣu (text: *gapādiṣu*; not corrected in Errata) ca nirvikalpakaṃ śabdānuvedhaśūnyaṃ ye jñānam icchanti, tān prati—yady api ṣaḍjādiṣu ṣaḍjādiśabdābhāve 'pi "gānam idam" ityādisāmānyaśabdānurodho 'sti; yady api ca nirvikalpake 'pi sūkṣmā vāg asti ity uttaram asti; tathāpi tanmatam upajīvya—sarvajñāneṣu prakārāntareṇa śabdānuvedham upapādayati—api ceti. atādṛktvam evāha—aviviktā hīti.

34. As suggested by MB, *PMM*, p. 55.

35. Brahmānanda Gupta, *Die Wahrnehmungslehre in der Nyāyamañjarī*, Diss. Bonn 1962 (Bonn: Rheinische Friedrich-Wilhelm Universitat, 1962), pp. 85-87; and *Nyāya-Mañjarī*, Vizianagram Skt. Ser., No. 10 (Benares: E. J. Lazarus, 1895), p. 98, 1.2: *vāgrūpam apare tattvaṃ prameyaṃ* (*nirvikalpasya*) *manvate*. Cf. Jayanta Bhaṭṭa's reply on p. 99, and his discussion of *śabdādvaita*, pp. 532-46. Note that Gupta's page references are to the Kashi Skt. Ser. ed. of the *Nyāya-Mañjarī*, which I have not been able to consult.

36. na brūmaḥ—śabdotthas tattvabodho vidhīyata iti; kiṃ tu pratyastamitabuddhibodhyabhedāvagrahaḥ. ataś cādvayo dvitīyatadvidhabodhābhāvād vā pramātṛprameyadvayavirahād vā tato 'nyaḥ...yato na śābdajñānaviṣaya ātmatattvam. vākyalakṣaṇo hi śabdaḥ pramāṇam. tasya ca viṣayo nānāpadārthasaṃsargātmā, tadanugamena pratīteḥ. tajjñānasya ca vividhārthamātrasaṃbhedāvabhāsasyātmatattvaṃ niṣprapañcaṃ dvaitaleśenāpy anavamṛṣṭaṃ kathaṃ gocaraḥ syād iti. S: etad apy asāram; yato yo 'sāv advayo

dvaitaleśasaṃsparśavikala ātmatattvabodhaḥ so 'vacchedavibhrāntivirahāt tasya svarūpāvasthānam.

37. *BS* 41.4-10. Cf. *SS* 19 and Par. 5.7-10 here.

CHAPTER V

1. *BS* 13.11-14.16: anyo 'rathaḥ—nāvidyā vidyārahitāsti. tathā hi—bhedadarśanam api na prakāśaśūnyam; tadabhāve na bhedaḥ prakāśeta. tasmāt para eva prakāśas tathā tathā prakāśate; yathoktam—"tam eva bhāntam anubhāti sarvaṃ tasya bhāsā sarvam idam vibhāti" (*KaṭhaU* 2.2.15) iti; kiṃ tu avidyānubaddhaḥ; yathoktam—"sarvaṃ darśanam anyūnam avikalpaṃ vikalpitam iva tv ayam āntaraḥ puruṣo 'bhimanyate". tathā na vidyā aikātmyaśravaṇādilakṣaṇā vināvidyayā, śrotṛśravaṇādivibhāgānubaddhatvāt; tatrāvidyayaiva vidyāpratyāsannayā vibhāgadarśanam avidyāṃ tīrtvā vidyālakṣaṇe nitye svarūpe 'vatiṣṭhate, pratibimbakaluṣitam ivodakaṃ tannivṛttau. P: syād etat—aikātmye vibhāgasyāsatyatvāt, tadadhiṣṭhānaśravaṇādayo 'py asatyāḥ kathaṃ kasmaicit kāryāya syuḥ? asatyāc ca satyapratipattir mithyaiva, yathā dhūma iti mithyāgṛhītād bāṣpād iti. S: ucyate; nāyaṃ niyamaḥ—asatyaṃ na kasmaicit kāryāya bhavatīti; bhavati hi māyā prīter bhayasya ca nimittam, asatyam ca satyapratipatteḥ, yathā rekhāgavayo lipyakṣarāṇi ca. P: syād etat—svarūpeṇedaṃ satyam, na śūnyam; aikātmyavādinas tu svarūpeṇāpy upāyānām asatyatā. S: ucyate—santu svarūpeṇa satyāḥ; yena tu rūpeṇa pratipādakāḥ tad asatyam; kāryopayogarahitā svarūpasatyatā vyarthā. api ca abhedadarśanopāyā api na svarūpeṇa mithyā, yato brahmaivaiṣāṃ svarūpam; tatra brahmaivāvidyānubaddhaṃ brahmaprāptyupāyaḥ, yathā rekhādayaḥ "kakāro 'yam, gavayo 'yam" ity avidyamānarūpeṇaiva varṇādīnāṃ bodhakāḥ. P: yo 'pi manyate—na rekhāgavayo gavayatvena gavayāntarāṇāṃ pratipattihetuḥ, na rekhā varṇatvena; kiṃ tu sādṛśyāt—etatsadṛśo gavaya iti, rekhā tu samayāt—īdṛśīṃ rekhāṃ dṛṣṭvāyaṃ varṇaḥ smartavya iti. S: tasya lokavirodhaḥ; tathā hi—bālā hi rekhāsu varṇatvenaiva vyutpādyante, loke 'bhedena ca vyapadeśaḥ—"ayaṃ gavayaḥ" iti ākhyātuḥ, pratipattuś ca—"gavayo 'yaṃ mayā dṛṣṭaḥ" iti. tathā asatyāt pratibimbāc cādṛṣṭasya pratibimbahetor viśiṣṭadeśāvasthasyānumānaṃ na mṛṣā; śabdāc ca nityād asatyadīrghādivibhāgabhājo 'rthabhedapratipattir na mithyā. tathā mithyāhidaṃśo maraṇahetuḥ; tataś ca maraṇamūrcchādyanumānaṃ na vitatham, kālādibhedayuktāt satyāhidaṃśād iva.—The second quotation (*sarvaṃ darśanam*...) is from *VPv* 1.9 (37.2), it is ascribed , along with a preceding quotation, to "the knowers of Brahman" (*api khalu brahmavida āhuḥ*—36.4).

2. *ŚV*, *Nirālambana*, 128c-129b: sarvathā sadupāyānāṃ vādamārgaḥ pravartate// adhikāro 'nupāyatvān na vāde śūnyavādinaḥ//.

3. Umbeka, *Śloka-Vārtika-Vyākhyā*, p. 244.

4. Ibid.

5. Ibid., pp. 224-32 passim.

6. *BS* 41.4-16: dṛṣṭaṃ ca hetutvenāpekṣitāyā api pūrvasyāḥ pratipatteḥ parasyāḥ balīyastvam; yathā dūrastheṣu vanaspatiṣu hastipratipattibhyo vanaspatipratipatteḥ; apekṣitā hi hastipratipattayo vyaktavanaspatipratipattyā hetutvena; na tasya indriyārthasaṃnikarṣamātrāj janma, āpāte 'bhāvāt; na

ca deśaviśeṣāt, taddeśasthasyaivotpatteḥ; tasmāt purovartiṣu vanaspatiṣu praṇihitamanasaḥ prācyaviparyāsānugatamatisaṃskārasacivendriyādisaṃyogakāritā seti mantavyam. evaṃ ekādisaṃkhyābuddhyupāyā viṃśatyādibuddhayo 'py udāhāryāḥ. evaṃ ca yad eke varṇayanti—svayam eva vyāhatā vedāntārthapratipattiḥ; nābhedo bhedam antareṇa śakyate 'vasātum; bhedopāyā hi tasya pratipattiḥ; tatrābhedaḥ samākṣiptabheda eva pratīyata iti vyāghātaḥ—tad apāstam; yata upāyam ākṣipati pratipattiḥ, no pāyasya paramārthatām, mithyājñānād api tattvapratipatteḥ. vyāvahārikaṃ ca bhedasya satyatvam iṣṭam eveti.

7. MB, *SS*, p. 40.

8. Iyer, *VPBH*, p. 87.

APPENDIX A

1. M. Biardeau, *PMM*, p. 1: 7th-8th c. A.D.; T.R. Chintamani, *JORM* 3 (1929), p. 43: A.D. 650-700; P. Hacker, *Vivarta*, p. 218: 7th c.; P. V. Kane, *JBBRAS* 1928, pp. 289-93, *History of Dharma-Śāstra*, (Poona: BORI 1962), V, p. 1191:fl. about 690-710; Kuppuswami Sastri, *BS*, p. lviii: 615-90; L. Schmithausen, *VV* 216, n. 150: 700, at the most a little earlier, in no case later; V. A. Ramaswami Sastri and K. A. Sivaramakrishna Sastri, *BV*, p. 89: later half of the 7th c.; T. Vetter, *MBS*, p. 15: around 700.

2. S. Das Gupta, *Hist.*, II, 87: 800; K. Kunjunni Raja, "Maṇḍana and Dharmakīrti", p. 250:fl. towards the close of the 8th c. and the beginning of the 9th.

3. *PV* (Gnoli's ed.) I.247cd equals *SS* (Biardeau's ed.) 99.7. *SS* 99.7-100.15 paraphrases *PV* I, 127.1-129.13. These correspondences were first noted by Gnoli, *PV*, p. xix, n. 2.

4. *Arthakriyākāritva* as the definition of existence: *BS* 85.12-16, 89.24-25, 90.19-91.6. For the concept in other contexts, see 49.19-20, 50.15-54.14, 73.4-8, 88.5-13.

5. Nagatomi, "Arthakriyā", pp. 57-63.

6. See *BS*, Appendix IV, pp. 48 and 50 for references. On p. 50, 55.8 is listed as one place where there is a quote from the *SV*. There is no quote there, and I have not been able to find any more *SV* quotes in addition to those listed on p. 50. All other references to *SV* and *TV* are correct.

7. *BS*, p. lvi. At *ViV* 281.4 Maṇḍana says *alaṃ vā gurubhir vivādena.* This does not seem to refer to Kumārila, since it closes a brief discussion (280.1-281.4) of the idea that there is an injunction for repetition of verbal knowledge, since it results in pure knowledge in which all mention of difference has been destroyed—not a doctrine of Kumārila's. In addition, immediately before and after this passage (278.8, 282.1), the specifically Prābhākara word *niyoga* is employed. Finally, Vācaspati Miśra in his gloss (282.10-11) says, "Being 'teacher' is metaphorical, because of the similarity (of the opponent to a teacher) in being worthy of highest honor". (*anuttarārhatāsāmyād aupacārikaṃ gauravam.*) While Vācaspati does not think that Maṇḍana is referring to his own teacher, and it is not impossible that he would know reliable traditions

on Maṇḍana's teacher (especially since they both seem to have come from Mithilā), it is still interesting to speculate whether Maṇḍana is referring to a teacher of his who held this doctrine. Unfortunately there is no way to tell. He could be, as Vācaspati indicates, merely showing respect to the adherents of an established tradition.

8. Frauwallner, "*Bhāvanā* und *vidhi* bei Maṇḍanamiśra", *WZKM*, 45 (1938), p. 231.

9. Compare *BS* 23-26, 75.4-12 and *Bṛhatī* (Madras University Skt. Ser. No. 3), pp. 20 and 22, as well as *ViV*, p. 109.3-4 and *Bṛhatī*, p. 38.3-5, as noted by KS, *BS*, p. lviii.

10. *BS* 82.12-118.14. Note the use of Prābhākara's technical term *niyoga* in this section, and in the title of this chapter (*Niyoga-kāṇḍa*). The aim of the *ViV* as a whole is the refutation of Prābhākara's theory of *niyoga* and the defense of Kumārila's *iṣṭasādhanatā* as the meaning of *vidhi*.

11. *BS* 136.18-150.24, *VV*, Vs. 37-120b.

12. LS, *VV*, pp. 239-41.

13. Ibid., p. 189, n. 95.

14. Hacker, *Untersuchungen*, pp. 1918-21.

15. Ingalls, "Śaṁkara's Arguments", pp. 293-94.

16. MB, *PMM*, pp. 1, 11, Kunjunni Raja, "Maṇḍana and Dharmakīrti", pp. 248-9. For references to the traditional lives see KS, *BS*, p. lvi.

17. KS, *BS*, p. lviii.

18. See Appendix B.

19. *BS* 32.17, Cf. 121.4.

20. KS, *BS*, pp. xlvi-vii; TV, *VV*, p. 113, n. 212.

21. Cf. Par. 1.66 and references there.

22. TV, *VV*, p. 113, n. 212.

23. *BSūB* 3.4.26 (898.8-9): vividiṣāsaṃyogāc caiṣām utpattisādhanabhāvo 'vasīyate; 3.4.27 (900.7-8): tasmād yajñādīni...sarvāṇy evāśramakarmāṇi vidyotpattāv apekṣitavyāni; 3.4.33 (905.2-3): tasmād utpattisādhanatva evaiṣāṃ sahakāritvavācoyuktiḥ.

24. Even Sureśvara says that works help towards the production of knowledge. See Hacker, *Untersuchungen*, p. 1994.

25. KS, *BS*, p. xlvii; Suryanarayana Sastri, "Maṇḍana and Bhāvādvaita", p. 283; TV, *BS*, p. 118, n. 224.

26. Ś does not actually use words along the line of *kāryasya kāraṇātmatvaṃ na tu kāraṇasya kāryātmatvam* in *BSūB* 2.1.14; he must be referring to the general trend of his argument there.

27. This is part of the P, but is based on what Ś would accept. For this and the previous quote from the *BS* I am indebted to TV, *BS*, p. 83, n. 138.

28. *TUB* 74.11-13 (on 2.6):...tan nāmarūpavyākaraṇaṃ brahmaṇo bahubhavanam. nānyathā niravayavasya brahmaṇo bahutvāpattir upapadyate 'lpatvaṃ vā. yathākāśasyālpatvaṃ bahutvam ca vastvantarakṛtam eva.

29. Hiriyanna, "Prapañca-vilaya-vāda", p. 110, n. 1.

30. Ibid., pp. 112-14.

31. Ibid., p. 110, n. 1. Other sources are: Sureśvara, *Sambandha-vārttika*, 378-426; Bhāskara, *Brahma-sūtra-bhāṣya*, 1.1.3-4, 1.4.21, 3.3.1; Rāmānuja,

Śrībhāṣya, 1.1.4 (Nirṇaya Sāgar ed. of *Catuḥ-sūtrī*, pp. 251-54); Vedānta Deśika, *Tattvamuktākalāpa*, 2.4.

32. *BS*, p. xlviii. KS also observes here that Amalānanda in the *Vedānta-kalpataru*, pp. 158-59, says that M refers to and rejects Śaṃkara's views on the *sthitaprajña* of *BG* 2.54. Amalānanda, like Śaṅkhapāṇi, is too late to be a strong witness for the relationship of M and Ś. According to Das Gupta, *Hist.*, II, 57-58, he lived in the 14th c., and in any case, he must have lived after Vācaspati, upon whom he comments. Ś's remarks on the *sthitaprajña* (*BSūB* 152.7-8 on 1.1.4 and 420.13 on 1.4.22, *BGB* II.54-72) do not have any significant resemblance to M's (*BS* 130.17-131.21).

33. As KS, *BS*, pp. lxxv-lxxvi, observes, in a MS of the *BS* in the Adyar Library, the *Śaṅkhapāṇi-vyākhyā* is given the name *Samīkṣāphakkikā* (see ref. 2 of phakkikā in Nyāyakośa: Tattvanirṇayārthapūrvapakṣādi-bodhakaṃ Vākyam), "the position of the *Samīkṣā*", that is, of Vācaspati Miśra's commentary on the *BS*, the *Tattva-samīkṣā*. (See *Bhamatī*, p. 1020, 1.19 [epilogic V. 3], and *Kalpataru* thereon, p. 1021, 1.9). This may be confirmed by the fact that at 291.14, after giving an analysis of the compound *abhūtakalpanopādānavyavahārasiddhārthagocaraḥ* of *BS* 151.11-12, Śaṅkhapāṇi says, *iti vṛttau vigrahaḥ*, which could be translated as, "thus the analysis in the *Vṛtti*", referring to a previous commentary. The complexity of the compound might have induced Śaṅkhapāṇi to give his authority for the analysis he gave. The fact that *vṛtti* is in the locative rather than in the genitive or in composition with *vigraha* leads me to prefer the translation given to "thus the analysis of the compound (*vṛtti*)" (literally, "in respect to the compound"), which is more forced. (The other two commentaries give no gloss of the compound at all.) I have not observed any other occasion on which Śaṅkhapāṇi says *iti vṛttau vigrahaḥ* after analyzing a compound instead of *iti vigrahaḥ*. On the other hand, it must be admitted that it would be strange for Śaṅkhapāṇi to refer to VM's work in this one place, yet not mention at the beginning or the end of his commentary that it was based on it. If the *Tattva-samīkṣā* were as bulky in relation to the text of the *BS* as the *Nyāyakaṇikā* is in relation to the *ViV*, it would be natural for someone to make an abridgement. But why not say so? On the other hand, there is reason to believe that Ānandapūrṇa had access to the *Tattva-samīkṣā*. In glossing the word *pratibhā* at *BS* 18.23, Ānandapūrṇa brings forward the *Yoga-sūtra*'s definition of *vikalpa*: *sabdajñānānupātī vastuśūnyo vikalpaḥ* (*BSV* 88.11). Now Vācaspati, in discussing the word *pratibhā* when it occurs in the *ViV*, 246.2 brings forward the same definition from the *YSū* (*ViV* 247.17-19). (MB, *PMM*, p. 87n, gives this as an example of VM's syncretism.) It is certainly likely that VM made the same identification in glossing this word when glossing the *BS*. Citsukha does not bring in the *YSū* quote when glossing *pratibhā*, but he does mention it a few lines later, explaining *vikalpa* when it occurs in 19.3. *BSV* 89.23), which proves little. If Ānandapūrṇa, who apparently knew VM's commentary, did not mention his use of it, Śaṅkhapāṇi could have done the same. On the other hand, this same point of interpretation counts against the possibility of Śaṅkhapāṇi's having followed the *Tattva-samīkṣā*, because he does not bring in the *YSū* definition in this context. The fact that no manuscripts are known of VM's commentary on the *BS*, while all his other works listed in the

final verses of the *Bhāmatī* have survived, gives a persuasive argument that the *Śaṅkhapāṇi-vyākhyā* is an abridgement of the *Tattvasamīkṣā*. I do not think people would have failed to have it copied otherwise. KS, *BS*, p. xviii, says, "All these commentators (Śaṅkhapāṇi, Ānandapūrṇa, and Citsukha) appear to have had access to Vācaspatimiśra's *Tattvasamīkṣā* and Śaṅkhapāṇi's commentary now published, is copious and lucid, though it happens to be the latest". Unfortunately KS does not tell us on what he bases these assertions. There are indeed places where two of the three commentaries resemble each other closely enough that one suspects either dependence of one on the other or dependence on an earlier work. I have not noticed any such place where all three agree as closely. On various occasions Citsukha or Ānandapūrṇa agree more closely with Śaṅkhapāṇi than with each other; in others they agree with each other against Śaṅkhapāṇi; therefore no two of the commentaries seem more closely related to each other than to the third. The resemblances could perhaps then best be attributed to following VM's commentary. I think the preponderance of the evidence is that Śaṅkhapāṇi's work is an abridgement of VM's, or at least follows it for the most part, although we are not yet able to reach certainty on this.

34. In commenting on *BSū* 4.1.15 Rāmānuja uses *pravṛtta*, but only because he needs a synonym to gloss *anārabdha* in the *sūtra*; so he glosses *anārabdhakārye* with *apravṛttaphale*. *Śrībhāṣya* 4.1.19 uses *ārabdha* throughout. Neither *pravṛtta* nor *ārabdha* occurs in *Śrībhāṣya* 4.1.18. The text of the *BSū* that Rāmānuja uses does not include 3.3.32 (*yāvadadhikāram avasthitir adhikārikāṇām*) of Śaṃkara's text of the *BSū*.

35. KS, *BS*, xxvi-1.

36. The following is what I hope is a nearly complete bibliography of the debate on the Maṇḍana-Sureśvara equation, including some articles on Viśvarūpa and Umbeka (or Uṃveka), since these writers enter into the question by having been identified with M or S or both:

N. S. Anantakrishna Sastri, *Two Commentaries on Brahmasiddhi*, Introd., pp. 7-18, Skt. Introd. 1-30.

R. Balasubrahmanian, "Identity of Maṇḍanamiśra".

D. C. Bhattacharya, "Maṇḍana, Sureśvara and Bhavabhūti; the Problem of their Identity".

S. Das Gupta, *History of Indian Philosophy* (Cambridge: Cambridge University Press, 1965), II, pp. 82-87.

M. Hiriyanna, "Sureśvara and Maṇḍana-Miśra", and "Śaṃkara and Sureśvara".

G. Jha, *Bhāvanā-viveka*, Intro. to Pt. 2, pp. 1-5, and "Is the Equation Maṇḍana=Sureśvara correct?"

P. V. Kane, "The Chronological Position of Maṇḍana, Umbeka, Bhavabhūti, Sureśvara", and *History of Dharmaśāstra*, V, 1188-98.

R. Krishnaswamy Aiyer, "Viśvarūpa-Sureśvara".

S. Kuppuswami Sastri, *Brahmasiddhi*, Introd., pp. xxi-lviii, and "Further Light on the Prābhākara Problem".

M. Ramakrishna Kavi, "Literary Gleanings No. XI, Identity of Suresvara".

S. K. Ramanatha Sastri, ed., *Ślokavārtikavyākhyā* (*Tātparyaṭīkā*) *of Bhaṭṭombeka*, Introd., pp. iii-li, and "Bhavabhūti and his Identity".

V. A. Ramaswami Sastri, ed., *Tattvabindu*, Introd., pp. 40-42.

P. P. Subrahmanya Sastri, *Brahmasiddhi*, ed. Kuppuswami Sastri, Foreword, pp. v-xix, and "Problems of Identity—Maṇḍana Miśra-Sureśvara", and "Viśvarūpa the author of the Bālakrīḍā and Viśvarūpa alias Sureśvarācārya".

S. S. Suryanarayana Sastri, "Maṇḍana and Sureśvara".

37. R. Balasubramanian, "Identity of Maṇḍanamiśra", *JAOS*, 82 (1962), pp. 522-32, is the latest attempt to defend the identity of Maṇḍana and Sureśvara. A few comments may be made on it: (1) In several places (pp. 523, 526, and 531) Balasubramanian calls the belief in their identity 'traditional'. It is true that this belief is favored by most of the biographies of Śaṃkara. But, as KS shows by listing many philosophical works which distinguish the two (*BS*, pp. l-lv), it is equally 'traditional' to deny their identity. Balasubramanian denies (pp. 527-29) that the fact that the authors of these works refer to 'Sureśvara' and 'Maṇḍanamiśra', or 'the *Brahmasiddhikāra*' and 'the *Vārttikakāra*' proves that they thought there were two different men. But if they did not believe they were different, why does not any of them say something like, "This is the opinion of Maṇḍana before he was won over by Śaṃkara"? (2) If M and S are the same, we must believe that his conversion to Ś's school was so thorough, and his repudiation of his past views so violent, that he was led to apply sarcasm to himself when quoting the doctrines he previously held (See Appendix A-25 and 26). (3) Balasubramanian, p. 531, says that the fact that S uses such a large amount of material from the *BS* without saying that he was borrowing it from another writer is evidence that he is the same man as M. But there is no reason why S should have felt compelled to draw attention to the fact he was borrowing. He was not citing opposing views, but only adopting what he could agree with. His making minor changes in the wording of the borrowed material without changing the arguments or their sequence seems to me to be a procedure more appropriate to someone borrowing from another writer than someone reworking his own material. M, for instance, when incorporating verses from the *VV* into the *BS*, leaves them unchanged. Besides, Dignāga gives an example of massive borrowing without attribution: his *Traikālyaparīkṣā* is made up entirely of verses from the third *kāṇḍa* of Bhartṛhari's *Vākyapadīya* and the so-called autocommentary on the first commentary. Finally, the intense dislike shown by S to M (see Appendix A-26-27) could explain why he did not mention that he was borrowing from M. He might have felt that he had incorporated what was of value in the *BS* into his own works, and that it was best not to lead anyone astray by drawing his attention to M's book. (4) Balasubramanian says, "It should be pointed out here that with regard to the Indian philosophical systems tradition is generally a surer guide than historical research" (p. 531). But, if we accept as a whole the tradition embodied in the biographies of Śaṃkara, we will have to believe not only that M and S are the same, but also that M-S is the same person as Umbeka and Vaśvarūpa. Yet Umbeka comments on M's *ViV* and notes variant readings of its text; and if these four figures are one, we will have to attribute to this hard-working man a prodigious output in Vedānta, Mīmāṃsā, linguistic philosophy, and Dharma-śāstra, not to mention literature, if we agree that S

or Umbeka is the same as Bhavabhūti. We will also have to accept the absurd and undignified story of Śaṃkara's entering into the body of a dead king to gain knowledge of the art of love so as to defeat M's wife in debate. (5) Finally, a point which no one seems to have mentioned before, M's style is very idiosyncratic—tense, abbreviated, telegrammatic—and is the same in all his prose works. But S's does not resemble it at all.

38. Most of the examples in this list were first assembled by M. Ramakrishna Kavi, "Literary Gelanings No. XI, Identity of Sureśvara", *J. of the Andhra Historical Res. Soc.*, 5 (1931), 190, n.6. Ramakrishna Kavi includes one parallel unaccountably omitted by KS, which I will reproduce here, on account of the rarity outside of India of the journal in which the article is printed: *BS* II.5c-6b: *pitrādiviṣaye 'pekṣā jananādiprabhāvitā| ekakriyāviśeṣeṇa vyapekṣā hrasvadīrghayoḥ||*; and *SV* 956: *satyaṃ vastu kathaṃ bhindyāt puṃvyapekṣāviṇirmitaḥ| bhedaḥ putrādibhāve tu janyatvam vastukalpitam||*.

39. Therefore, at least as regards their doctrinal content, they do not give evidence for the M-S identity.

40. Ramakrishna Kavi, op. cit., p. 192; S. K. Ramanatha Sastri, "Bhavabhūti and his Identity", *JAHRS* 1 (1926), p. 128; Balasubramanian, pp. 529-30. For Śālikanātha's references to M, see KS, *BS*, Appendices, pp. 51-2.

41. D. Bhattacharya, *History of Navya-Nyāya in Mithilā* (Darbhanga; Mithila Institute, 1958), p. 27, says he was "only slightly senior to Vācaspati". L. Schmithausen, "Vorstellungsfreie und Vorstellende Wahrnehmung bei Śālikanātha", *WZKSO*, 7 (1963), p. 115, n. 27, says the two were more or less contemporary, Kane, *Hist.*, V, 1190-92, on the other hand, maintains that Śālikanātha was a direct pupil of Prābhākara, as does Kuppuswami Sastri, "Further light on the Prābhākara Problem", p. 478.

42. Frauwallner, "Kumārila's Bṛhaṭṭīkā", *WZKSO*, 6 (1962), pp. 88-90.

43. As noted by KS, *BS*, Appendices, p. 53, who does not however include B and the parallels to it given here. Hiriyanna, 'Brahmadatta'; p. 4, attributes A to Brahmadatta on the authority of Jñānāmṛta's commentary on the *NS*, *Vidyā-surabhi* (MS, Govt. Or. Lib. Madras). But Jñānāmṛta lived in the 18th or 19th c. (Potter, *Bib.*, p. 354), so we need not be bound by his opinion.

44. Another position in which repetition of knowledge is said to be necessary appears in *NS* III.88-93, 123-26. This does not appear to represent M, since the opponent stresses the importance of repeated *reasoning*, which M does not do. A similar position occurs in *SV*, 818-49.

45. *BS*, Appendices, p. 53.

46. *Ad* 796: brahmaṇi kāryakāraṇabhāvaḥ sāmānyaviśeṣabhāvaś ca vastuno 'stīti bhartṛprapañcapakṣe prajñākaraṇavākyavyākhyā pratyuktā saṃpraty akāryakāraṇasāmānyaviśeṣaṃ pratyagbrahmety upagacchatāṃ maṇḍanādīnāṃ tadvyākhyām utthāpayati.

47. *BUBV* 4.4.887=*GK* 2.38, *BUBV* 4.4.888=*GK* 3.46. Ānandagiri, *ad BUBV* 4.4.889, says: *tatraiva vaiyāsikam vākyadvayam āha*. Because not all the volumes of the Pratīka-Index to the crit. ed. of the *Mahābhārata* have been available to me, I have not been able to find *BUBV* 4.4.889 and 890 in the *MBh*. However, V. 889ab is found in a different context in *MBh* crit. ed., 13.295*1 post (Vol. 17, Pt. 1, p. 260).

48. KS, *BS*, pp. xxx-xxxi, translates *dhīrāḥ* by 'courageous', and says it

is a sarcastic reference to what S would consider M's timid accommodation of the Naiyāyikas by saying that verbal knowledge must have a relational content. But the opponent in this passage does not say or imply that it must have relational content, though the one in the passage from the *BUBV* discussed just previously does. Therefore I prefer to translate *dhīrāḥ* by 'wise'.

49. Although Ānandagiri, *ad* 876, says: *svayūthyānām eva matāntaram āha*, "He states another opinion of those who belong to his own group".

50. *BUBV* 4.4.876: asaṃtoṣād ato 'nye 'tra bhūridoṣadarśinaḥ/ vyākhyānād anyathā cakrur vyākhyāṃ vedārthaniścitāḥ//.

51. KS, *BS*, pp. xxvi-l, gives a number of doctrinal points on which M and S disagree, but in none of the others does S seem to me to give M's position as a *pūrvapakṣa*.

52. Frauwallner, loc. cit.

53. Ibid., "Landmarks in the History of Indian Logic", pp. 137-38.

54. LS, *VV*, p. 189, nn. 95 and 96.

55. Kunjunni Raja, "On the Date of Śaṃkarācārya", pp. 134-8; Ingalls, "Śaṃkara's Arguments against the Buddhists", p. 292, n. 2.

56. S. K. Ramanatha Sastri, ed., *Ślokavārtikavyākhyā*, Introd., pp. xviiiff.

57. TS text, p. 812: *uveyakas tv āha na bodhātmakam nāma jñānānām prāmāṇyam. kiṃ tarhi? arthāvisaṃvāditvam.* The name is spelled differently, but as Jha notices (*BV*, pt. 2, Introd., p. 2) there are several ways of spelling it. In any case, this appears to be a quote of the *Śloka-vārttika-vyākhyā* (as noticed by LS, *VV*, p. 216, n. 150). See the last two lines of *Ślokavārtikavyākhyā*, p. 53: *tasmād ayam arthaḥ—pratyakṣādīnām pramāṇānām anvayavyatirekābhyām arthāvisaṃvāditvam prāmāṇyam avagamyate, na bodhakatvamātram.* These are, it might be added, appropriate sentiments for a follower of Maṇḍana. Cf. *BS* 106.22-107.5, 155.18-21, where he says that other sorts of cognition besides *pramāṇa* are also 'knowledge' (*jñānapratīti*).

58. Demiéville, *Le Concile de Lhasa*, p. 177.

59. Frauwallner, 'Landmarks', pp. 143-44.

APPENDIX B

1. Gnoli, *The Pramāṇvārttikam*, p. xvi, n. 2.

2. *VV*, pp. 1; 76; 218, n. 152.

3. Ibid., p. 218, n. 152. On page 61, LS says that *VV* V. 80 refers to some other work ("Worauf Maṇḍana hier verweist, vermag ich nicht zu sagen)". To quote the verse and his translation: *ālambanārthas tadyuktavyahārasya yogyatā/ anyasyāpi hi naivānyas sa ity eva hi darśitam//* "(Dass die Perlmuschel) Objekt (der Silbererkenntnis) ist, würde bedeuten dass sie möglicher Gegenstand des von ihr hervorgerufenen Handels ist. Denn es ist gezeigt worden, dass es auch in anderen Fällen nichts anderes bedeutet". I do not think this is a reference to another work. LS's translation does not take into account that there are two *hi*'s in the second half of the verse, nor that there is naturally a caesura after *anyas*, which both the MS and LS's own reading accentuate by breaking the *sandhi*. The first *hi* must indicate that *pāda* c gives a reason

for the definition of *ālambana* in the first half, and second *hi* that *pāda* d gives a reason for what is said in *pāda* c. Therefore, I would translate it thus: "The meaning of 'objective support' is suitability for the activity that belongs to it (e.g., reaching out for it or talking about it—see LS, *VV*, p. 116). For there is no other (meaning) even for the other (for right knowledge as well as for error—*VV*, p. 117), because what is manifested is just 'this here' (not silver which is somewhere else, and therefore is not the *ālambana*)".

4. Although MB, *PMM*, p. 315n, says that because M does not actually mention that the verses in the *BS* that are also found in *VV* are borrowed from the *VV*, we cannot say that the *BS* is later.

5. MB, *SS*, p. 68. Iyer, *SSMM*, pp. 27-8, discusses only the possibility that the *vākya-sphoṭa* is referred to.

6. MB, *SS*, pp. 91.9 and 99.7-102.28, *passim*.

7. MB, *SS*, p. 68.

8. MB, *PMM*, p. 86.

BIBLIOGRAPHY

BOOKS

Amalānanda. *Vedāntakalpataru.* See Śaṃkara, *Brahmasūtra Śāṅkara Bhāṣya.*

Ānandapūrṇa. *Bhāvaśuddhi.* See Anantakrishna Sastri, ed. *Two Commentaries on Brahmasiddhi.*

Anantakrishna Sastri, N.S., ed. *Two Commentaries on Brahmasiddhi: Bhāvaśuddhi of Ānanadapūrṇamuni and Abhiprāyaprakāśikā of Citsukhamuni (Brahmasiddhi-vyākhye).* Madras Government Oriental Series, No. 161. Madras: Government Oriental Manuscripts Library, 1963.

Balasubramaniam, R. *A Study of Maṇḍanamiśra's Brahmasiddhi.* Diss. Madras 1960.

Belvalkar, S. K. *Shree Gopal Basu Mallik Lectures on Vedānta Philosophy.* Poona: Bilvakuñja Publishing House, 1929.

Bhartṛhari, *Mahābhāṣya Ṭīkā,* Vol. 1. Ed. V. Swaminathan. Hindu Vishvavidyālaya Nepal Rajya Sanskrit Series, Vol. 11. Benares: Benares Hindu University, 1965.

——— *Vākyapadīya: A Treatise on the Philosophy of Sanskrit Grammar, with a Commentary by Puṇyarāja.* Ed. Gaṅgādhara Śāstrī Mānavallī. Benares Sanskrit Series, Nos. 11, 19 and 24. Benares: Braj B. Das and Co., 1887. (The commentary ascribed by the title to Puṇyarāja is actually an abridged form of the *Vṛtti.* See Biardeau, *Vākyapadīya Brahmakāṇḍa,* p. 2n.)

——— *Vākyapadīya of Bhartṛhari,* Ed. K. V. Abhyankar and V. P. Limaye. University of Poona Sanskrit and Prakrit Series, Vol. 2. Poona: University of Poona, 1965.

——— *Vākyapadīya of Bhartṛhari with the Commentaries Vṛtti and Paddhati of Vṛṣabhadeva: Kāṇḍa I,* Ed. K. A. Subrahmania Iyer. Deccan College Monograph Series, 32. Poona: Deccan College. 1966.

——— *Vākyapadīya of Bhartṛhari with the Commentary of Helārāja: Kāṇḍa III. Part I.* Ed. K. A. Subrahmania Iyer. Deccan College Monograph Series, 21. Poona: Deccan College. 1963.

Bhāskara, *Brahmasūtrabhāṣya.* Ed. P. V. Dvivedi. Chowkhamba Sanskrit Series, 20. Benares, 1915.

Bhatt, Govardhan P. *Epistemology of the Bhāṭṭa School of Pūrva Mīmāṁsā*. Chowkhamba Sanskrit Series, Vol. 17. Benares. 1962.

Bhattacharya, Dineshchandra. *History of Navya-Nyāya in Mithilā*. Darbhanga: Mithila Institute. 1958.

——— "Maṇḍana, Sureśvara and Bhavabhūti: The Problem of their Identity." *Indion Historical Quarterly*. 7 (1931), pp. 301-8.

Bhattacharya, Vidhushekhara. *The Āgamaśāstra of Gauḍapāda*. Calcutta: University of Calcutta, 1943.

Biardeau, Madeleine. *La Philosophie de Maṇḍana Miśra, vue à partir de la Brahmasiddhi*. Publications de l'École Française d'Extrême-Orient, Vol. 76. Paris, 1969.

——— *Sphoṭa-siddhi* (*La Demonstration du Sphoṭa*). See under Maṇḍana Miśra.

——— *Théorie de la Connaissance et Philosophie de la Parole dans le Brahmanisme Classique*. École Pratique des Hautes Études—Sorbonne, Sixième Section: Sciences Economiques at Sociales, Le Monde d'Outre-Mer Passé et Présent, Première Série: Études. 23. Paris and the Hague: Mouton and Co., 1954.

——— *Vākyapadīya Brahmakāṇḍa avec la Vṛtti de Harivṛṣabha* (*Texte Reproduite de l'Édition de Lahore*). Publications de l'Institut de Civilisation Indienne, Série in-8°, Fascicule 24. Paris: E. de Boccard, 1964.

Cammann, K. *Das System des Advaita nach der Lehre Prakāśātmans*. Münchener Indologische Studien, Band 4. Wiesbaden: Otto Harrassowitz, 1965.

Chatterjee. S. C. *The Nyāya Theory of Knowledge: A Critical Study of Some Problems of Logic and Metaphysics*. Calcutta: University of Calcutta, 1939.

Citsukha. *Abhiprāyaprakāśikā*. See Anantakrishna Sastri. ed. *Two Commentaries on Brahmasiddhi*.

Dasgupta, Surendranath. *A History of Indian Philosophy*. 5 vols. Cambridge: Cambridge University Press. 1922-55.

Demiéville, Paul. *Le Concile de Lhasa*. Bibliothèque de l'institut des Hautes Études Chinoises. Vol. 7. Paris: Imprimerie Nationale de France. 1952.

Dharmakīrti. *Dharmakīrti's Pramāṇavārttika with a Commentary by Manorathanandin*. Ed. Rāhula Sāṅkṛtyāyana. *Journal of the Bihar and Orissa Research Society*, 24 (1938), Appendix.

Frauwallner, E. *Geschichte der indischen Philosophie*. 2 vols. Salzburg: Otto Müller, Band I, 1953, Band II, 1956.

Ganguli, Hemant Kumar. *Philosophy of Logical Construction: An Examination of Logical Atomism and Logical Positivism in the light of the Philosophies of Bhartṛhari, Dharmakīrti and Prajñākaragupta*. Calcutta: Sanskrit Pustak Bhandar, 1963.

Gauḍapāda. *Gauḍapādakārikā*. See Śaṃkara, *Gauḍapādakārikā-bhāṣya*.

Gaurinath Sastri. *The Philosophy of Word and Meaning: Some Indian Approaches with Special Reference to the Philosophy of Bhartṛhari*. Calcutta Sanskrit College Research Series, No. 5, Studies No. 2. Calcutta: Sanskrit College, 1959.

Gnoli, Raniero, ed. *The Pramāṇavārttikam of Dharmakīrti: The First Chapter with the Autocommentary*. Serie Orientale Roma, 23. Rome: Instituto Italiano per il Medio ed Estremo Oriente, 1960.

Gupta, Brahmānanda. *Die Wahrnehmungslehre in der Nyāya-mañjarī*. Diss. Bonn 1962. Bonn: Rheinische Friedrich-Wilhelms-Universität, 1962.

Hacker, Paul. *Untersüchungen über Texte des frühen Advaitavāda. I. Die Schüle Śaṅkaras*. Akademie der Wissenschaften und der Literatur, Abhandlungen der Geistes-und Sozialwissenschaftlichen Klasse Jahrgang 1950, No. 26. Wiesbaden: Franz Steiner Verlag, 1950.

——— *Vivarta: Studien zur Geschichte der illusionistischen Kosmologie und Erkenntnistheorie der Inder*. Akademie der Wissenschaften und der Literatur, Abhandlungen der Geistes- und Sozialwissenschaftlichen Klasse, Jahrgang 1953, No. 5. Wiesbaden: Franz Steiner, 1953.

Hasurkar, Shrinath S. *Vācaspati Miśra on Advaita Vedānta*. Mithila Institute Series 3. Studies in English, No. 2. Darbhanga: Mithila Institute, 1958.

Hattori, Masaaki. *Dignāga, On Perception, being the Pratyakṣa-paricheda of Dignāga's Pramāṇasamuccaya from the Sanskrit Fragments and the Tibetan Versions*. Harvard Oriental Series, Vol. 47. Cambridge, Mass.: Harvard University Press, 1968.

Ingalls, Daniel Henry Holmes. *Materials for the Study of Navya-Nyāya Logic*. Harvard Oriental Series, Vol. 40. Cambridge, Mass.: Harvard University Press, 1951.

Jayanta Bhaṭṭa. *Nyāyamañjarī*, Ed. Gaṅgādhara Śāstrī Tailaṅga.

Vizianagram Sanskrit Series, No. 10 (Vol. 8, Pt. 1). Benares: E. J. Lazarus, 1895.

Jhā, Gaṅgānātha, trans. *Ślokavārttika, translated from the original Sanskrit with extracts from the commentaries of Sucarita Miśra (the Kāśikā) and Pārthasārathi Miśra (the Nyāyarathākara)*. Bibliotheca Indica, N.S., No. 965, 986, 1017, 1055, 1091, 1157 and 1183. Calcutta: Asiatic Society of Bengal, 1907.

——— *Pūrva-Mīmāṁsā in its Sources* (with a critical bibliography by Umesh Mishra). Library of Indian Philosophy and Religion, 1. Benares: Benares Hindu University, 1942.

———, Trans. *Tattvasaṅgraha*. See Śāntarakṣita, *Tattvasaṅgraha*.

Kane, P. V. *History of Dharmaśāstra*. Government Oriental Series, Class B, No. 6. 5 vols. Poona: Bhandarkar Oriental Research Institute, 1930-62; 2nd ed. of Vol. 1, Pt. 1, 1968.

Keith, Arthur Berriedale. *Indian Logic and Atomism: An Exposition of the Nyāya and Vaiśeṣika Systems*. Oxford: Clarendon Press, 1921.

——— *The Karma-Mīmāṁsā*. London: Oxford University Press, 1921.

Koelman, Gaspar M. *Pātañjala Yoga*. Poona: Papal Athenaeum, n.d.

Kumārila Bhaṭṭa. *The Mīmāṁsā-Śloka-Vārtika of Kumārila Bhaṭṭa, with the commentary called Nyāyaratnākara by Pārthasārathi Miśra*. Ed. Rama Sastri Tailanga. Chowkhamba Sanskrit Series, No. 11. Benares, 1898-99.

Kunjunni Raja, K. *Indian Theories of Meaning*. Adyar Library Series, Vol. 91. Madras: Adyar Library, 1963.

Kuppuswami Sastri, S., ed. *Brahmasiddhi by Ācārya Maṇḍanamiśra with commentary by Śaṅkhapāṇi*. Madras Government Oriental Manuscripts Series, No. 4. Madras: Government Press, 1937.

——— *A Primer of Indian Logic According to Annambhaṭṭa's Tarkasaṃgraha*. 3rd ed., Madras: Kuppuswami Sastri Research Institute, 1961.

Lévi, Sylvain. *Vijñaptimātratāsiddhi: Deux Traités de Vasubandhu: Viṃśatikā et Triṃśikā*. Bibliothèque de l'École des Hautes Études, Sciences Historiques et Philologiques, Fascicule 245. Paris: Honore Champion, 1925.

Maṇḍana Miśra. *Bhāvanāviveka with Viṣamagranthabhedikā*.

Ed. V. A. Ramaswami Sastri and K.A. Sivaramakrishna Sastri. Annamalai University Sanskrit Series. No. 16. Annamalainagar: Annamalai University, 1952.

——— *The Bhāvanāviveka of Maṇḍana Miśra with the Commentary of Bhaṭṭa Umbeka.* Ed. Gangānātha Jhā. Princess of Wales Saraswati Bhavana Sanskrit Texts, No. 6. Benares, 1922-23.

——— *Brahmasiddhi by Ācārya Maṇḍanamiśra with Commentary by Śaṅkhapāṇi.* Madras Government Oriental Manuscripts Series, No. 4. Madras: Government Press, 1937.

——— *The Mīmāṁsānukramaṇikā of Maṇḍana Miśra, with an original commentary Mīmāṁsāmaṇḍana by M. M. Gaṅgānātha Jhā.* Ed. Pandit Ḍhuṇḍhiraja Śāstrī. Chowkhamba Sanskrit Series, No. 68. Benares, 1930.

——— *Sphoṭasiddhi (La Démonstration du Sphoṭa).* Ed. and trans. Madeleine Biardeau. Publications de l'Institut Fraçais d'Indologie, No. 13. Pondichéry, 1958.

——— *Sphoṭasiddhi of Maṇḍana Miśra (English Translation).* Trans. K. A. Subrahmania Iyer. Deccan College Building Centenary Series, 25. Poona: Deccan College, 1966.

——— *The Sphoṭasiddhi of Ācārya Maṇḍanamiśra with the Gopālikā of Ṛṣiputra Parameśvara.* Ed. S. K. Ramanatha Sastri. Madras University Sanskrit Series, No. 6. Madras: University of Madras, 1931.

——— *Vibhramaviveka.* Ed. S. Kuppuswami Sastri and T. V. Ramacandra Dikshitar. Madras Oriental Series, No. 1. Pub. in *JORM*, 1932.

——— *Vidhiviveka.* Ed. with Vācaspati Miśra's *Nyāyakaṇikā* by Rama Sastri Tailanga. Benares: Medical Hall Press, 1907. Reprinted from the *Pandit*, N. S., 1903-6.

Matilal, Bimal K. *Epistemology, Logic, and Grammar in Indian Philosophical Analysis.* Janua Linguarum, Series Minor, 111. The Hague: Mouton, 1971.

Mookerjee, Satkari. *The Jaina Philosophy of Non-Absolutism: A Critical Study of Anekāntavāda.* Calcutta: Bhāratī Jaina Pariṣat, 1944.

Murti, T.R.V. *The Central Philosophy of Buddhism: A Study of the Mādhyamika System.* 2nd ed. London: George Allen and Unwin, 1960.

Patañjali. *Vyākaraṇa-Mahābhāṣya.* Ed. F. Kielhorn. 3rd ed.

K. V. Abhyanakar. 2 vols. Poona: Bhandarkar Oriental Research Institute, 1962 (Vol. 1) and 1965 (Vol. 2).

Potter, Karl H. *Bibliography of Indian Philosophies.* The Encyclopedia of Indian Philosophies, Vol. 1. Delhi: Motilal Banarsidass, 1970.

Prābhākara. *Bṛhatī.* Madras University Sanskrit Series, No. 3. 3 pts. Madras, 1934.

Rāmānuja. *Śrībhāṣya.* In *Śrī Bhagavad Rāmānuja Granthamālā.* Ed. Sri. Kanchi P. B. Annangaracharya Swamy. Kanchipuram: Granthamala Office, 1956.

Ruegg, David Seyfort. *Contributions a l'Histoire de la Philosophie Linguistique Indienne.* Publications de l'Institut de Civilisation Indienne, Série in-8°, Fascicule 7. Paris: E. de Boccard, 1959.

Śaṃkara. *Bhagavadgītābhāṣya—Śrīmadbhagavadgītā Śāṅkarabhāṣyānandagiriṭīkāsaṃvalitā.* Ed. K. S. Āgāśe. 3rd ed. Ānandāśrama Sanskrit Series, No. 34. Poona, 1936.

——— *The Brahmasūtra Śāṅkara Bhāṣya with the Commentaries Bhāmatī, Kalpataru and Parimala.* Ed. Anantakrishna Śastri. 2nd ed., ed. Bhārgav Śāstri. Bombay: Nirṇaya Sāgar Press, 1938.

——— *Bṛhadāraṇyakopaniṣat Ānandagirikṛtaṭīkāsaṃvalitaśāṃkarabhāṣyasametā.* Ed. K. S. Āgāśe. 5th ed. Ānandāśrama Sanskrit Series, No. 15. Poona, 1953.

——— *Chāndogyopaniṣat Ānandagirikṛtaṭīkāsaṃvalitaśāṃkarabhāṣyasametā.* Ed. K. S. Āgāśe. 5th ed. Ānandāśrama Sanskrit Series, No. 14. Poona, 1934.

——— *Gauḍapādakārikābhāṣya—Sagauḍapādīyakārikātharvavedīyamāṇḍūkyopaniṣat Ānandagirikṛtaṭīkāsaṃvalitaśāṃkarabhāṣyasametā.* Ed. A. Kathavate. 6th ed. Ānandāśrama Sanskrit Series, No. 10. Poona, 1936.

——— *Taittirīyopaniṣat Ānandagirikṛtaṭīkāsaṃvalitaśāṅkarabhāṣyopetā.* Ed. V. S. Islampurkar. 5th ed. Ānandāśrama Sanskrit Series, No. 12. Poona, 1929.

Śaṅkhapāṇi. *Śaṅkhapāṇi-Vyākhyā.* See Maṇḍana Miśra, *Brahmasiddhi.*

Śāntarakṣita. *Tattvasaṅgraha of Śāntarakṣita with the Commentary of Kamalaśīla.* Ed. Embar Krishnamacharya. 2 vols. Gaekwad's Oriental Series, Nos. 30 and 31. Baroda: Central Library, 1926.

——— *The Tattvasaṅgraha of Śāntarakṣita with the Commentary of Kamalaśīla.* Trans. Ganganatha Jha. 2 vols. Gaekwad's Oriental Series, Nos. 80 and 83. Baroda: Central Library, 1937.

Schmithausen, Lambert. *Maṇḍanamiśra's Vibhramavivekaḥ, mit einer Studie zur Entwicklung der indischen Irrtumslehre.* Österreichische Akademie der Wissenschaften, Philosophisch-Historische Klasse, Sitzungsberichte, 247. Band, 1. Abhandlung. Vienna: Hermann Bohlaus, 1965.

Srinivasachari, P. N. *The Philosophy of Bhedābheda.* Madras: Srinivasa Varadachari and Co., 1934.

Stcherbatsky, Th. *Buddhist Logic.* 2 vols. Bibliotheca Buddhica, Vol. 26. Leningrad: Academy of Sciences of the U.S.S.R., 1930-32. rpt. New York: Dover, 1962.

Subrahmania Iyer, K. A. *Bhartṛhari: A Study of the Vākyapadīya in the Light of the Ancient Commentaries.* Deccan College Building Centenary and Silver Jubilee Series, 68. Poona: Deccan College, 1969.

——— Trans, *Sphoṭasiddhi of Maṇḍana Miśra (English Translation).* Deccan College Building Centenary Series, 25. Poona: Deccan College, 1966.

Subrahmania Iyer, K. A. *The Vākyapadīya of Bhartṛhari with the Vṛtti: Chapter I, English Translation.* Deccan College Building Centenary and Silver Jubilee Series, 26. Poona: Deccan College, 1965.

Sureśvara. *Bṛhadāraṇyakopaniṣadbhāṣyavārttikam Ānandagirikṛtaśāstraprakāśikākhyaṭīkāsaṃvalitam.* Ed. K.S. Āgāśe. Ānandāśrama Sanskrit Series, No. 16. 3 vols. Poona, 1892-94.

——— *Naiṣkarmyasiddhi with a commentary by Jñānottama Miśra, also Brahmāmṛta by Jaikrishna Brahmatīrtha.* Ed. R. S. Mānavallī. Benares Sanskrit Series, Nos. 38, 41, 43 and 88. Benares: Vidyavilas Press, 1904.

——— *Saṃbandhavārttika.* Vol. I of *Bṛhadāraṇyakopaniṣadbhāṣyavārttika,* q.v.

——— *Śrītaittirīyopaniṣadbhāṣyavārtika and its commentary by Śrīmat Ānandāśrama.* Ānandāśrama Sanskrit Series, No. 13. Poona, 1889.

Thibaut, George, trans. *The Vedānta Sūtras of Bādarāyaṇa with the Commentary by Śaṅkara.* 2 vols. Sacred Books of the East, Vols. 34 and 38. Oxford: Clarendon Press, 1890 and 1896. rpt. New York: Dover, 1962.

Umbeka. *Bhāvanāvivekaṭīkā*. See Maṇḍana Miśra, *Bhāvanāviveka*.

——— *Ślokavārtikavyākhyā* (*Tātparyaṭīkā*) *of Bhaṭṭombeka*. Ed. S. K. Ramanatha Sastri. Madras University Sanskrit Series, No. 13. Madras: University of Madras, 1940.

Vācaspati Miśra. *Bhāmatī*. See Śaṃkara, *Brahmasūtra Śāṅkara Bhāṣya*.

——— *Tattvabindu*. Ed. V. A. Ramaswami Sastri. Annamalai University Sanskrit Series, No. 3. Annamalainagar: Annamalai University, 1936.

——— *Le Tattvabindu de Vācaspatimiśra*. Ed. and trans. Madeleine Biardeau. Publications de l'Institut Francais d'Indologie, No. 3. Pondichéry, 1956.

——— *Nyāyakaṇikā*. See Maṇḍana Miśra, *Vidhiviveka*.

Vedānta Deśika. *Tattvamuktākalāpa with Sarvārthasiddhi*. Benares: Medical Hall Press, 1900. Reprinted from the *Pandit*, 1896-1900.

Vetter, Tilmann. *Erkenntnisprobleme bei Dharmakīrti*. Osterreichische Akademie der Wissenschaften, Philosophisch-Historische Klasse, Sitzungsberichte, 245. Band, 2. Abhandlung. Vienna: Hermann Böhlaus, 1964.

——— *Maṇḍanamiśra's Brahmasiddhiḥ, Brahmakāṇḍaḥ: Übersetzung, Einleitung und Anmerkungen*. Osterreichische Akademie der Wissenschaften, Philosophisch-Historische Klasse, Sitzungsberichte, 262. Band, 2. Abhandlung. Veröffentlichungen der Kommission für sprachen und Kulturen Süd-und Ostasiens. Heft 7. Vienna: Hermann Böhlaus, 1969.

Woods, James Haughton. *The Yoga-System of Patañjali, or the Ancient Hindu Doctrine of Concentration of Mind*. 2nd ed., Harvard Oriental Series, Vol. 17. 1927; rpt. Benares: Motilal Banarsidass, 1966.

ARTICLES

Balasubramaniam, R. "Identity of Maṇḍanamiśra." *JAOS*, 82 (1962), 522-32.

Biardeau, M. "Quelques réflexions sur l'apophatisme de Śaṅkara." *Indo-Iranian Journal*, 3 (1959), 81-101.

Chintamani, T. R. "Date of Śrī Śaṁkarācārya and some of his Predecessors." *JORM*, 3 (1929), 39-56.

Frauwallner, E. "Bhāvanā und Vidhi bei Maṇḍanamiśra" *WZKM*, 45 (1938), 212-32.

——— "Dharmakīrtis Saṃbandhaparīkṣā: Text und Übersetzung." *WZKM*, 41 (1934), 261-300.

——— "Dignāga, sein Werk und seine Entwicklung." *WZKSO*, 3 (1959), 83-164.

——— "Kumārila's Bṛhaṭṭīkā." *WZKSO*, 6 (1962), 78-90.

——— "Landmarks in the History of Indian Logic." *WZKSO*, 5 (1961), 125-48.

Hacker, Paul. "Eigentümlichkeiten der Lehre und Terminologie Śaṅkaras: Avidyā, Nāmarūpa, Māyā, Īśvara." *ZDMG* 100 (1950), pp. 246-86.

——— "Jayantabhaṭṭa und Vācaspatimiśra, ihre Zeit und ihre Bedeutung für die Chronologie des Vedānta." *In Alt- und Neu-Indische Studien: Beiträge zur Indische Philologie und Altertumskunde—Festschrift Schubring*. Hamburg, 1951. pp. 160-69.

——— "Die Lehre von den Realitätgraden im Advaita-Vedānta." *Zeitschrift für Missionskunde und Religionswissenschaft*, 1952, pp. 277-93.

——— "Relations of Early Advaitins to Vaiṣṇavism." *WZKSO*, 9 (1965), 147-54.

——— "Śaṅkara der Yogin und Śaṅkara der Advaitin: Einige Beobachtungen." *WZKSO*, 12/13 (1968/69) (*Festschrift Frauwallner*), 119-48.

——— "Vedānta-Studien." *Welt des Orients*, 1948, pp. 240-49.

Hasurkar, Shrinath S. "Maṇḍana Miśra's Views on Error." *Adyar Library Bulletin*, 23 (1959), 19-38.

Hiriyanna, M. "Bhartṛ-Prapañca: An Old Vedāntin." *Indian Antiquary*, 53 (1924), 439-50. Reprinted in *Indian Philosophical Studies* I. Mysore: Kavyalaya Publishers, 1957. pp. 79-94.

——— "Brahmadatta: An Old Vedāntin." *PAIOC* 4 (1925), 78-98. rpt. *JORM*, 2 (1928), 1-9.

——— "Fragments from Brahma-Nandin." In *K. B. Pathak Commemoration Volume*. Government Oriental Series, Class B, No. 7. Poona: BORI, 1934. pp. 151-58.

——— "Fragments of Bhartṛ-Prapañca." *PAIOC* 3 (1924), 439-50.

——— "Prapañca-vilaya-vāda—A Doctrine of Pre-Śaṅkara Vedānta." *JORM*, 1 (1927), 109-16.

——— "Śaṃkara and Sureśvara." In *Dr. C. Kunhan Raja Presentation Volume*. Madras: Adyar Library, 1946. pp. 1-4.

——— "Sureśvara and Maṇḍana-Miśra." *JRAS*, 1923, pp. 259-63.

Ingalls, Daniel H. H. "Śaṁkara on the Question: Whose is avidyā?" *Philosophy: East and West*, 3 (1953), 69-72.

——— "Śaṁkara's Arguments against the Buddhists." *Philosophy: East and West*, 4 (1954), 291-306.

Jhā, Gaṅgānātha. "Is the Equation Maṇḍana-Sureśvara Correct?" *Mīmāṁsā Prakāśa*. 1 (1936), 7.

Kane, P. V. "The Chronological Position of Maṇḍana, Umbeka, Bhavabhūti, Sureśvara." *JBBRAS*, N. S. 3 (1928), 289-93.

——— "Vedānta Commentators before Śaṅkarācārya." *PAIOC* 5 (1930), pp. 937-52.

Krishnaswamy Aiyer, R. "Viśvarūpa-Sureśvara." *Journal of the Śrī Śaṃkara Gurukulam* (Srirangam), 2 (1940-41), pp. 39-42.

Kunjunni Raja, K. "Maṇḍana and Dharmakīrti." In *Essays in Philosophy Presented to Dr. T. M. P. Mahadevan on His Fiftieth Birthday*. Madras: Ganesh and Co., 1962, pp. 249-51.

Kunjunni Raja, K. "On the Date of Śaṃkarācārya and Allied Problems." *Adyar Library Bulletin*, 24 (1960), 125-48.

——— "A So-called View of Maṇḍana on Word-Meaning Discussed by the Navyanyāya School." *Proceedings of the All-India Oriental Conference* 26, *Summaries*. New Delhi, 1964, p. 199.

Kuppuswami Sastri, S. "Further Light on the Prābhākara Problem." *Proceedings of the All-India Oriental Conference* 3. Madras, 1925, pp. 475-81.

Lienhard, Siegfried. "Einige Bemerkungen über Śabdabrahman und Vivarta bei Bhavabhūti." *WZKSO*, 12/13 (1968/69) (*Festschrift Frauwallner*), 215-19.

Mayeda, Sengaku. "The Advaita Theory of Perception." *WZKSO*, 12/13 (1968/69) (*Festschrift Frauwallner*), 221-39.

——— "The Authenticity of the Bhagavadgītābhāṣya ascribed to Śaṅkara." *WZKSO*, 9 (1965), 155-97.

Nagatomi, Masatoshi. "Arthakriyā." *Adyar Library Bulletin*, 31/32 (1967/68) (*Dr. V. Raghavan Felicitation Volume*), 52-72.

Ramakrishna Kavi, M. "Literary Gleanings No. XI: Identity of Sureśvara." *Journal of the Andhra Historical Research Society*, 5 (1931), 187-92.

Ramanatha Sastri, S. K. "Bhavabhūti and his Identity." *Journal of the Andhra Historical Research Society*, 1 (1926), 125-29.

Ramaswami Sastri, V. A. "Bhāvanā, the Leading Concept of Verbal Cognition." *Bhāratīya Vidyā*, 8 (1952). 1969-76.

——— and Sivaramakrishna Sastri, K. A. "Maṇḍanamiśra's Bhāvanāviveka—a Study." In *A Volume of Studies in Indology Presented to Prof. P. V. Kane, M. A., LL.M., on His 61st Birthday, 7th May* 1941, ed. S. M. Katre and P. K. Gode. Poona Oriental Series, No. 75. Poona: Oriental Book Agency. 1941. pp. 408-10.

Ruegg, David Seyfort. "On the Term *buddhivipariṇāma* and the Problem of Illusory Change." *Indo-Iranian Journal*, 2 (1958). pp. 271-83.

——— Rev. of *Vivarta, Studien zur der illusionistischen Kosmologie und Erkenntnistheorie der Inder*, by Paul Hacker, *JAOS*, 78 (1958), pp. 81-83.

Footnote to above. *JAOS*, 78 (1958), p. 140.

Schmithausen, Lambert "Vorstellungsfreie und vorstellende Wahrnehmung bei Śālikanātha." *WZKSO*, 7 1963), pp. 104-15.

Stcherbatsky, Th. "Über die Nyāyakaṇikā des Vācaspatimiśra und die indische Lehre vom Kategorischen Imperativ." in *Beiträge zur Literaturwissenschaft und Geistesgeschichte Indiens: Festgabe Hermann Jacobi*, ed. Willibald Kirfel. Bonn: Kommissionsverlag Fritz Kloff, 1926, pp. 369-80.

Subrahmania Sastri, P. P. "Brahmādvaita of Maṇḍana Miśra." *Kalyāṇa Kalpataru*, 3 (1936), pp. 504-07.

——— "Problems of Identity—Maṇḍana Miśra-Sureśvara." *Journal of the Śrī Śaṃkara Gurukulam* (Srirangam). 2 (1940-41), p. 5.

——— "Viśvarūpa the author of the Bālakrīḍā and Viśvarūpa alias Sureśvarācārya." In *A Volume of Studies in Indology Presented to P. V. Kane*. Poona Oriental Series, No. 75. Poona: Oriental Book Agency, 1941. pp. 405-7.

Suryanarayana Sastri, S. S. "Maṇḍana and Bhāvādvaita." In *Collected Papers of Professor S. S. Suryanarayana Sastri*. Ed. T. M. P. Mahadevan. Madras: University of Madras, 1961. pp. 272-81. First pub. *Philosophical Quarterly* (Amalner), 12 (1936).

——— "Maṇḍana and Sureśvara." In *Collected Papers of Professor S. S. Suryanarayana Sastri*. Ed. T. M. P. Mahadevan. Madras University of Madras, 1961. pp. 281-91. First pub. *Journal of Madras University*, 11 (1939), pp. 30-40.

Vetter, Tilmann, "Zur Bedeutung des Illusionismus bei Śaṅkara." *WZKSO*, 12/13 (1968/69) (*Festschrift Frauwallner*), pp. 407-23.

INDEX

A. Aklujkar 135-36
abhāva 19, 34
Abheda 10, 35, 55-56, 60, 77-78, 83, 89, 132, 148
abheda-darśana 11
abhedāvabhāsa 146
Abhinavabhāratī 129
Abhinavagupta's 129
Abhyāsa 34, 125
absence of / apprehension 72
absence of / cognition 71
absence of / discrimination 64
absence of the error 98
ācchādikā 34, 73
activity of consciousness 68-69, 94
activity of / knowledge 68
adhyāropa 64
adhyasya 23, 33, 54, 57, 63-64, 146
Advaita 1, 8, 24, 32, 35-36, 67, 70, 72, 77, 98, 105
Advaitāvadin 105, 121
Advaitin 1, 29, 37-38, 45, 113
Advaita of Śaṁkara 41
Advaita-vedānta 8, 112
adventitious / conjunction 68
affirmation 81
āgantuka 126
āgantukacaitanya 147
agrahaṇa 33, 71, 73
ajāti-vāda 23, 49
ajñāna 59, 126
akhyāti 35, 64, 72
akhyātivādin 37, 141
ākhyeyarūpa 91
akṣara 132
ālambana 22, 56, 105
Amalānanda 154
aṃśa 14
anādi 57, 58
anākhyeya 89, 91, 140
anākhyeyau 3
anākhyeyaśabda 90, 149
Ānandagiri 124, 126, 158
Ānandapūrṇa 44, 144, 154-55
Anantakrishna Sastri 121
anirvacanīyatva 1, 2, 5, 8, 18-19, 25, 36, 38, 47-48, 106
anirvacanīya-khyāti-vāda 24-25, 27, 31, 141
anirvacanīya 1, 4-5, 9-10, 18, 29, 37-39
anirvacanīyakhyāti 20-21, 32, 35-37, 130
anirvacanīya-khyāti-vādin 23, 64
antaḥkaraṇa 40
anupākhyāta 16, 17
anupākhyeya 15, 17-18, 20, 89
anupākhya 20, 141
anyathā-khyāti 19, 24-25, 32-38, 59, 63-64, 70-73, 83, 87, 105, 107, 109
anyathā-khyāti-vāda 28, 130
apekṣā-buddhi 109
apprehension 33, 64, 75, 97, 102, 106-08, 132
appearance 2, 3, 6, 21, 34, 39, 41, 43, 45, 47-49, 54, 58-59, 86
aprapañca 23
arabdha 120
āropaṇīya 64
āropasya viṣaya 64
artha 80
arthakriyā 65
artha-kriyākaritva 111, 152
arthamātra 77, 79, 97
asat 16-17
asatya 21, 47, 61, 101
asat-khyāti 19-20, 22, 23
asat khyāti vāda 37, 141
āśraya 62, 66, 148
atheistic 132
Ātman 14, 45-46, 83-84, 119, 132, 145, 147
ātma-khyāti 27, 37
Aupaniṣadātmaparīkṣā 5
Authenticity 147
avabhāsa 40-41, 43, 48
Āvaraṇa 70, 74
āvaraṇa-śakti 70, 72
āvaraṇa-śakti-agrahaṇa 71
avastu 8, 11, 15, 19
avidyā 1-7, 9-11, 13-14, 18, 20, 21-23, 25-31, 33-35, 45, 48, 51, 53-64, 66, 70-75,

84, 87, 99, 100-02, 106, 114, 119, 126, 137-38, 141-42, 146-47
avidyā-kalpita 5, 30
avikalpa 92
avikalpam 101
avikalpa / knowledge 91
avidyāsaṃskāra 57
avidyātmaka 5
avidyāmāyā 31
avidyātmikā 66
avikalpa / *jñāna* 91-92
avyakta 15
ayathārtha-grahaṇa 33

Bādarāyaṇa 113, 140, 143
Bālakrīḍā 156
Balasubramanian 156-57
bandha 51
Bhagavadgītā 62
Bhagavadgītā bhāṣya 146-47
Bhāmatī 154-55
Bhartṛhari 16-17, 45, 53, 80, 84, 88, 90, 93, 109, 134-36, 140, 145, 148-49
Bhāskara 113, 115, 153
Bhāṣya 120
Bhāṭṭa 127
Bhāṭṭa Mimāṃsā 19, 32
Bhaṭṭombeka 155
bhāva 26, 34
Bhavabhūti 155-57
Bhāvādvaita 153
bhāvanā 15, 112, 153
Bhāvanā viveka 112, 128, 129, 155
bhāvaśūnytvam 19
bheda 10, 24, 51-52, 65, 77-78, 148
bhedāḥ 14
bhedābheda 4, 13, 30, 66, 70, 113, 115
bhedābheda-vāda 45, 66, 136
bhedādarśana 59
bhedavikalpa 56
bhoktṛśakti 147
Biardeau 17-19, 49, 91, 109, 135-36, 140, 146, 149-50, 152
bīja-śakti 30, 66
bīja-nidrā 72
bimba 144
Brahmadatta 157
Brahma-siddhi 1, 3, 31-32, 34, 39, 68, 77, 87, 101, 111, 114, 121, 128-29, 148, 155-56
Brahmasiddhikāra 156
Brahma-sūtra-bhāṣya 153
Brahma-sūtras 112-13
Brahman 1-8, 11, 20-23, 28-32, 35, 44-45, 48-49, 56, 60-63, 65-71, 73-74, 77-78, 80, 83-87, 96-99, 102-03, 105-07, 113-15, 117-19, 121, 123, 126, 132, 136, 143, 145, 147-48, 151
Brahmānanda / Gupta 150
Bṛhadāraṇya-kopaniṣad-bhāṣya-vārttika 124
Bṛhatī 153
Bṛhaṭṭīkā 122, 127
Buddhi 40-41, 45
buddhivipariṇāma 146
Buddhism 47-49
Buddhist Logic 138, 146, 148-49

Caitanya 68
Causa materialis 56
Chain of Cognition 7
cidātman 46
citi 25
citiśakti 68, 70, 147
Citsukha 144, 149, 154-55
Cognition 2, 6-8, 13, 15-16, 18-21, 23-24, 27, 32-33, 52, 68, 72-73, 75, 78, 80-82, 86, 93, 97, 99, 103, 107-08, 147, 149, 158
Council of / Lhasa 127
Concept of / Superimposition 64
Conjunction 123
Consciousness, 1, 14, 19, 21-24, 26-28, 40-41, 44-48, 50, 68-69, 72, 88, 94-95, 106, 147
Complex / cognition 93
Contradiction 107
Constructive 80
Constructive cognition 42, 82, 86, 93, 95
Correct / cognition 108
Cosmological 1, 5, 30-31, 143

Dasgupta 145, 154-55
D. Bhattacharya 157
D.C. Bhattacharya 155
definition of / existence 152
Demiéville 127, 158
Deśika 154
dharma 12
Dharmakīrti 10, 25, 46, 55, 80, 111, 122, 126-27, 145, 152-53
Dharma-śāstra 156

dhvani 15, 18, 145
dhyāna, bhāvanā, upāsanā 97
Difference 10-16, 19, 24, 27-28, 31, 41, 45, 49, 53-55, 59, 77-79, 81, 83, 86, 95, 97, 101, 107, 113, 121, 132, 145, 148-49, 152
Dignāga 25, 46, 80, 136, 145, 156
direct / awareness 98-99
direct / knowledge 84
draṣṭṛ 68
dravya 80, 148
dṛkśakti 65-68, 70, 147
dṛśya 41
duality 34, 67, 69, 71, 97-98, 114

efficient cause 53
empirical error 32
empirical reality 9
entity 2, 6, 11, 19, 58
epistemic 62
epistemology 31, 41, 107
epistemological 4-5, 58
error in perception 53
errorneous / cognition 74, 87, 99
essence 1, 11
essence of Brahman 1, 3
essence of the / word 132
eternal / consciousness 147
eternal knowledge 1, 46
eternal metaphysical 58
external / objects 67, 89

false 3, 8, 14, 34, 58
false appearance 1, 3, 4, 59-60, 96
false cognition 35, 75
false knowledge 59, 113
false perception 140
false snakebite 102
final/knowledge 106
Fourth state 71, 74
Frauwallner 127, 136, 157-58

Ganges 124
Gauḍapāda 23, 71, 74, 126
Gauḍapāda-kārikās 71, 112
G. Jha 155
Gnoli 152, 158
Gopālikā 132, 140
Grammanans 23
G.S. Mānavalli 150

guṇatva 148

Hacker 4, 30, 47, 54, 58, 136-39, 141, 143-47, 152-53
hare's horn 19-20, 42
Harivṛṣabha 4, 17, 49, 91-93, 108, 135, 144
hetu 53
Hetuprakaraṇa 127
Hiriyana 119, 155, 157
History of / Dharmaśāstra 155
Hsüan Tsang 127

illusionistic 47-48
imagined / *bheda* 148
imagined / snakebite 104
impression beginningless 58
indescribability 6, 9, 12-13, 18, 136
indistinct apprehension 64
inexpressibility 1, 5, 14, 17, 22-23, 25, 27-28, 31-32, 35, 47, 138
inexpressibility of error 38
inference 81, 99, 101-02, 104
Ingalls 4, 136, 143, 148, 153, 158
injunction 72-73, 93, 97
injunction of knowledge 73, 121
intuition 90
iṣṭasādhanatā 153
īśvara 29, 62
īśanaśakti 65 66, 70
Īśvarapratyabhijñāvivṛtivimarśinī 129
Īśvara Saravaśakti 65
I Tsing's 127
invocations 132-33
Iyer 89, 135-36, 140, 148-50

Jayanta Bhatta 95, 141, 150
Jha 137-38, 148-49, 158
jīva 4-5, 51, 57, 60-61, 113
jñāna 51
Jñāna-Karmasamuccaya-vāda 32
Jñānāmṛta's 157
jñānaśakti 70

K.A. Subramania Iyer 17
K.A. Sivaramakrishna-Sastri 152
kaivalya 68, 147
kalpanā 8-10, 12, 25, 58-59, 61
Kalpataru 154
Kamalaśīla 4-5, 7-8, 11, 127
Karma-mīmāṃsā 38

kārya 145
K.A.S. Iyer 135
Keith 148
Kevalādvaita 113, 115
K. Kunjunni Raja 152-53, 158
Knowledge of Brahman 71-72, 83, 97, 99
Koelman 147
Kumārila 24, 36, 82, 93, 95, 103-05, 111-12, 122, 126-27, 131, 136, 148, 152
Kumārila's Bṛhaṭṭīkā 157
Kuppuswami Sastri 26-27, 114-15, 119-21, 123-24, 149, 152, 154, 155, 157

Lambert 23
laya 74
liberation 1, 6-9, 21-22, 33, 69, 96, 98, 113, 117
liberating / knowledge 98
limitation 119
limitation of / Brahman 119
loka 14
L. Schmithausen 130, 152

Madeleine 49
Madhyamika 11, 19, 23, 141
Mahābhāṣyadīpikā 135
mahāsāmānya 80, 82
mahiman 65
malcontent 126
Mandana-Sureśvara 155
Maṇḍana's *vastu-mātra* 89
manifestation 108
manifoldness 119
māyā 1-2, 5, 29-31, 59-62, 119
māyākāra 60
māyā-prakṛti 45
māyā-avidyā 1, 62, 65
māyā-mayi 30
māyā-śakti 29
mental / impressions 106
metaphysical 33
metaphysical / ignorance 140
Mīmāṃsā 38, 156
Mīmāṃsā-sūtras 144
Mīmāṃsāka 24, 36-37, 132
Mīmāṃsānukra maṇikā 37, 130, 133
mokṣa 99, 147
mother-of-pearl 2, 26, 28, 79, 97
M. Ramakrishna Kavi 155, 157
mirage 22, 30
misapprehension 64, 108
mithyā 20, 61
mithyāvabhāṣa 1, 34, 48, 59-60
mithyādarśana bhyāṣa 57
mithyājñāna 59
mithyājñānanimitta / dharmas 117
mutual / non-existence 78
mystic state 7

Nagatomi 152
naisargika 57-58
naisargikī 57
Naiyāyikas 158
nāmā-rūpa 5, 29, 62
nescience 1, 3, 10-11 13-14, 34, 49, 60, 73-74
negation 81
nibandhana 53
nidrā 72
nihilism 23
nimitta 23, 53, 89
Nirālambana 151
nirupākhya 19-20, 26
nirupāphyatva 19
nirvacanīya 26
nirvikalpa 80-81, 83, 85, 90-93, 96, 98
nirvikalpa jñāna 87, 91, 93, 95, 98
nirvikalapa pratyakṣa 82, 89
nirvikalapa / sāmadhi 98
N.S. Anantakrishna Sastri 155
niścaya 52, 88
nisargajā 57
nitya 47, 145
niyoga 35, 152
Niyoga-kāṇḍa 32, 34, 97, 144
Nyāyakaṇikā 154
Nyāyakośa 154
Nyāya-Mañjarī 150
Nyāya-Vaiśeṣika 82, 149

object / support 159
objective / illusion 59-60

padārthasaṃsarga 124
pañjikā 5, 47, 127
paramārtha 9, 10, 46
paramārtha-sat 2, 103
pāramārthika 80
pariṇāma 40-41, 44, 46-50, 113
pariniṣpanna paramārtha 2

Pārthasārthi Miśra 81
partibimba 145
Particular / universals 82
Patañjali's 68
Pātañjala Yoga 147
Perception 10-11, 13, 16, 18, 77-78, 80-83, 85-87, 95, 99-100, 105, 149
Perceptual / cognition 95
phakkikā 154
Phenomental / diversity 100, 117
Phenomental / existent 143
Phenomental / world 117
positive / existence 118, 142
P.P. Subramanya Sastri 156
Prabhākara 23, 32, 112, 127, 152, 157
Prabhākara theory of 35
pradhāna 55
Prajñā 71, 74
prakṛti 5, 41, 44, 55, 62, 68, 87, 143
prakṛti-pradhāna 56
pramāṇa 52, 59, 100
pramāṇavārttika 111, 127
Pramāṇavārttikam 158
prapanca 20, 51, 86, 119
Prapañca-vilaya-vāda 119, 153
Prapañcavilaya-vādin 119
pratibhā 84, 90-91, 154
Pratibimba-vāda 145
pratyakṣa 51, 57, 77, 80-83, 93, 95-96, 100, 106, 145, 149
pratyakṣa-buddhi 80
pravilaya 73
pratyayapravāha 124
primordial substance 5
Projective / nescience 73
puruṣa 68, 147
purusacit 68
Pūrva-Mīmāṃsā 24, 32, 37, 132, 148
Purvapakṣa 5
P.V. Kane 155

regressus ad infinitum 67
rūpa 10, 24, 142
Ruegg 144, 146

Śabara-bhāṣya 130, 144
śabda 20, 41, 46, 87, 96, 98-99, 106-07
Śabda-brahman 4-5, 7, 68
Śabda-brahma-parīkṣā 8
Śabda-brahma-vāda 8, 18, 22
śabdātmans 145
śabdādvaita 46, 49-50, 84, 88, 92-93, 132, 150
śabda-tattva 99
śabdadhātusamīkṣā 136
śabdapūrva 137
sādhya 34
sad-rūpa 77
sākṣātdarśana 125
śakti 4-5, 18, 30-31, 60, 62, 65-70, 148
śakti of Brahman 4
sākaṣātkāra 20
Śālikanātha 121, 122, 157
sāmānya 14, 78, 83, 85, 149
sāmānya-viśeṣas 82
Saṃbandha-samuddeśa 135
Sambandha-vārttika 153
sāmarthya 65
sāmarthyātiśaya 65
samāropa 63-64
Sambandhavārttika 121
Samīkṣāphakkikā 154
Śaṃkara 1-2, 4-5, 8-9, 15, 21, 28-31, 34, 38, 53-54, 57, 62, 64, 99, 103-04, 111, 113-15, 117-20, 123, 125-26, 135-36, 140, 143, 145-48, 155-56
Śaṃkaran 119
saṃskāra 52, 59, 72, 120, 125
saṃsāra 51, 57-58
Śaṃkaracarya 158
Sāṃkhya 41, 55-56, 147
Sāṃkhya-yoga 143
saṃsarga 78, 123
sāṃsārika 117
saṃtati 8, 146
saṃvṛti 9
samvṛti-sat 103
samavāya 78
Śaṅkara 18, 143, 147
Śaṅkhapāṇi 44, 94, 119-20, 130, 138, 144, 149-50, 154-55
Śaṅkhapāṇi-vyākhyā 154-55
Śaṅtarakṣita 5, 46-47, 78, 127, 145
sarga 51
sarvaśakti 66, 70
sat 77, 79, 143
sattā 77-78, 82, 85, 148
sattā-lakṣaṇa 84
Sautrāntikas 11
savikalpa 80-81, 83, 87, 91-93, 95-96
savikalpa / cognition 89

savikalpa / jñāna 91
savikalpa pratyakṣa 80, 82
Schmithausen 23, 25, 32, 37, 64, 131, 157
Seminal Power 66
Seminal Sleep 71-72
Siddhi-kāṇḍa 85
Śloka-vārttika 81, 103, 111, 122, 127, 149
Śloka-vārttika-vyākhyā 127, 151, 155, 158
Sphoṭa 15-17, 107-08, 132, 145
Sphoṭa-siddhi 3, 15, 107, 111, 131
S.K. Ramanatha Sastri 155, 157-58
Śribhaṣya 155
śrutī 39, 43, 70, 73, 96, 101, 145
Stcherbatsky 138, 146, 148-49
sthitaprajña 154
summum genus 82
Śūnyavāda 19-20, 23, 25, 38, 105-06
Śūnyavādins 1, 64, 103
Śūnyatā 22, 33
Śūnya 19-20, 25
Superimposition 21, 23, 33, 35, 54, 63-64
Sureśvara 56, 111, 113, 121-23, 125-26, 153, 155-57
Sureśvarācārya 156
S.S. Suryanarayana Sastri 115, 153, 156
svabhāva 1, 11, 14, 79
Svābhāvika 57
svalakṣaṇa 10, 55, 81
svarupapratistha 147
svarūpāvasthāna 147
svarūpābhivyakti 147
svarūpaprāpti 147
svātmasthiti 147
svavṛtti 3
Śvetāśvatara 62
Syncrétisme invertébré 49
syntax 91

Taijasa 74
tamas 57
Tantravārttika 112
Tarka-kāṇḍa 77-78, 83, 86
tat 29
Tātparyaṭīkā 155
tattva 29
Tattvabindu 156
tattvagrahaṇa 33
Tattvamuktākalāpa 154
Tattva-Saṃgraha 5, 46, 48, 127, 145
Tattvasamīkṣā 154-55
theory of *anyathā-khyāti* 108
theory of the causality 33
theory of error 74-75, 99, 101, 112
theory of inexpressibility of 37
theory of injunction 112
theory of wrong cognition 75
Thibaut 28, 140, 143
Traikālyaparīkṣā 135, 156
Triṃśikā 44
turīya 71

Umbeka 81, 105, 127, 148, 155-57
upādāna 44, 54-56, 144, 146, 148
upādhis 119
Upaniṣad 62, 85, 99, 102, 113, 125, 132
Upaniṣadic 35

Vācaspati Miśra 36, 55, 119, 122, 141, 145, 152, 154
Vaisesika 109, 147
Vākśakti 66, 69-70
Vākyapadīya 3, 8, 16, 41, 88, 107
vākśaktir 94
vākya-sphoṭa 132
Vākyapadīya-vṛtti 68, 88, 107, 135
V.R. Ramaswami Sastri 152, 156
vāsanā 55
vastu 6, 9, 11, 14, 20, 78, 80
vastu-bheda 14
Vasubandhu 44, 46, 49
vastu-Mātra 80
vastu-sat 12
vastusvarūpamātra 89
Veda 32, 99, 106
Vedānta 1, 5, 8, 21-22, 32, 34-36, 38, 46-48, 50, 65, 70, 77, 81, 84, 107, 112, 154, 156, 120
Vedānta-Sūtras 140, 142
Vedānta-kalpataru 154
Vedāntic 10, 28, 136
Vedāntin 23-25, 32, 34, 36, 77, 81, 104, 119, 141
vedya-vastu 20
Vetter 114-15, 152
vibhrama 13-14, 22, 26, 51, 57, 59, 141-42, 147
Vibhrama-viveka 8, 19-20, 32, 35, 38, 46-47, 64, 130
vidhi 153
Vidhi-viveka 32, 35, 128-29
vidyā 8-9, 11, 27, 34, 66, 87, 101, 105
vijñāna 1, 46

Vijanavada 9, 27, 45-49, 105
Vijñānavādin 1, 10, 105
Vijñānadvaita 41, 45, 47
Vijñaptimātratāsiddhi 144
Vijñāmātra 105
Vikara 43-44, 49
vikalpa 9-10, 25, 52, 77-78, 81, 88, 90, 96-98, 154
vikalpa-buddhi 80, 82, 95
vikalpapratyaya 42, 93
vikalpavāsanā 57
vikalpa-vāsanā 10
vikṣepa 70-71, 74
vikṣepikā 34, 73
vikṣepa-śakti 70-71
vimuktatman 141
vipariṇāma 42-43
viparīta-khyāti 17, 74
viparyaya-grahaṇa 33, 73
viparyāsa 17, 59
viparyāsa-jnana 34
viśeṣa 11-12, 14, 55, 78, 80, 82
viśva 74
Viśvarūpa 155-56
vivarta
vivartaḥ 3
vivartana 39, 46
viveka 36
void—*śūnya* 25
Vṛṣabhadeva 89
Vṛtti 8, 16-18, 21, 41, 45, 48-49, 89-90, 135-36, 145-54
Vṛttikāra 113, 115, 120
vyakta 16, 18
vyakti 78
Vyāsa 68
vyavahāra 2, 9, 25
vyāvahārika 20, 37, 51
vyavahāra saṃvarti 2
vyāvahārika-sat 2

Wrong apprehension 114
Wrong cognition 34-35, 73, 75

Yoga 8, 143
Yogacara 11, 81
Yogadarśana 64
Yogasutras 68, 147, 154
Yoga-sūtra-bhāṣya 68-70
Yogin 7-8, 137-38, 147
yogitvāvasthā 7